WITHDRAWN
L. R. COLLEGE LIBRARY

401
L14m

31249

| DATE DUE | | | |
|---|---|---|---|
| Aug 15 '73 | | | |
| Oct 31 '73 | | | |
| Dec 11 '73 | | | |
| Feb 24 '76 | | | |
| Aug 9 '77 p | | | |
| Apr 8 78 | | | |
| Sep 26 '80 | | | |
| | | | |
| | | | |
| | | | |
| | | | |
| | | | |

# THE
# MIRACLE
# OF LANGUAGE

# THE MIRACLE OF LANGUAGE

## Charlton Laird

*University of Nevada*

Cleveland  New York

## THE WORLD PUBLISHING COMPANY

Carl A. Rudisill Library
LENOIR RHYNE COLLEGE

*Library of Congress Catalog Card Number:* 53–10610

401
L 14 m
31249

FIRST EDITION

March 1954

HC 953

*Copyright* 1953 by Charlton Laird.

All rights reserved. No part of this book may be reproduced in any form without written permission from the publisher, except for brief passages included in a review appearing in a newspaper or magazine. Manufactured in the United States of America. Design and typography by Joseph Trautwein.

*For*

L I L L I A N  E.  G E N T

*who made a son of me*

8832  73

# CONTENTS

vii

viii                    *Contents*

# Contents

# PREFACE

A preface should not dwarf the book, and this one shall not.

The volume is not intended mainly as a text, although it grew in part from my difficulties as a teacher. Language is so entrancing that all sorts of people want to know about it, and yet, except for classroom texts which have limited usefulness outside the classroom, I found difficulty naming a book to which I could gladly refer the curious for a ready answer to anything linguistic. Accordingly I tried to ask myself all the most important questions about language, answering those for which the present state of our scholarship provides answers and guessing at the rest, labeling my guesses for what they are. In the belief that promoting the popular understanding of language is a worthy endeavor, I have tried to write so that a dogged person can understand me and a charitable reader can stay awake. Popularization has necessitated simplification; I hope it has not led me into downright error.

That I am indebted to thousands of students of language, living and dead, goes without saying. Many of the deepest debts are acknowledged by inference in the bibliographical note at the end of the book, but in a popular survey most scholarly indebtedness must pass unacknowledged. At least one name not mentioned there should be added, that of Professor R. D. Harriman of Stanford University, whose lectures have been invaluable. I am indebted also to those who have read the book in manuscript, especially to my colleague, Professor Robert M. Gorrell, Mrs. Patricia Martin Gibby, Professor Margaret M. Bryant of Brooklyn College, Dr. Sven Liljeblad of Idaho State College, and Mr. David B. Guralnik of The World Publishing Company. They are not responsible for anything I have said, least of all for my approach, which probably lacks a becoming decorum. My greatest debt is to my wife, Helene Laird, who has served as typist, editor, and laboratory canine—when I had a notion, I "tried it on the dog."

No one who knows anything of language will suppose that this volume purports to be a contribution to scholarship. A work of this sort should rely on the tested results of scholarship, and where tested results were available, I have tried to employ them. Some of the material concerning Noah Webster is new, but I trust not exceptionable—I am here indebted to Mr. Ben Grauer for his very kind loan of Webster's rare *Philosophical and Practical Grammar of the English Language*. My treatment of grammar in Chapters 10 to 13 of necessity embodies my own versions of attitudes widely held.

CHARLTON LAIRD

*University of Nevada*
*Reno, Nevada*
*1953*

# THE
# MIRACLE
# OF LANGUAGE

# ❦ 1 ❦

## THE MIRACLE OF THE DESART

THE LONESOME LAND—THE MECHANICS OF A MIRACLE—THE
END AND MEANS OF MEANING—THE MIRACLE AND THE NA-
TURE OF MAN—THE MIRACLE WILL HAVE NO NOSTRUMS—DIA-
LECT: THE MIRACLE IN THE MAKING—MIRACLE WITH DUAL
CONTROLS

*The Lonesome*
*Land*
To MOST of us a desert is a place with too
little water and too much sand, but to our
ancestors a "desart" was any wild place
where no one lived, presumably because no
one would want to.

Imagine that you live in such a place. No other human being
is near, and you have never seen anything human except the
reflection of yourself in a pool. You suppose you are as unique
as the sun and the moon.

You live in a world of sight and sound, but sounds of a limited
sort. You know the rushing wind, the pattering sleet. You know
the lonesome and terrifying howls of the wolves, the insane
laughter of the loons, the chattering of chipmunks and squirrels.
You can extract meaning from these sounds. You know that after
the wind may come rain or snow or hail to beat upon you. You
know that with the wolves abroad you want a good fire at night,
and that with the loons crying a certain season of the year has
come. You can guess that if the chipmunk chatters and jerks his
tail with uncommon violence he is probably either hungry or
angry. But to none of these sound makers, wind or wolf or chipmunk, can you say anything. Nor do they mean to say anything to you; not even the loon, in whose voice there is a human

3

note, means to discuss the weather. You are living in a world almost devoid of communication.

And so one evening you are lonely and empty because the moon is shining and there is a strange beauty over the land. Being sad, you imagine the nicest thing that could happen to you—that there might be another creature such as you, such as you are though a little different, for there seem to be two chipmunks and numerous loons. Except that this creature, since it would be like you, would not scurry off to hide in a hole, nor disappear with a whirring of wings. It would come and want to live with you, and the two of you could do everything together. And if you happened to like each other very much—well, you could look at each other in the moonlight and feel good inside. You might even touch each other, very intimately. Beyond that you could not go, for how can any creature, you would assume, let another know how he is feeling or what he is thinking?

Oh, you could rub your belly if you were hungry, smile and nod your head if you wanted to agree, and bellow if you were angry or got burned. But if you looked at another creature and felt very loving, how could you let the other creature know it? Or how could you find out if the other creature felt the same way? Or maybe a little bit different?

Since you have already imagined the impossible, and in the moonlight with the strange shapes and shadows everywhere it is very pleasant and strangely comforting to imagine nice and impossible things, you imagine something more. You imagine that by some sort of magic, whenever you want the other creature to know what you are thinking, your thoughts will appear in the other person. This creature, too, can give you his thoughts just by wanting you to have them. Then, if you love each other, you can tell each other all about it, only by wanting the other one to know.

But that could not happen. That would be a miracle and, being a practical fellow who takes little stock in miracles, you go off and try to drown your lonely feeling in fermented goat's milk.

Far from being fantastic, this miracle is occurring at the moment. Anyone reading this page knows essentially what I was thinking when I wrote it. Wherever this page goes, to Denver or Dublin, people will know what I was thinking, and if by some waywardness in fashion this book should have more than momentary life, people as yet unheard of will know. Similarly if any of these people were here in this room, and instead of writing I were to start creating, with my tongue and my teeth and the holes in my head, the intermittent sounds which we call speech, they would know immediately what I am thinking. Furthermore, for all or any of this to occur, neither you nor I need be conscious of the way it occurs. I need only want you to know, and you need only refrain from leaving the room or throwing down the book.

In short "the miracle of the desert" can and does occur; it occurs so commonly that most of us never give it a thought. The very babes learn to take advantage of it, just as they learn to walk or to hold a spoon. The miracle is the subject of this book. We call it language.

*The Mechanics of a Miracle*

THE MIRACLE of speech does not grow less if we examine it. Let us consider what happens. At first let us take the simplest sort of instance, in which one person speaks a word and another hears it. Any word would do, but let us use the word *wrist*.

What has the speaker done when he utters this word? By gentle pressure of the diaphragm and contraction of the intercostal muscles he has emitted a little air, scrupulously controlled, although the muscles which expelled the air are so strong they could shake his whole body if they were used vigorously. He has slightly tightened some membranes in his throat so that the column of air has forced the membranes to vibrate. Meanwhile a number of minute movements, especially of the tongue, have caused the center of vibration to spread sideways across the tongue, move suddenly forward, concentrate just back of the upper teeth, and then cease. With the cessation of this voiced sound, the column of air hisses against the upper teeth and gums, and is suddenly and momentarily stopped by a flip of the tongue. The tongue strikes the roof of the mouth with the portion just back from the tip, and spreads so that the whole column of air is suddenly dammed up and then released. All this must be done with the muscles of the throat relatively relaxed, and when the little explosion has taken place, everything must stop at once.

Now the word *wrist* has been spoken, only a word, but the whole operation is so complex and delicately timed that nobody could do this by thinking about it. It can be done successfully, in the main, only when it is done unconsciously. In part it can be learned, and people having speech defects sometimes learn part of the practice by laborious study, but good speech is always mainly unconscious speech. Any tennis player, even if he could not explain this enigma, could provide an analogy for it. When he sees a rapidly flying tennis ball coming toward him, he knows what he must do. He must maneuver himself into the proper position, be poised with his weight properly distributed, meet the ball with the proper sweep of his arm and with his racket held at just the right pitch, and all this must be timed to stop the flying ball at a precise point. But if the tennis player pauses to think of all these things which must be done and how he will do them, he is lost. The ball will not skim back over the net, building air pressure as it goes until it buzzes down into the opponent's corner. If the tennis player thinks about anything except where he wants the ball to go and what he plans for the next stroke, he will probably become so awkward that he will be lucky to hit the ball at all. Rapid, precise muscular actions can be successfully carried out only by the unconscious part of the brain. And so with the speaker. He cannot speak well unless he speaks unconsciously, for his movements are as precise, as complicated, and as exactly timed as those of the tennis player. Anyone who doubts it need only observe the distress of a speaker who has not learned English as a child trying to say the word *clothes.*

So much for the speaker. Now for the hearer. Sound waves which are set in motion by humming, purring, and hissing in the speaker's throat and head penetrate to the listener's inner ear,

and there set up kindred vibrations. At once that marvelous agglomeration of nerves, nuclei, and whatnot which we call the
brain makes the hearer aware that a familiar sound has been
produced, and presents him with various concepts associated
with the sound. And here we are in the presence of meaning.

*The End and
Means of
Meaning*
How is it possible that two people who
may never have seen each other before, or
who may not even live on the same continent, or be alive in the same century have
immediate, similar, and complicated ideas
in the presence of a sound? Especially is this event amazing
when we consider that there are hundreds of thousands of these
sounds with millions of meanings and still more millions of im-
plications so delicate that they cannot be defined. Somehow hundreds of millions of people have agreed, at least roughly, as to
the meaning of the word *wrist* and the other countless words in
the language, and this in spite of the fact that the human animal
is so varied and contentious a creature that seldom will two
human beings agree about anything, whether the subject be religion, politics, or what will "go" with that hat.

Of course when the word *wrist* is spoken by one person and
heard by another, communication has not as yet taken place in
any very elaborate or precise way. The single word raises almost
as many questions as it answers. Is the speaker thinking that his
wrist is arthritic, or that certain brush strokes can best be made
with the wrist? These questions can be partially answered by
adding a few more words, but in spite of anything he can do the
speaker is likely to remain to a degree ambiguous. He cannot be
precise because the syllable he is uttering has no precise meaning.

Thus "the miracle of the desart" is far enough from the divine
to exhibit a human flaw. Exact communication is impossible
among men. Gertrude Stein may have felt that "a rose is a rose
is a rose," but our speaker, if he considers the matter carefully,
must know that a wrist is not necessarily a wrist. It may be some
bones hung together by ligaments. It may be the skin outside

these bones. It may be the point which marks the end of the sleeve. If the speaker is a tailor, *wrist* may be a command to hem a glove. But even granted that both speaker and hearer agree that *wrist* is here associated with the bones, flesh, and skin at the juncture of the human hand and arm, they may still associate highly varied feelings with this part of the body. The speaker may have big, bony wrists, and have hated them all her life. The hearer may have been forced out of an Olympic skiing contest when he fell and broke a wrist. There is no one thing which *wrist* calls up in exactly the same form to everyone; there are not even areas of meaning which are the same for everybody. Meanings exist only in minds, and minds result from beings and experiences; no two of them are alike, nor are the meanings they contain. Still, granted that meaning is not and never can be exact, there remains a body of agreement as to the association to be connected with certain sounds which is staggering to anyone who will contemplate it.

But we have only begun, for we started with the simplest sort of example of spoken language. A word like *no* can mean *no*, *damn it*, or *yes*, or dozens of things between and among these meanings, depending upon the way in which the word is pronounced and the sounds modulated. The emission and comprehension of words, furthermore, become immeasurably complicated as soon as a speaker starts running them together into sentences. But let us ignore those possible ramifications and complicate the situation only slightly by making the speaker also a writer, and let him make a few marks on any sort of impressionable object. These marks can now take the place of sound and can call up the concepts associated with *wrist* wherever they go. They can continue calling up these concepts long after the man who made them is dead; they can do so for hundreds, even thousands, of years. Clay cones and slabs of stone, scratched with marks which were long undecipherable, were still able to produce something like their original meaning when their language was rediscovered, although no living man had known how to speak or write or think the language for thousands of years.

Man, then, can be defined, if one wishes, as a languagized mammal. A cow may be able to communicate in a cowlike way by bawling and dogs may be able to express themselves to a degree by looking soulfully from one end while wagging the other, but man is probably more significantly distinguished from his fellow creatures by his complicated means of communication than by any other difference. In short, man as we know him could not exist without language and until there was language. Civilization could not exist until there was written language, because without written language no generation could bequeath to succeeding generations anything but its simpler findings. Culture could not be widespread until there was printed language.

In the beginning was the word. Or, if in the beginning was the arboreal ape, with the word and an opposable thumb he scrambled down from the trees and found his way out of the woods.

*The Miracle and the Nature of Man*

Now HAVING said so much, we have implied a great deal more. If language is intimately related to being human, then when we study language we are, to a remarkable degree, studying human nature. Similarly we may expect language to be what it is because human beings are what they are. But we should not expect to study language by making inferences from other fields of study. That way madness lies—or at the least, monumental blunders. For instance, in the nineteenth century, students of society assumed that since the theory of evolution revealed new truths about human anatomy the same theory working in the same way should reveal new truths about human society. It did not. It led folklorists and anthropologists into one misbegotten generalization after another, and scattered the pages of a monumental work like *The Golden Bough* with errors which must now be patiently corrected. Any field of study which does not have principles of its own is a poor study, and surely no one can accuse language of paucity. We must expect language, however it is rooted in mankind and civilization, to have principles of its own, and we shall doubtless find ourselves in trouble unless we respect them.

Men have not always done so. There was, for instance, a serious group of enthusiasts for language who hoped to reform national conduct and international manners, to harden sloppy thinking and to clear muddy expression by reforming our vocabulary. These people were well intentioned, and certainly their ends were desirable. If we could stop an international gangster with a few well-chosen words, that would be an admirable stroke. But it does seem a good bit to achieve with nothing more tangible than a refurbished vocabulary, particularly since a large number of learned and eloquent people have been laboring for a long time, using the excellent disciplines of grammar, rhetoric, and lexicography, to encourage the precise use of language, and in spite of them national and international hoodlums are still with us. But let us see what these people proposed by way of method.

They recognized, first, that words have many usages, and that unless we are sure in what sense a word is being used we are likely to misunderstand one another. Furthermore, they recognized that many serious arguments, even fights and wars, grow out of misunderstandings, and that these misunderstandings may rest on various usages of words. Our language is so lacking in precision, they felt, that communication with any exactitude is impossible. Could exact communication be achieved, they trusted, we should find ourselves in complete harmony.

To follow their reasoning we might take a simple sentence like the following: *Civilized man cannot live without religion.* Obviously this sentence means many things depending upon the definition of the words. When is a man civilized? When can he be said to live? What degree of withoutness is *without?* By *religion* do you mean belief in a supernatural and omnipotent being, adherence to a recognized church, the practice of an abiding faith, a conviction that there is order and purpose in the universe. or what? A word like *religion* can have a score of meanings, or more, and even seemingly unequivocal words like *can* and *not* have various uses. Accordingly, some of the reformers decided to make American diction so precise that words could be used with mathematical exactness, and to do this they planned a dictionary. In this work all words would be defined in all uses and each would be given a label. To be clear, one need only affix the label.

According to the New Dictionary, the sentence above would read something like the following: Civilized$_{10}$ man$_8$ can$_2$ not$_1$ live$_{14}$ without$_3$ religion$_9$. Now the statement has become clear and precise. As soon as the reader has looked up each of these words in the New Dictionary and learned that *religion* here means "conviction of the existence of a supreme being," and that *live* means "enjoy one's powers to the fullest," he will be approaching some certainty as to the meaning of the sentence, and be the readier either to agree with it or to dispute it more violently than before.

*The Miracle*      UNDOUBTEDLY if this method were feasible
*Will Have*       it would promote the precise use of language. But the procedure has faults and
*No Nostrums*     they are pretty obvious. Not the least of them are these: nobody would be willing to use this method, and nobody could use it if he wanted to, because it ignores human nature and because it defies fundamental principles of human language.

It ignores, for instance, the fundamental principle that language constantly changes. So far as we know, it always has changed; it is changing now, and we have good reason to suppose it will continue to change in spite of handbooks on usage, the grade school teacher, and the National Broadcasting Company. A dictator like Hitler can influence language considerably; if he wishes to jail everybody caught using the Greek roots in the word *telephone* and let them out only if they will use the equivalent German roots in *Fernsprecher*, most of them will say

*Fernsprecher.* But not even a dictator with a concentration camp can keep language from changing, because it changes in more ways than any dictator could detect. The guards in the concentration camp themselves would be changing it unconsciously. So would the dictator. Before we could decide which was $religion_{21}$ and which $religion_{22}$ and print a dictionary with those decisions, the language would have changed.

No writer would use this language and no speaker could speak it. Would Mr. Hemingway consent to write about an old man and the sea, looking up in his dictionary every time he used the word *sea* to discover whether this was $sea_{15}$ or $sea_{18}$? Would the president of the National City Bank require all his letters to be written with it? I doubt it. Bankers, as far as I have observed them, are even more conservative with their language than with their loans.

In short, this system could not be used for many reasons, but mainly because it ignores the nature of the human mind, as the mind expresses itself in language. We have no difficulty distinguishing between the words *religion* and *theology* because we have differences in form and sound with which to associate differences in meaning, but if *theology* were $religion_{21}$, we never could remember whether it was religion-sub-twenty-one, religion-sub-twenty-two, or religion-sub-twelve.

If a language like this is unusable in writing, it is worse than unusable in speaking. The new language might reduce gossip, but ordinary conversation would cease altogether and that would be a pity. To speak at all in the new language, all of us would have to wheel monumental dictionaries about with us, using something like a self-serve grocery cart. Talk would however die in a good cause, for it would carry this artificial language along with it. No language has ever been able to survive unless rooted in common speech. Language is a product of the human mind and the human vocal organs; it follows the ways of the human mind and the human larynx. For the moment, let us postpone consideration of larynxes and speculate a little about brains and language.

*Dialect: The
Miracle in
the Making*

WE HAVE already agreed that every speaker or writer uses words as they exist for him; figuratively, he picks them out of his own brains. The Anglo-Saxons had a fine phrase for speaking, "to unlock the word-hoard," just as though each person about to speak his mind would first go to his great safe-deposit box of words, and pick out those he wanted to present to you on this occasion. Many of these jewels and pieces of old linguistic treasure would be similar to other word-jewels in other people's word-hoards, but each is an individual piece with its own background and character, made anew though on a familiar model. Quite literally each of us has his own word-hoard, be it large or small, and every word in that treasury is a little different from any word owned by anyone else, different in meaning, in pronunciation, and in the manner in which its owner uses it.

Now, since each of us owns his own words and uses them in his own way, it follows that each of us speaks a dialect. More properly, each of us participates in a number of ways of speaking and has what is sometimes called an *idiolect*. Each of us has an individual way of speaking, shares family speech habits, shares also a neighborhood dialect or several neighborhood dialects, and has occupational speech peculiarities, perhaps of several sorts. For instance, an old lady of my acquaintance was fond of the word *pesky* and unconsciously bequeathed it to all her children, along with a good many other words she had made her own when she was a girl. These children grew up with their family peculiarities, but added to them the community speech common in Iowa. They say *goin'* and *doin'*. One left home early and his speech is tinged with pronunciations from San Antonio, Texas. One became an engineer and his language is spattered with *pylons* and *safety factors*. Another became a labor leader and the jargon of his job is all over his talk. That is, each of these children of the old lady now speaks a dialect which reflects his home, his family and acquaintances, his occupation, and dozens of other things.

Some people, of course, suppose that dialects are shameful, or at least unfortunately conspicuous like a large Adam's apple, and they try to "correct" their dialectal peculiarities. But how can we decide which is the "correct" dialect? It used to be easy. We used to assume that the New England dialects were better than the others, because most of the lexicographers came from New England, and they put their own pronunciations into the dictionaries. Noah Webster, in prescribing a pronunciation, remarked that he knew the word was pronounced differently in the South. "But in Connecticut," he added, "we pronounce it this way." Apparently he assumed that in matters of speech, a New Havenite could do no wrong; a Yankee was born a linguistic standard. But lexicographers are no longer so provincial—besides, a considerable number of them come from the Middle West and the South. They are inclined to ask why is it better to pronounce *idea* with the sound of an *r* at the end and *mother* without it, than to change one nasal for another at the end of *going?* Students of language now tend to find all dialects equally interesting, and to write those into dictionaries which incline to be central.

When people try to "correct" their speech, they often succeed only in mixing up their dialects more than they were mixed before, or they develop a stilted pronunciation. A friend of mine was born in a little community of Latter Day Saints, and acquired the dialect peculiar to that group, in which the sounds customarily heard in *harm* and *warm* are transposed. My friend discovered to his horror that he was saying *form* where other people said *farm*. This was a serious matter, for he had to work with agricultural people, and he carefully taught himself to say *farm* with a fine, broad *a*. But he did not learn the related words; he still says *farmer formers* when he means *former farmers*, and he talks about the *business of forming* on farms. Personally, I preferred the speech of another of my Mormon friends, who was more forthright. She was a dean of women and, feeling responsible for the conduct of the students, was outraged when they stormed, shouting, into the college dining hall. "Why," she said, "they act as if they were barn in a born." We all liked her, more so because her speech was redolent of her background and character.

Basically all speech is dialectal. It exists as dialects, and if it is to be understood, it must be studied as dialects. This is one reason that there are, at this writing, at least two zealous efforts to study local American speech. One program is dedicated to preparing a linguistic atlas of the country, tracing dialects and their movements by careful study of a relatively small number of locutions. Dialect maps have already been prepared for New England, and are in process elsewhere; they are modeled upon some excellent European dialect maps. A second project envisages a monumental dialect dictionary. Both works will be fascinating, if and when they can be finished. Meanwhile anyone interested in language can have fun with two excellent albums of dialect records; one for the United States, *The Linguaphone Language Records,* and one for the British Isles, *British Drama League Dialect Records,* both available through the Linguaphone Institute, RCA Building, New York City.

*Miracle
with Dual
Controls*

WE MAY now observe a curious paradox, a paradox embodied in the apparently diametric statements in the earlier and later parts of this chapter. First we noticed that language relies upon a body of human agreement bewildering in its complexity. Human beings can speak, and can be understood, only because they have at their call millions of meanings and countless ways of putting these meanings together to produce larger and more exact meanings. These meanings and means of meaning, although they may eventually become codified, rest in reality upon an agreement unconsciously entered into, signed, and sealed by all of us. Language is language only because it has currency; the giving of currency is an act of social faith, the utilizing of the common by-product of many minds busy with their own affairs. Thus looked at from one point of view, language is a common product made by all of us, in process of being remade by all of us, existing in any real sense because it is made by all of us, and understandable only if studied as the commonality of many minds over many generations.

On the other hand we have seen that language as it exists is always the possession of individuals. Vocabularies are individual vocabularies, and ways of speaking are always the ways of individuals. A man's speech is as peculiar to him, as inseparable from him, as is his own shadow. It has grown with him, and most of it will die with him; like his shadow, it is to a degree made anew every day. He inevitably speaks a dialect, his own dialect, which is in turn compact of many regionalisms, a sort of linguistic goulash, made of many ingredients and stewed in a man's own way. Looked at from this point of view, language becomes a pattern of dialects, myriads of dialects infinitely blending into one another.

Philosophically, here is a dualism strange indeed. Like the higher forms of life, language results from engendering by opposites. But unlike mammalian life, it never becomes either male or female; it carries always with it the impress of this curious duality, and it must always be studied as at once general and particular, common and individual. This is not the least of the curiosities of language.

Nor is it the only one.

## THE BEGATS OF THE SONS OF OG

WHERE DID YOU COME FROM, BABY DEAR?—THE SONS OF OG—
THE WANDERINGS OF THE BEGATS OF OG—THE CURSE OF GOOD
BISHOP LITTLE WOLF—ROBBER BARONS AMONG THE VIKINGS
—HENGIST AND HORSA, LINGUISTIC IMPORTERS

*Where Did You Come From, Baby Dear?* BABIES AND language are the essential ingredients of civilization, and speakers of language no more know where it came from than babies know where they come from. Oh, in a sense we know. We know that we are all inventing it every day of our lives, and that everybody always has been, since before somebody grunted the first meaningful grunt. As language we know a great deal about it, but as an invention—perhaps the greatest invention of all time—we know almost nothing. In the sense in which the word *invention* is commonly used—something devised by an individual or individuals, by known means, at a given time and place—we have not even a plausible guess. We know only that there must have been a time when there was no language, and then there was a time when there was a language, but we do not know how, when, where, or by whom language came into being.

Not that we have lacked for theories. Sir Thomas Browne supposed that Hebrew was Adam's language, that it was native in mankind, and that a child reared in solitude would speak it naturally. Other early writers assumed that man did not invent language, but received it as a direct gift from God. Johann Herder, whose inclinations as a German romanticist did not becloud his critical mind, disposed of that supposition by point-

17

ing out that language is so illogical and capricious that only a blasphemer could attribute it to the Deity. His contemporary, Rousseau, in his concern for the origins of society, thought that primitive men, seeing the need of language, sat down and deliberately evolved one, which they then used by mutual agreement. Herder saw what was wrong with that notion, too—primitive men are very ingenious getting themselves into trouble and then getting out of it, but they have shown very little aptitude in laying plans for the future. Herder himself thought that language was due to an inner impulse, from something like "a mature embryo pressing to be born." In this he may have been right, but he was certainly not very specific. Others were more so. If we are to believe all the theories that followed Herder's during the nineteenth and early twentieth centuries, language arose from efforts to imitate birds and animals, from wordless cries of pain and joy, from the misunderstood babblings of playful children, from an economical desire to make more use of the voice. And the theorists found handsome names for their theories and satiric names for the rival theories, so that there was the Ding-Dong Thesis, the Ee-Ee Thesis, the Bow-Wow, the Pooh-Pooh, the Whistle and Grunt, or as many more as you like. But the proponents of one thesis were not able to convince the proponents of any of the other theses, and of late years the whole subject as a field for speculation has, by tacit agreement, been pretty much dropped.

Nor have we lacked investigations. Anthropologists have combed the backward corners of the earth for a people speaking a primitive language. They have found none. If they had they might not have been able to prove much; given a primitive language, we should not know that all primitive languages had been like it. But even so, a simple-minded language would have been handy to have. None has survived, not even among the most simple-minded people. The aborigines of central Australia have such elementary concepts that they profess to have noticed no causal relationships between sexual intercourse and birth—though some ethnologists doubt they are that naïve. The Sari of Lower California lived by digging up clams, but it seems never to have occurred to them that if they would fasten a clamshell to a stick they could dig more easily. Yet the languages of the bushmen and the Sari, like the languages of all other backward peoples, are elaborate, and show evidences of decay.

In short we know nothing about how language started, and we have not even the materials from which we might hope to find out. Logically, of course, there must have been a time when some primordial creature—let us call him Og—opened his carnivorous jaws and said, "Bup," or "Ickey,' and his bored wife, or his Electra-complex-ridden daughter, or his worst enemy in the next cave, or somebody, understood him, and language was born. Something of the sort there must have been. Theoretically and symbolically there had to be an Og.

*The Sons*
*of Og*

BUT IF Og himself is speculative, what happened to the language he might have invented is not. We know a great deal about that. At least we know about the more recent descendants of Og's original language, and recent, when it refers to languages, can concern thousands of years. To understand what has happened to these descendants, let each one of the dots below represent a language spoken today, a language like English or Bantu or Arapaho, and assume that the line of dots extends not only across this page but across many pages.

. . . . . . . . . . . . . . . . . . . . . . . . . . . . . . . . . . . .

Now assume that the first dot stands for Modern English, and the second for Modern German. Their relationship can be represented as follows:

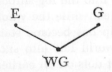

That is, we know that both Modern English and Modern German come from a language no longer spoken which we call West

Germanic. Now assume that the next four dots stand for Danish, Swedish, Norwegian, and Modern Icelandic, which descend from North Germanic. But North Germanic and West Germanic both descend from Proto-Germanic (Teutonic). Accordingly these six languages can be plotted as follows:

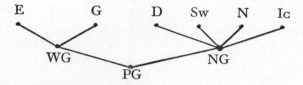

And so on. For example, French, Italian, Spanish, Portuguese, and Romanic descend from Latin; but Latin came from Italic, which with Proto-Germanic had a common ancestor, Indo-European, so that the diagram would now look something like this:

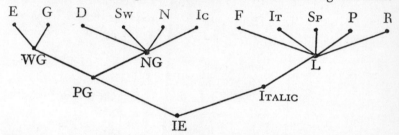

How long can this go on? There are limits. We soon come to languages so remote that we cannot even guess intelligently. Of the languages in the figure above, five of the six below the top line exist in no written form and never did. What we know of them we must infer. The more we know the more we can infer, and each year inference can be pushed further, but even so, we come eventually so far into the fog-shrouded past that we must wait for more light. Meanwhile the whole pattern of language growth and relationship has become startlingly clear. Most of the languages of the world fall into such consistent language families that the row of dots on an earlier page can be made to look something like this:

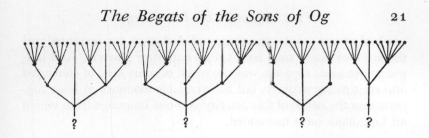

*(Remote time, about which we know little linguistically as yet)*

It is as though you sat looking out from an upstairs room with
high windows. You see twigs which run down to branches,
branches which run down to bigger branches, big branches
which join at limbs. And then the window sill cuts you off. Is
this one mammoth tree, spreading from one trunk? You cannot
tell. It looks like one tree. But of course it could be several trees.
Theoretically it could even be a hedge.

What we know is this. The languages of the world fall into
linguistic groups, which are parts of linguistic families, which
belong to tribes of families, so that all languages appear to have
descended from one universal parent language. The evidence
looks as though there was only one primordial Og blurting "Bup."
But we do not know.

There is some analogy for this guess. Most of the great inventions about which we know anything were made only once and
spread from this single invention. The wheel, presumably, was
invented but once or, at most, a very few times, but has so spread
that a world without wheels is now inconceivable. And the wheel
was pretty obvious. People must have been rolling on rocks and
falling on bottoms from the dawn of time. More than one of
them might be expected to have said, "If that round thing moved
me, why won't it move my load?" But few of them did. The
others just picked up themselves and the load, and went trudging
on. Need we be surprised if language was invented only once?

Of course the process was probably not so simple as one Og
blurting one "Bup." Most complicated inventions have been the

work of many people; the theory of evolution, for instance, was the work of many men both before and after Darwin. And language, we must suppose, was the result of some kind of concerted and continuing activity, but the available evidence at least suggests that the result of this activity was one language from which all languages have descended.

*The Wanderings of the Begats of Og*

So Og begat sons and daughters, and they peopled the earth with languages. The languages spoken by the North American Indians, for instance, can be divided into perhaps fifty groups, a number which may be reduced as anthropologists discover more relationships. The great Algonquian language family stretched from Labrador south and west, and can be divided into a half-dozen subfamilies. The Athapascan family includes the speech of tribes from Alaska south and east. The Uto-Aztecan Indians (of which the northern division is often called Shoshonean) liked the high mountain valleys, and are strung from central Idaho to the Valley of Mexico. A score of language families are represented in California. And so on. South American Indians spoke languages belonging to another half-hundred families. Similar linguistic groups can be identified in Africa and the islands of the Pacific.

We who speak English are most interested in the ancestry and relationships of our own language. It is an illustrious ancestry with important relationships. The diagram on page 26 indicates that English came from a long-extinct tongue called Indo-European, which is one of the great language families of the Eurasian land mass, accounting for most of the languages now spoken in Europe and some in southern Asia. In eastern Asia is the great Sinitic language, which includes the various divisions of Chinese speech. The Semitic-Hamitic group dominates the Near East. An eastern form of Semitic-Hamitic, Babylonian-Assyrian, has been long extinct. Hebrew was the language of the writers of the Old Testament and Aramaic the language of many writers of the New. Both languages were superseded by

Arabic, another language from within this group and still one of the great languages of the world. Among adjacent language groups are Finno-Ugric, which includes Finnish and the Lapp dialects, and Altaic, which includes Turkish. By all odds the most important body of modern languages, whether one counts the number of speakers of the language, the social and political importance of these speakers, or the areas in which the languages are dominant, are the descendants of Indo-European.

We do not know who the Indo-Europeans were. Even our name for them was certainly not theirs, and we know them only by the languages which have sprung from their language. In fact we have no recorded sample of Indo-European—if it was ever written we have no direct evidence. But by comparative linguistic study we have a mass of information, both general and detailed, concerning the Indo-Europeans and the language they spoke. They were a relatively primitive people. All of their descendants, even in historic times, were crude fellows—hunters, nomadic herdsmen, primitive farmers. At some prehistoric time they must have been living in east central Europe, well north in the Temperate Zone. How do we know this? In a number of ways, but here are two. First, draw a line from the Adriatic to the Baltic Sea. Roughly speaking, the Indo-European languages east of this line resemble each other more closely than they resemble the languages west of this line. Similarly the languages to the west resemble one another and not those to the east. The inference obviously is that the descendants of the Indo-Europeans migrated east, south, and west. The languages of these people broke up as they went, following the dialectal tendencies we have noticed in Chapter 1.

Second, the vocabulary of the Indo-Europeans reveals that they lived in a temperate climate. If a single word occurs in all branches of the Indo-European family, it probably came down from the original language. If this happens repeatedly in words of a certain type, we can assume that whatever caused those words was part of the aboriginal Indo-European experience. Conversely, if certain sorts of words have no common occurrence among the Indo-European languages, we can assume that the experiences which brought these words into being were relatively late. Now, any search of a good etymological dictionary will reveal that the words for the flora and fauna of the temperate climate include many which are so widely scattered among the Indo-European languages that they must have come from the parent word stock. For instance most Indo-European languages have common words for animals like bears and wolves, for plants like pine trees, for phenomena like snow. But there are no common words for rhinoceroses, elephants, crocodiles, or palm trees. That is, the aboriginal Indo-Europeans tracked bears in the snow, feared wolves, and sat under conifers, but they knew nothing about living in the tropics.

There were, then, some thousands or tens of thousands of years ago, a body of people with a common language, living in temperate east central Europe, perhaps about where Czechoslovakia is now. They were apparently cattle-raising nomads, and they were living in a stone-age culture. They spread. One group got as far as southeast Asia, coming into the Indian peninsula through the Khyber Pass in the second millennium before Christ, probably earlier than 1500 B. C. This group spoke a language which in a later state is known as Sanskrit, and which also was the ancestor of the classical Prakrit and a multitude of Modern Indic tongues. They must have left northern Europe a long time before they arrived in India; when is anybody's guess. There is a large body of literature preserved in Sanskrit, and the *Rig-Veda* supposedly dates about 1220 B. C. On their way southeast, these Indo-Europeans split up enough so that they left several related languages scattered along their route, in Afghanistan, Baluchistan, and modern Persia.

Other Indo-European peoples went in other directions. The Slavic languages of modern Russia and the Balkans represent one large division, somewhat related to Baltic languages like Lithuanian. The Hellenes went into what is now southern Russia, then down into the Balkan Peninsula, and gave us classic and then Modern Greek. The Italic people pushed south from the Alps; from them we have Latin, and a number of extinct languages like Umbrian and Volscian. The Celts were once in much of central Europe, but their languages survive now only in a fringe by the sea: Gaelic (which includes Irish and Scottish Gaelic), Breton, Welsh, and Manx. The Proto-Germans followed them and left their languages all over northern Europe. There were other members of the Indo-European language family that fared worse. Thraco-Illyrian survives in Albanian; Anatolic gives us Armenian. Tocharian was once sufficiently distributed in the Gobi Desert to be recorded in two forms, Tocharian A and Tocharian B, but it died with the cities buried in the desert sands. Others must have disappeared completely. We know little of Macedonian except that it was apparently related to Greek.

The result of all this is that in recent centuries the civilized world has been predominantly Indo-European speaking. At this writing the great powers seem to be Russia, the British Commonwealth of Nations, and the United States. They all speak Indo-European languages. The languages of the whole New World descend from Indo-European, except for American Indian languages which are either dying out or apparently about to do so. Most of the currently important nations of Europe speak an Indo-European tongue: France, Germany, Italy, Spain, the Low Countries, the Scandinavian and most Balkan countries. India is a linguistic babel, but the important Indic tongues stem from Indo-European. China, potentially a great power, speaks a Sinitic tongue. Turkish derives from Altaic. Arabic states and others speaking Semitic-Hamitic tongues may grow into importance. But at this writing, Indo-European languages carry the bulk of the communication in the civilized world, more than all languages derived from all other parent tongues whatever.

Ignoring branches of Indo-European which are either now extinct or, like Anatolic, but scantily represented, a chart of the Indo-European family tree would look about like the one on the following page.

Does the growth represented in this chart still continue? Are the linguistic family trees of the world sending out more twigs to become more branches? Possibly. The forces which make new languages are still at work; they are the forces of regional dialect, but to create a new language they must operate for many cen-

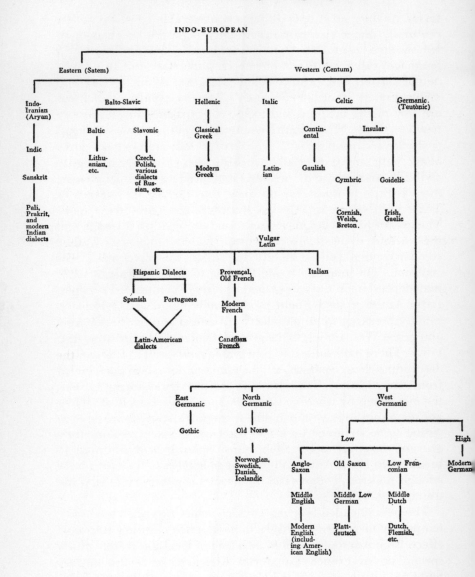

turies, or they must operate for a considerable time, say a few centuries, under circumstances highly favorable to change. In two or three centuries Anglo-Saxon became Middle English, a language which would not have been understandable to a continental Saxon. But primitive languages are dying so fast and civilization is standardizing men's lives so rapidly, that there are few places in the world today which seem to promise any new languages. Most primitive languages and languages of small or backward peoples will probably be exterminated in time, along with any potential offspring. The closely knit, highly civilized countries will probably not produce new languages; there is little prospect, for instance, that the regional speech of Texas will become a language. But there are a few likely spots. The great Chinese language has already broken up so much that the various dialects are sometimes called languages. Unless standardization comes rapidly in China, this divergence will continue. The making or obliterating of new languages there may depend upon the success and rigidity of communist regimes. Latin America, also, might produce new languages. Spanish is rapidly breaking up into dialects in Central and South America and in the West Indies, to the great detriment of Latin American unity. There may some day be a whole new family of languages descending from Spanish, as the Romanic languages descended from Vulgar Latin. Some teachers are now endeavoring to stem the movement by teaching Castilian Spanish in the schools. They are not likely to have much effect; linguistic movements are too strong to be stemmed by a few teachers, however zealous they are and however noble their aims. Spanish will continue to break up in Latin America until our neighbors to the south have enough political, commercial, and social community to stop the trend.

The new so-called languages which sometimes arise to answer temporary needs are not likely to have much of either future or effect. Monokoutouba, said to be a sort of local Esperanto which sprang up in French Equatorial Africa to serve the natives building a railroad from the Congo river town of Brazzaville to the coast, has sufficed for a translation of a Molière play, but will probably not spread widely nor long endure.

*The Curse of*
*Good Bishop*
*Little Wolf*

Of the languages descended from Indo-European we are most interested in those related to our own language, the descendants of Proto-Germanic or Teutonic. It differs enough from other Indo-European languages—Greek, for instance—so that some scholars have guessed that it may stem from Indo-European as that language was learned by a conquered people. Of East Germanic, a body of dialects spoken in what is now central Europe, we have only one exemplar, a fragmentary translation of the Bible into Gothic, represented mainly in the unique *Codex Argentius* at Uppsala University, Sweden. During the Thirty Years War it was either "saved" or "stolen," depending upon the point of view, from the library at Prague, and deposited at Uppsala. Later it was re-stolen, rediscovered in Holland, repatriated by a Swedish nobleman, and redeposited at Uppsala.

The story of this precious body of linguistic knowledge takes us back to the fourth century of our era, when much of western Europe was disturbed because all sorts of people were hunting homes, driven from homes they had by other people, who in turn had been displaced by hordes moving west from the Asiatic plains. Our bit of transcribed Gothic, the most archaic and, linguistically, probably the most interesting document written in a language descended from Proto-Germanic, is a bit of flotsam on those turbulent waves.

It happened this way. Various divisions of Goths were living, more or less at peace with the Romans and the Greeks to the south, more or less at war with the Slavs to the east, in what is now the upper Balkan peninsula and central Europe. When hordes from the east hit western Europe, they hit the Goths first. The easterners were Huns, and among the sufferers were the West Goths, under Athanaric. Athanaric responded by moving south upon the Arian Goths, who had been glossed over with a thin film of Christianity. The Arian Goths turned to the new religion for help, and specifically to their consecrated bishop, one Ulfilas, which is Gothic for Little Wolf. Ulfilas was a man of parts. Born in Asia Minor, he had brought to Europe with him one of the Christian sects of the day, Arianism, which denied that Christ was part of the Trinity, admitting him only as Jehovah's only-begotten Son. In the fourth century Christian dogma had not yet become standardized, and few people cared much that the bishop was an Arian. He could preach eloquently in Latin, Greek, or Gothic, an ability more important than the mildly heretical nature of his beliefs. Somebody, presumably Ulfilas, obtained sanctuary for the Arian Goths in Greece.

Now, supposedly, the great work began. Missionaries from time out of mind have given their hearts and their candle-lit hours to translating the Word into a language understandable to their charges. The Bible has been set into some thirty-two Indian languages north of Mexico; on the east coast of North America John Eliot finished a translation into Natick by 1663, and on the west coast the Reverend Henry H. Spalding was murdered by his charges after he had translated part of the Gospels into Nez Percé and printed the sacred Word on a hand press lugged across the mountains. Ulfilas was no exception to this passion for spreading the Gospel. Apparently with the help of many hands, he translated the Bible, almost complete, from Latin into Gothic. According to hearsay—only fragments exist—he left out the Book of Kings. What he had against Kings, we do not know.

Germanic storytellers were fond of the literary theme in which a hero gives his people a great boon; but the boon is cursed, and it brings with it destruction. This is the theme of the Nibelung-Volsung story, the original of Wagner's *Ring Cycle;* it is the theme of much of *Beowulf.* In the sense that Ulfilas fitted into this theme, he was a typical Germanic hero, in spite of his Asiatic background. Or because of it. Through him and his Bible the Goths became Christians of a sort; that is, ostensibly they were Arians. They were Arians when they moved down into the Balkan Peninsula. They were still Arians when they moved west, sacked Rome in 410 A. D., and still Arians when they moved across southern France, the Spanish peninsula, into North Africa, and eventually back into southern France again to settle down. There hundreds of years later, after the Roman world had fallen apart, a splendid cultural revival, often called the Twelfth Century Renaissance, was in progress, and the descendants of the Arian Goths had their share in it. Some scholars believe that if this revival could have continued the whole history of the western world would have been shoved ahead by centuries. But it did not continue. It was wiped out in a series of ruthlessly competent butcheries few savages could match.

Not that the descendants of the Goths, now called the Albigensians from their center at Albi, had done anything overt. They merely happened to be handy victims in a situation that needed victims. Tens of thousands of crusaders were back from the Holy Wars; years of campaigning had bred a love of war in them, and a propensity for appropriating things. The respectable folk who had stayed home and prospered were wondering what might happen if these hordes of returned soldiers of the Lord, doubtless to be rewarded in heaven, should decide to be rewarded also on earth. A new crusade was needed to keep the soldiers occupied, to supply the King of France with gold. The Albigensians had gold, plenty of it. They were certainly sinners, for they had preserved Bishop Ulfilas's once-tolerated but now abhorred Arian heresy. Accordingly a crusade was declared against them, and the returned soldiers were happily diverted, murdering, raping, and pillaging the made-to-order victims.

Thus, indirectly and unintentionally, the good bishop with his precious gift of the Word in Gothic brought destruction to the peaceful citizens of southern France. Without him and his Bible, Modern French might have stemmed, not from the dialect of Paris, but from the dialect of Toulouse, Montpellier, or Marseille in the south. But that is speculation. The fact is that without him we would know practically nothing of the descendants of the Germanic language in anything like the archaic form in which he preserved it in Gothic. The grammar and vocabulary of his translation have been of inestimable value in revealing the relationships of Proto-Germanic to other Indo-European tongues.

*Robber Barons
Among the
Vikings*

VARIOUS distant relatives of the Goths lived
to the north, contiguous to the Baltic and
the North Seas. These people were fond of
avenging their family deaths, going to Val-
halla when they died, and speaking an an-
cestor of Old Norse in the meantime. During the course of their
tribal brawls, one political incident had far-reaching linguistic
results. Norway had been largely ruled by a number of *jarls*,
rugged individualists who believed in every jarl's right to tell his
neighbor what to do, and to charge for this advice by appropriating the neighbor's property. This pleasant state of affairs
was interrupted by one Halfdane the Black, who started a New
Deal by enlisting various lesser folk and using them to discomfit
his fellow jarls. The movement was brought to conclusion by
Halfdane's son, Harold Fairhair, who became the great liberator
or the great dictator, the epithet depending upon one's political
views. As a result, a number of jarls lost their heads and others
lost their taste for Norway and became Vikings, which is often
a polite term for international pirates. Some of the Vikings emi-
grated to the bleak island of Iceland, previously inhabited only
by a few Celtic anchorites, pious folk who were in no position to
resent sudden guests.

The new culture throve in Iceland. The immigrants were an
exceedingly competent, and even a rather well-educated lot, as
educated people went under the Arctic Circle in those days.
They could fish, or fight, or farm, and they did all of these. Iceland became a key station in the settlement of Greenland and
in the eventual discovery of the continent of North America.
Icelanders developed a relatively representative government, a
stable and prosperous community, and a great love of the culture
they had brought with them. They went their own hearty way,
too distant and too insignificant to be much bothered by the rest
of Europe. Icelanders had gone west in order to get away from
Harold Fairhair and all his deals, old and new, and they did.

Meanwhile the continent of Europe was being ravaged. The
Vikings who had not gone to Iceland did part of the job, plundering France, the British Isles, and large areas of Middle Europe.

They only continued what other Teutons like the Goths and Burgundians had begun. There were generations of feudal wars. There was the Black Death. And most destructive of all—at least to pagan culture—there was Christianity. As a result, many of the great peoples of northern Europe have disappeared without leaving behind them one written scrawl. Most are represented only by a few carvings in stone. Of the great Burgundian people, nothing. Of the conquering Franks, a late governmental scrap and nothing else earlier than a saint's legend. Even of Anglo-Saxon, which is relatively well represented, there are only a few important pieces which are not mainly inspired by Christianity.

But not so in Iceland. Icelanders preserved much of the lore they brought with them. They developed a vigorous saga literature of their own, and they imported the literature of the Continent, translating it into their tongue. In Iceland more than the robber barons found a home; literary works lost on the Continent can be reconstructed from their Icelandic translations. For to Iceland most things went, and in Iceland much was preserved. Here came no hostile Vikings to burn the monasteries, and the manuscripts along with them. Here was no early Christianity, busy to root out evidences of paganism, including pagan languages and pagan letters. Here was no Henry VIII, to close the religious houses and incidentally to doom tens of thousands of manuscripts with his edict. As a result more language and literature were preserved on the rocky little island of Iceland than in all other early Germanic areas combined, incomparably more. Today any serious student of the English language must study the dialect of those émigrés who preferred the fogs of Iceland to the New Deal in Norway.

*Hengist and*      WHILE ALL this was going on, there had
*Horsa, Linguistic*      been developments to the west. When
*Importers*      Julius Caesar came in his campaigning to
the North Sea, he made a reconnaissance in
force to the neighboring island of Britain,
but he was too busy dividing all Gaul into manageable parts to

be bothered conquering an island just then. In the next century, however, the Romans started taking over, and built a considerable culture in Britain before trouble at home forced them to abandon their paved streets and their tile-floored villas, and go home. They left a void. The native Celts had become civilized, law-abiding people, accustomed to government and reliable police, nearly as helpless before an invading host as most modern civilian populations would be. Germanic pirates from the Continent started raiding the Celts, and when the pirates found that the local people could offer only sporadic resistance, they moved in. They were followed by professional soldiers and, eventually, by ordinary farmers.

We do not know in detail what happened. Pirate bands do not usually include many scholars, writers, or librarians, and in those days generals seldom wrote books. These people left behind them few records but their bones, their moldering gear, their offspring, and their language. But from these we can infer something. There are also legends. Centuries later a descendant of the first imperious visitors, the Venerable Bede, said the invaders came because a local Celtic king, one Vortigern, invited two hardy fellows, Hengist and Horsa, to help him in a fight. Hengist and Horsa won Vortigern's battle for him, and then saw no reason to go home. They took over; they invited their friends, who proceeded to make life unpleasant for the Celts.

There is no good reason to believe this. The Venerable Bede had no reliable sources. Much of what he reported was certainly folklore, and this tale has a fine folkloristic ring to it. On the other hand, there is no good reason not to believe it. Basically the story is plausible enough, and just this sort of thing has certainly happened, times without number. At best, of course, the tale must be a vastly simplified account of what was certainly a many-pronged invasion lasting for a century or more. But in one form or another there must have been a Hengist and Horsa, if we think of these two gentlemen as symbols for the West Germanic tribesmen who occupied an island that looked good to them.

From Bede's point of view the invasion was important because "as the event still more evidently showed, it appears to have been done by the appointment of our Lord himself, that evil might fall upon them [the Celts] for their wicked deeds," the Celts having "cast off the light load of Christ." From a linguistic point of view, however, the importance of the invasion is this. Hengist and Horsa brought with them the English language. It has since grown to such proportions that it is now the standard speech of two of the great world powers, and has become the nearest thing to a common language that our disunited world has yet been able to achieve. But at that time it was an insignificant confusion of the speech of a few seaside-dwelling West Germans, the Angles, part of the Saxons, and perhaps a few other errant Germans, renegades and freebooters most likely.

# ❧ 3 ❧

## ENGLISH: HIS SISTERS AND HIS COUSINS
## AND HIS AUNTS

THE OMNIPRESENT ANGLO-SAXONS—ANGLO-SAXONS MAKE
THEMSELVES AT HOME—THE ENGLISH LANGUAGE ENTERTAINS
SOME STRONG-MINDED RELATIVES—AND NOW THE SOPHISTI-
CATED COUSINS COME—THE PEACEFUL COUSINS

*The Omni-*
*present*
*Anglo-Saxons*

"WHO SEES things grow from their origin,"
Aristotle says, "will have the most advantageous view of them." No arch-Methuse-
lah has seen language grow from its origin,
but we have now glimpsed the origin and
growth of English and its sister languages from Indo-European.
Without this fundamental understanding—that English is one
of a family of languages and partakes of the qualities of that
family—no one can ask significant questions about the background of our speech. But now we can propound some of the
most searching questions. Let us try to do so.

*What is the nature of the English language, and how did it
acquire this nature?*

This question is too large to answer all at once, but we can
start on it by breaking it down a bit. Pretty clearly English, like
most languages, is made up of symbols for meaning (words), and
some method of putting these words together so that they convey
enlarged meaning (grammar). Of these two, the words are the
more obvious; everybody is aware of words, whereas much grammar is unconscious. Accordingly let us start with words, and ask

35

ourselves where our words came from—later we can ask how they came to be what they are today.

In view of the previous chapter, part of the answer must be obvious. If English came from Anglo-Saxon, and Anglo-Saxon came from Indo-European, at least part of our vocabulary must descend to us from Indo-European through Anglo-Saxon. How much of it, and which parts of it? To start an answer, one might start counting the words in ordinary prose, dividing them into those which came from Anglo-Saxon and those which did not. On the assumption that the stuff you are now reading is ordinary prose, the next paragraph will be printed with *as* for *Anglo-Saxon* over the words which come from that language, and *o* for *other* over the remaining words.

   *as*   *as* *as*   *as*   *as*    *o*      *o*    *as* *as*   *o*
There is, of course, a preliminary question. Did the Anglo-

 *o*   *as* *as*  *o*   *as*   *as*   *o*   *o*   *as* *as*  *o*   *as*
Saxons get all their words from Indo-European, or did they have

 *as*   *o*    *o*  *as* *as*   *as*   *as*  *o*   *as*     *o*
some secret cache of words from which they could surreptitiously

   *o*    *o*   *as*   *as*    *o*   *as*   *o*   *as* *as*
augment their word stock? Presenting the evidence for an

 *as*    *as*   *o*   *as*   *as*   *as*   *o*   *o*   *as* *as*
answer would require our going into Anglo-Saxon as a lan-

 *o*   *as* *as* *as* *as*  *o*   *as* *as*   *o*   *as* *as*  *o*
guage, and that, at the moment, we are scarcely in a position

*as* *as* *as*   *o*   *as*   *as*  *as* *as* *as*  *o*   *as*  *o*
to do. But fortunately the answer is not in dispute. The Angles

 *as*   *as*   *o*   *as*   *as*   *o*    *o*    *o*    *o*
and the Saxons came from relatively isolated Germanic peoples.

*as*      *as*   *as*      *o*      *as*      *o*      *o*      *o*      *as*      *as&o?*
Having been in contact with Roman traders, they had picked

*as as as*      *o*      *as*      *as*   *o*      *as*      *as*      *as*      *o*
up a few Latin words. All their neighbors spoke some derivative

*as*      *o*      *o*      *as*      *as*      *o*   *as*      *o*      *o*      *as*
of Indo-European, and from them the Anglo-Saxons borrowed

*as as*      *as*      *as*      *as*   *as*   *as*      *as*      *as*      *as*      *o*
a few more words. Thus even the borrowed words in Anglo-

*o*      *as*      *as*      *o*      *o*      *as*   *as*      *o*      *o*   *as*
Saxon came from Indo-European, but the important fact is

*as*      *as*      *as*      *as*   *as*      *o*      *o*      *as&o?*
that although speakers of West Germanic acquired scattered

*as*      *as*   *as*   *as*   *as*   *as*      *o*   *as*      *o*      *as*      *as*      *as*
words here and there, the great bulk of their word stock came

*as*      *o*      *o*      *as*      *o*      *o*   *as*      *as*      *as*      *o*
to them directly from Proto-Germanic, and most of Proto-

*o*      *as*      *as*      *o*   *o*
Germanic came from Indo-European.

We are now ready to look at the paragraph above. The first
result is obvious; the *as*'s predominate. That is, in this passage
more words come from Anglo-Saxon than from all other sources
combined. The subject matter influences these results a little;
had the subject been *pterodactyls* instead of *words*, the *pterodactyls* would have been marked *o*. On the other hand, had the subject been *farm grains and animals*, there would have been still
more words marked *as*. The linguistic habits of the writer make
some difference, also. The writer could have changed *would require our going* to *would necessitate going*, and thus drop out
one *as* word. Or he could have written *we should have to go*, and

thus drop out one *o* word. But he could not have changed the result much if he had tried, because of the nature of the words themselves.

A little study of this passage will reveal the reason. The bulk of the words marked *o* fall into a few categories. They are learned words, like *Proto-Germanic* and *language;* they are qualifying words, like *fortunately, relatively, surreptitiously;* they are the sort of words used in sophisticated discussion, like *preliminary, question, derivative,* and *dispute.* The words marked *as* include the bulk of the common names for things, like *word* and *neighbor;* the words for customary actions, like *go* and *speak;* the words which have little meaning in themselves, but which are essential to any coherent use of the language, like *a, the, of, from, get, do, had, there.* In short, most of the common words of the language come from Anglo-Saxon; most of the words not from Anglo-Saxon are comparatively uncommon. There are exceptions, of course. *They, their,* and *them* are the most striking exceptions; there are special circumstances accounting for them, to which we shall return. Some borrowed words, like *question,* have become relatively common. But the exceptions are obviously exceptions; the core of functioning English vocabulary is Anglo-Saxon vocabulary.

Just to keep the record straight, we might remind ourselves that counting words in a piece of prose is not the only plausible check of vocabulary. We might, for instance, count a page in a dictionary. Were we to do so, we should get another answer, but we might postpone that test until we have followed further the Anglo-Saxons and the linguistic habits they brought with them.

*Anglo-Saxons* WE HAVE already observed that the some-
*Make* what barbaric farmers who came to the
*Themselves* island of Britain in the fifth and sixth cen-
*at Home* turies were a mixture of West Germanic-
speaking lowlanders, mostly Angles and Saxons. Strictly speaking their language was not Anglo-Saxon and no such language existed; there were only Anglian dialects,

Saxon dialects, and other Germanic dialects, which have descended with variations until this day. But Anglo-Saxon is a convenient term; not everybody knows what it means, but nobody confuses it with anything else, as they do its synonym, *Old English.* "Oh, I just love those Old English novels," an acquaintance of mine gushed, in speaking of Thomas Hardy. At least, nobody thinks Thomas Hardy wrote Anglo-Saxon. Roughly, then, the Hengist and Horsa of the Venerable Bede and all their rude pirate friends spoke what we may call Anglo-Saxon.

They continued to speak it for some hundreds of years, disturbed by nothing more than a few obstreperous Celts and one another's battle-axes. It took them a century or so to drive out or to pacify the Celts. Some of these Celts died in battle; others took sanctuary on convenient islands, Ireland and the Isle of Man, for instance. Some fled to the continent and founded a colony in what is now Brittany—named, presumably, from the British immigrants. But probably most of them stayed on the island of Britain. Those who could not live with the Germans fled to the mountains of Scotland and Wales where the invaders were not disposed to follow. The invaders were farmers, and wooded mountains are not good farming country; besides, it is often unhealthy to go among mountains if somebody on top of the mountain does not like you.

Many Celts stayed where they were, reduced to subsidiary or servile positions under the invaders. Apparently the Germans were not shockingly hard on them, provided they would surrender anything the Germans wanted, especially the best farming land. The Celtic graveyards of the period are in villages up on the hilltops, connected by the ancient Celtic trackways. Down in the rich valleys are the Germanic graveyards. In defense of the invaders one should add, perhaps, that the Celts had not bothered with that land; it was covered with oak trees, which were hard to get rid of, and the Celts had not taken much to farming anyhow. But whether they were treated badly or not, the Celts did not love their Germanic fellow Indo-Europeans. In fact, they seem to have hated them so much that although the

Celts had become Roman Christians they took no chances of seeing any Germans in the Christian heaven. They declined to
convert them to Christianity, thereby dooming them expedi-
tiously to hell.

So the invading Germans fought a slow war of conquest with
the native Celts, and continued fighting small dynastic wars
among themselves after they had subdued the natives. They settled down and became natives themselves, and soon an ancestor
of the English language was the native speech. In all this, they
absorbed almost no Celtic language, as they absorbed no Celtic
religion. Many Celtic names for places survive, mostly old Celtic
roots with Latin endings, now changed beyond all ready recognition; for instance, *Eboracum* became *York*, and *Caer Lugu-
valium* became *Carlisle*. But you can search for hours through a
dictionary without finding any other sort of word which the
Anglo-Saxons in the valleys got from the Celts on the hilltops or
the Celtic servants in the kitchen. A few Celtic words we have.
A few words for place names have become common nouns, *down*
for *hill*, for instance. Later we acquired Celtic words with Celtic
goods. We borrowed Celtic *whisky*, and corrupted the Celtic
word for it, *usquebaugh* (water of life), but all that happened
long after. The early Celts had no whisky to lend. The explanation for the meager Celtic influence upon English supposedly is
that the invaders conquered slowly, keeping their own ranks
intact, taking new land only when they needed it; hence there
were never a few conquering Germans surrounded by large
numbers of native Celts. The Celts who stayed had to learn
Anglo-Saxon; the Germans never bothered to learn Celtic. The
experience of the white people in what became the United States
is somewhat analogous; since on the whole the whites drove the
Indians before them, and kept the Indians in a servile position
and few in number when the two peoples mixed, relatively few
Indian words except place names have found their way into
standard English. Many of our Indian words date from the day
when a small number of white trappers or traders lived in a
predominantly Indian culture. That seemingly did not happen

in Britain; any German who found himself in a predominantly
Celtic culture did not live long.

*The English*
*Language*
*Entertains Some*
*Strong-Minded*
*Relatives*

THUS THE Angles and the Saxons, their
friends and their dialects, became established in England. Christianity eventually
found its way to them in spite of the native
Celts, partly from Ireland and partly from
the Continent. Several relatively large political areas, or kingdoms, took something
like shape on the island. To the north and east were Northumbria
and Mercia, mainly Anglian areas; to the south and west were
various divisions of Saxons; at the extreme southeast tip were the
descendants of the Jutes—whoever they were. They were apparently the first comers among the Germanic people. The Venerable Bede, with a handy etymological guess, said they came
from Jutland, but we now know they did not. The best guess
seems to be that they were professional soldiers—that is, professional international robbers; anyhow, their descendants lived
mostly in what is now Kent. This was the situation when some
strong-minded relatives of the Germanic invaders came to visit.
They announced their arrival by sacking the Abbey of Lindis-
farne late in the eighth century, and not until about the year
900 did the Anglo-Saxons have reason to hope they had stopped
coming.

These guests were some of the same Vikings who figured in
the previous chapter. They came mainly from Norway and Denmark, and they brought with them techniques which the intrepid
northern sailors had worked out. They possessed long, open
boats, pushed by crude sails or manned with long oars. If the
oarsmen were hardy enough, these boats could be taken across
the Atlantic Ocean. And they were, for the oarsmen were hardy.
The combination of boats and boatmen constituted the best navy
in Europe. It constituted, also, a threat to the very existence of
the civilization of western Europe, for once again offense had

advanced faster than defense, and civilization appeared helpless
before the onslaughts of the Nordic seafarers.

They had a tactic. A few boats with a few hundred armed
men would sail into a harbor or row up a river—the shallow
draft of the boats permitted entry, especially at high tide, into
many rivers. The men would land to murder, rape, burn, or
do what they pleased; mainly, of course, they wanted to
rob, but other inconveniences usually attended the robbing.
Before the residents could muster a fighting force, the marauders had filled their boats with plunder and were gone,
ready to sail into another harbor or up another river and repeat
the process.

Against this attack Europe had little defense. The Vikings
overran Ireland, they pillaged all over France, they sacked in
Spain and the Mediterranean areas. For a time they held most
of England. They swept in from the north and east, butchering
and plundering. Men hid in the woods, eating what they could
find, and there were no virgins in the land. How all this was
stopped is not to be told here. Partly, of course, it stopped because
the North ran out of excess Vikings, for in spite of their prowess,
Vikings tended to die suddenly. In England the Norsemen were
stopped partly because King Alfred built a better navy than they
had. On the Continent the feudal system, based upon the fortress,
deterred the Vikings, or Creek Men, by providing a refuge near
the creek. It was a long, complicated, bloody business. But we
are concerned with linguistics, not with bloodletting.

By the end of the ninth century, King Alfred and his West
Saxons had stopped the Vikings in England. By beating them in
battle, by outsmarting them in geopolitics, by converting them
to Christianity and threatening them with the terrors of hell, he
got them to agree, sporadically, to stop looting and settle down.
They had come in such great numbers that they could not be
driven out. They were mostly Danes and, like the Anglo-Saxons,
they were mostly farmers who wanted land. The habitable parts
of the island of Britain—the outlying areas harbored only wolves,
Welshmen, and Scotsmen, who did not count—were divided

along a line running roughly from modern London to modern
Liverpool, which just happened to be about the line between the
Anglian-speaking and the Saxon-speaking groups. The area to
the northeast of this line became Danelaw, the country in which
the law of the Danes was the law of the land, the country in
which the Vikings could do as they pleased; the area to the southwest remained Saxon.

This line is the line of cleavage of British dialects until this
day. To the south and west are forms descending from the Saxon
dialects. To the north and east the forms descend from Anglian,
as these have been altered, corrupted, and augmented with influence from Old Norse. Most medieval works composed in the
north can be recognized at once, not only by grammatical differences, but also by the Norse words in the vocabulary. Many
of these words have been lost in Modern English or are preserved
only in certain dialects not now considered standard English,
which has descended mainly from the dialect of London (*bushy*
in southern England can be *bosky* in the north), but to see how
Viking influence upon vocabulary has persisted, one has only
to look at a map of Britain. In Anglo-Saxon a common word for
an inhabited place was *tun,* which in Modern English can appear as *town, ton, don, dun,* and the like. A corresponding word
in Old Norse is *ham.* A glance at the map will show that southern
and western areas are seeded with *Wimbledon, Brighton, Taun-
ton, Swindon.* In the occasional occurrences of *ham* in the south,
as in *Hampton, Southampton, ham* is presumably the Anglo-
Saxon word for *home,* or a similar word meaning "meadow" or
"river land," which did not come from Old Norse. To the north
are *Nottingham, Birmingham, Durham,* and *Bullingham,* and
in a truly Danish area, *North Ham, South Ham,* and *West Ham*
surround *Ham.*

In this manner the Vikings left a lasting imprint upon the
language of Britain, partly because so many of them stayed, and
stayed clustered in their own little groups, partly because they
were so important—after all, King Canute was King of Denmark
before he was King of England—and partly because the lan-

guages of the invaders and the invaded were so similar that subsequent inhabitants of Britain did not always know whether they were talking North Germanic Old Norse or West Germanic Anglo-Saxon. Nor do we always know. For instance, most dictionaries say that the origin of our word *gutter* was Old French *goutiere*, from a word meaning "a drop" (Modern French *goutte*), which has certainly given us English *gout*. But it could also have come from an Old Norse word. When Robert Mannyng of Brunne wrote:

"He toke the gate and went thru the gate"

he means to say that a man walked along the path (Old Norse *gata*) and went through the gate (Anglo-Saxon *gæt*).* We should note, furthermore, that the nominative masculine form of the word *gata* in Old Norse ended in *r*, that is, *gatr*, and that if Robert Mannyng had been trying to write this sound he would probably have written *gater* or *gutter*, just as we do. Did the Old Norse word for path, *gatr*, become the path along the side of the street, where, when there was water, the water ran? Or did the Old French *goutiere*, a trough to catch the drops from the eaves, become a place for water to run along a road as well as a way for water to run along a house? The answer is not easy. Often we do not know whether we are speaking Old Norse or not.

The most spectacular borrowing from Old Norse is probably that to be found in the Modern English plural third person pronoun. The Anglo-Saxon pronouns *hie, hiera, heom, hie* became so corrupted that they were readily confused with singulars (the nominative plural became *he*, identical with the masculine singular; the possessive became *her*, identical with the feminine singular; the dative and accusative merged and became *hem*, identical with a variant spelling of *him*). When this happened, speakers of Middle English gradually adopted the Old Norse plural pronoun, which has given us our *they, their, them*.

---

* The ligature *æ* is an Anglo-Saxon spelling roughly equivalent to the modern sound of *a* in *hat*.

*And Now the*
*Sophisticated*
*Cousins*
*Come*

No SOONER had the Angles and Saxons learned to live more or less at ease with their obstreperous relatives from the North, than more relatives arrived, beginning in the summer of 1066. These, too, were Vikings, but they had been living in France and had become sophisticated. Or somewhat sophisticated. They had not been tractable folk when they arrived. They had harried widely and laid siege to Paris. They finally agreed to being bought off, accepting a large chunk of France on the promise of keeping other Vikings out of that country. The story is that when their leader was asked to kiss the French king's foot in sign of fealty he picked it up so high the king went over backward. After they settled in France these reformed Vikings learned to talk French of a sort, greedily acquired the advantages of western European culture, and proceeded to set up a Norman empire which was eventually to stretch from Scotland to Sicily. They took advantage of some dynastic changes on the neighboring island of Britain—their home was just across the channel from England in what is still called Normandy—moved in rapidly, defeated a hastily gathered army near Hastings, and established themselves, under William the Conqueror, as rulers of the country.

The victors acted like the winners in a political election. There was little raping or pillaging. Anybody who accepted the results of the hustings at Hastings was allowed to go about his business. Many an Englishman probably did not notice the change much more than many a Democrat does when the Republicans come in. Of course the winners appropriated all of the best jobs, including the important posts in the church and in education, which was part of the church, as well as in government. Norman Frenchmen became the governors, the administrators, the preachers, the teachers, the big landowners, and the like. These people used French, and forced those who dealt with them to use French —or rather, the Scandinavianized French which we call Anglo-Norman. Meanwhile, intellectual matters were in the hands of the Universal Church, which wrote and even spoke Latin. English, as a written language, almost disappeared.

Anyone examining the preserved writings of this time, and making up his mind solely on bulk and importance of written work, would inevitably conclude that the English people must thereafter have spoken French or Latin or some kind of mixture of them. Letters were written in French, cases at law were conducted in French, sermons were delivered in French, handbooks of agriculture and conduct were written in French, stories were told in French. Meanwhile, learned disquisitions were conducted in Latin, the schools were based upon Latin, and great international works like Geoffrey of Monmouth's *History of the Kings of Britain*, which was known and venerated all over Europe, were written in Latin. Only stray pieces of script have been preserved from that time of anything that stems from Anglo-Saxon, and these, like Lawman's *Brut*, were even then little known.

But what happened? English survived to become again the official language of England, and all the works written in French or Latin, if they any longer had an importance, had to be translated into Middle English. Obviously most Englishmen must have gone right on talking Anglo-Saxon while they wrote French. Or at least their wives went on talking Anglo-Saxon, and little Athelwold learned Anglo-Saxon as he learned to toddle. Little Athelwold's daddy, if he had to sue his neighbor, may have sued him in French, and he prayed to the Virgin Mary in Latin; but when he spanked little Athelwold he spanked him in Anglo-Saxon, and the evidence that he did is all over the language. The words *bottom*, *buttocks*, *butt*, and *rump* are all from Germanic roots, along with some other terms now considered vulgar.

Furthermore, the impact of the Norman French upon the English language was much slighter than is commonly supposed. A very large percentage of the words in any dictionary came into English from Latin or Greek, and many of them by way of French. The natural assumption has been that William the Conqueror and his Normans brought these words along with him. The argument—or the presumption, for supposed truth was long taken for granted—ran somewhat as follows: English vocabulary is heavily French; the Normans conquered England; the Normans spoke French; *ergo* the conquering Normans forced their

French vocabulary upon the English people. This assumption is written into many conventional reference works and assumed in most of the others. The most interesting fact about it is that it is not true.

Doubtless the Normans would have been glad to fasten their language on the country. Within limits they tried to. But they were too few, and they were too remote from English life. After a while everybody forgot who had been Normans and who had been Anglo-Saxons, and most people did not care. But meanwhile, little Athelwold had been whopped in Anglo-Saxon, and he learned the language with a sense of intimacy which he never acquired for French. Anyhow, only relatively few Englishmen ever learned French, even Anglo-Norman. Educated people did, of course, but not many people were educated.

This sounds like theorizing. How can we know that French vocabulary in English does not come mainly and directly from the Norman Conquest? In several ways, but here are two.

Comparatively few French words were borrowed into English during Anglo-Norman times, and the great bulk of them were borrowed after French ceased to be spoken as a native language in England. For instance, the following is a tabulation of about a thousand words selected objectively, and arranged by the half century of their first appearance in English, so far as the word is recorded in the *New English Dictionary*. The *New English Dictionary* (1928), in its revised re-issue (1933), called the *Oxford English Dictionary*, is the monumental thirteen-volume work which is the standard authority for the history of English words.

The study was begun many years ago by the distinguished Danish grammarian, Otto Jespersen, and concluded by Professor Albert C. Baugh of the University of Pennsylvania. These men would be the first to point out that the figures cannot be taken at their face value. By these figures, less than one percent (9 out of 1000 words) were borrowed from French into English during the first 134 years of Norman occupancy. This is obviously not correct. Part of the paucity of Anglo-Norman words results, surely, from the scarcity of written Middle English from that

| Date of first appearance in English* | Number of words | Date of first appearance in English | Number of words |
| --- | --- | --- | --- |
| 1050 | 2 | 1451–1500 | 90 |
| 1051–1100 | 0 | 1501–1550 | 62 |
| 1101–1150 | 2 | 1551–1600 | 95 |
| 1151–1200 | 7 | 1601–1650 | 61 |
| 1201–1250 | 35 | 1651–1700 | 37 |
| 1251–1300 | 99 | 1701–1750 | 33 |
| 1301–1350 | 108 | 1751–1800 | 26 |
| 1351–1400 | 198 | 1801–1850 | 46 |
| 1401–1450 | 74 | 1851–1900 | 25 |

period. Furthermore, the results of the *New English Dictionary*, though they reveal a mine of information, are far from complete. The *Middle English Dictionary* now being published will certainly increase this percentage somewhat. But even after all possible qualifications, exceptions, probable errors, and the like have been allowed for, the basic fact remains obvious. The bulk of French words appeared in the English language long after Anglo-Norman was no longer spoken as a native tongue.

Now for the second piece of evidence, which perhaps need not be labored, the more because the evidence requires going into grammatical forms. The words which were borrowed appear mostly in the dialect of the French of Paris, not in the dialect of Normandy, the home of the conquerors. Evidence for a statement like this must inevitably be detailed, but the following may provide an index which is roughly reliable. Anyone who knows Modern French recognizes most of the French words at once. These French words are recognizable because they come mostly from the French of Paris, and standard Modern French also stems from the French of Paris. Words which came into English from Anglo-Norman are often not readily recognizable as French. For instance, our word *carrefour*, a square or crossroads,

* From *History of the English Language* by Albert C. Baugh. Copyright 1935 by Appleton-Century-Crofts, Inc. Used by permission.

comes to us from something like standard Old French. But the main intersection in the old town of Oxford, England, is called Carfax, somewhat to the wonder of some local people who associate the word by folk etymology with *car tracks*, although there are no car tracks there. The explanation is that this place name preserves the Anglo-Norman form, sometimes spelled *carfoukes*, from Medieval Latin *quadrifurcus*, having four forks. And so it goes. The bulk of the French words which we use today did not come into English in Anglo-Norman times, and when they did come, they came in a form the Normans in England would never have used—the whole of France laughed at the way those Hrolf-come-lately Norsemen tried to talk French. Only the exceptions, like *Carfax*, are Anglo-Norman.

The Norman Conquest ended the direct invasions of the English language by military means. The effects of both the Viking and Norman invasions, as invasions, were meager in language, much more meager than most people suppose. The Viking invasion eventually affected the language, not because the Danes invaded, but because so many of them settled down. The Norman Conquest had great indirect effect, because Normans cemented English connections with the Continent; the invasion was followed by a flow of Continental goods and fashions, and these eventually brought their words along with them. But the evidence in England as elsewhere is that conquest alone seldom influences language very much. Language is too fundamental, too much rooted in childhood, in the family, in eating and sleeping and making a living, ever to be directly influenced much by war. Language grows from life, not from death.

*The Peaceful Cousins*   MOST OF the relatives of English have remained peacefully at home, minding their own meanings. If they have come to English speech, they have done so through the ordinary channels of interlingual exchange. To understand their impact upon our language we must become acquainted with the concept of *cognates*. The word means "born together," and it refers specifically to words which have descended in various languages from a common parent. Naturally, any word in English which has descended through Anglo-Saxon from Indo-European is likely to have sisters, cousins, and aunts scattered over a fair share of the civilized world. Any of tens of thousands of examples would suffice, but let us take the word *mother*.

This word certainly occurred in Indo-European, supposedly in a form something like *\*mater.\** If so, Latin has preserved it intact. The Greek *meter* is not much different, nor is the Celtic *maither*—Celtic is etymologically close to Latin. Sanskrit has *matar;* Slavic, *mati* and *mote*. The Proto-Germanic form must have been something like *\*modor*, judging from the occurrence of the word in Old High German, Plattdeutsch, and Old Norse; German *Mutter* and English *mother* develop from Old High German *mouter* and Anglo-Saxon *modor* respectively. Thus, modern equivalents of *mother* like French *mère*, German *Mutter*, and Spanish *madre* are cognates, distant cousins which have all descended from old great-grandmother Indo-European, each through its own line of descent by the various aunts and uncles.

Sometimes the cousins go visiting, in entirely peaceful ways. *Maternal* obviously comes from *mater*, and thus an English-speaking mother can have either of two cognate forms applied to her; she may be *maternal* from the Latin or *motherly* from the English. The synonyms *matriarchy* and *Mutterrecht* are cognates from Greek and German respectively. *Maiden* and *matron*, though to a degree antonyms, can probably be traced to the same root. Our dictionaries and our language are scattered with the cousins, the second cousins, the third, eighth and tenth cousins of English, many of them readily recognizable, but many of them obscure to all but the experts. They are numerous, so numerous that most of the English vocabulary which has not come directly from Indo-European by way of Anglo-Saxon has come indirectly from Indo-European by way of some more or

* The asterisk before *\*mater* is intended to indicate that the form does not occur in any extant manuscript, but has been inferred from what it has done, very much as atoms are inferred from what they do. In this book all inferred forms will be preceded by an asterisk.

less distant relative. English is deeply indebted to its far-flung linguistic family.

To understand what has happened to these distant cousins of English and to our native words, we should inquire a little more into the ways of a man with a word.

## ℳ 4 ℳ

## AMOEBAS IN THE DICTIONARY

OUT OF ONE, MANY—THE WAY OF A MAN WITH A WORD—
AMOEBAS AND REVERSE AMOEBAS—SELF-DETERMINATION FOR
AMOEBAS—MORALS AND THE PRIVATE LIFE OF THE AMOEBA
—THE AMOEBA AND GOOD CLEAN FUN—AMOEBAS AT WORK
AND PLAY

*Out of One,*
*Many*

ANYONE who has considered the statements at the end of the previous chapter must realize that something extremely important has been omitted. Vocabulary, and especially English vocabulary, cannot be so simple as those statements imply.

Whether the English word stock is or is not the largest, most varied, and most exact body of words which has ever been available to the speakers of a single language, we need not inquire. Certainly, the English vocabulary is one of the extraordinary achievements of the human mind, far more awesome—wonderful in the pure sense of that word—than were the seven wonders of the world recognized by the ancients. How large is it? No one knows, but a good so-called unabridged dictionary contains approximately half a million entries. This list contains only a modest proportion of the words recorded in all dictionaries—law dictionaries, scientific dictionaries, technical dictionaries, dictionaries of colloquialisms, and the like.

Three quarters of a million? That would seem conservative, and we still have to define *a word.* Some of these so-called "words," forms which have come to us with some continuity, have many uses. If one thinks of these words as the carriers of units of meaning, then many of the words single in form become multiple in use and meaning. Many words have dozens of meanings. If anyone has seriously tried to total all the words, in the sense of named meanings, in the language, this writer is unaware of the effort. A rough check of random sections in various dictionaries suggests that we may safely say there are more than twice as many named meanings in English as there are recognized words. How many named meanings does a writer of English have before him, then, when he tries to compose a sentence? Two million? Certainly there are many times what any human being could ever learn, or learn to use. And yet we are constantly obtaining new words.

Nor is our vocabulary remarkable only for its size. Probably no other language has had so many and such varied synonyms. Practically speaking, English is the only language which has supported separate books of synonyms. We have synonym books of several sorts, and Roget's *Thesaurus*, an awkward book nowhere nearly so easy to use as it could be, has been sold in millions of copies. In most languages, on the other hand, there are no synonym books. Most speakers of other languages are not aware that such books exist. Even for French and German, for which books of synonyms have been prepared, few prospective users have bothered to buy even one synonym book. An American editor is likely to have several on his desk.

And has this wealth and variety of vocabulary come mainly from Indo-European? If so, strange doings must be implied in those innocent-looking words, *come from*, because the Indo-European vocabulary could not have been large. Primitive peoples generally show great ingenuity in saying anything they have to say, but they do not usually have large vocabularies with which to say it. That the Indo-European vocabulary was small we infer, just as the language itself is inferred. But survivals through extant languages permit us to assert with great confidence that our inference is correct.

How, THEN, have these few thousand Indo-European words, based upon a few hundred Indo-European roots, been blown up into hundreds of thousands of named meanings?

The answer is that this is the sort of thing human beings do. Creating new meanings and juggling old words so that they can bear these meanings are part of the whole complex of being human. It is the way our minds and our social intercourse work. Much speculation and investigation have gone into the understanding of this process; in any final sense we do not understand it, and probably never shall, but we have an immense body of fact concerning it, and we have plausible statements of what seem to be the laws governing these mountains of fact and the principles which bring order among them.

Before we talk about principles, we should perhaps look at a few of the words which illustrate those principles. Any common word would suffice for our first example, one such as *tap*. Presumably the syllable came from an Indo-European base resembling *\*dap*, "something cut out," from a base like *\*dai*, "to cut" or "to tear." By the time this word got into Anglo-Saxon as *tæppe*, it meant "something cut out and used to stop a hole." Anglo-Saxon also had a verb form corresponding to this, as did many other Germanic languages, which meant "to draw forth liquid by means of a tap." By Middle English times the situation had become complicated, for a new word *tappe* appeared, a noun meaning "a light sound," or "a light blow which would produce the sound"; there was also a verb meaning "to give a light blow." Thus, when King Arthur split a giant from head to crotch with one stroke, and buried the axe deep in the ground, the writer could remark, "It was not a light tap." No one knows where this word *tap* came from. In Middle English it was imported from Old French *tapper*, but where did the French get the word? They may have used it in imitation of the sound of a light blow, but there are, in various Germanic dialects, enough similar words meaning "to strike a blow" so that there is at least strong suspicion that the French word came from a Germanic dialect, perhaps by way of the Low Countries. Meanwhile, a *tap* in a bunghole had to be pounded in, and usually *tapped* sideways to get it out; no doubt the association helped.

Thus, by Middle English times the word *tap* could mean "to pound in" or "to draw out" and it could mean also the names of these actions and the names of a number of things connected with these actions. Now things start happening to this word. The sort of tap which is also a spigot was so convenient that it started replacing other taps, and when running fluids became essential to industry and to modern living, taps became faucets but were still called taps, and the stuff which comes out of taps, *tap water*. These taps are not tapped at all, in the sense of being pounded; they are screwed with a thread. Consequently we now have implements for inside threading, whether or not a tap in the sense of "a faucet" is to be attached by the threads, and these implements are taps: *hand taps, machine taps, taper taps, plug taps, bottoming taps, pipe taps, collapsing taps, tap chucks, tap extractors, tap reamers, tap grinders, tap gauges,* and so on, ad infinitum, even to *tapper taps,* in which the two types of *tap* fall together again. A *tapping hole* can be distinguished from a *clearing hole*—it is now a question of size—and a *taplet* is at first a small tap, and then becomes no tap at all, but an insulator. Meanwhile in England, the place where liquor is drawn becomes a *tap,* a *taphouse,* or a *taproom,* the woman who draws the liquor a *tapstress,* and the imbiber who swallows too much is in slang *tap-shackled.* To acquire liquid refreshment surreptitiously is to *tap the admiral,* the legend being that a dead admiral was brought home by sea preserved in alcohol, or rather he was preserved until the sailors drew off the liquor and consumed it.

But this is only the beginning. Not only are there many more sorts of tap which represent objects, sights, or sounds; the word *tap* is used figuratively. One can make an opening in order to *tap.* A railroad *taps* a productive area, and the railroad line which runs into the area is called a *tap line.* Resources can be *tapped.* Even mental, moral, and physical resources can be tapped. A water main can be *tapped* to divide its flow, and a telephone wire can be *tapped* to obtain information. Because the funeral sound for a soldier was a tap on a drum, a bugle call became *taps,* a

piece of music became *taps,* and *it's taps for him* can be an indication of certain death. A patch fastened on the bottom of a shoe
with taps became a *tap,* a leather-thick layer of liquor in the
bottom of a glass a *heeltap,* and the dancer who taps with the
metal taps on his shoes is a *tap dancer.* One was *tapped* for Bones,
the senior society at Yale, physically tapped, and now one can be
*tapped* for any kind of appointment, and the *tapping* can be done
by long-distance telephone. Anything ready to be tapped is
*on tap,* whether the commodity be beer or gossip. And so it goes.

One meaning of a word leads to another meaning; words
which were separate fall together and become indistinguishable;
new meanings lead to other new meanings. Some meanings disappear, and from some meanings, perhaps very minor meanings
on the periphery of the whole body of meaning of a word, will
suddenly blossom new meanings of various sorts and in considerable number. A change in society has created a demand for
new words; we get the new words by juggling the old ones.

Psychologically, what has happened? How have we been able
to make an old word serve a new purpose, take on a new meaning? Scrutiny of the uses of *tap* will suggest that two complementary changes operate with overwhelming frequency. For
instance, to *tap* means to draw liquor out of a barrel by means
of a bung-stop. By extension, by generalizing this idea, to *tap*
means to draw upon any resources whatever by making an actual
or an imaginary opening into these resources. That is, a concrete
or specific object or action has been seen in its general aspect,
and the word for the concrete thing now becomes a word for
a generality.

This tendency can be observed constantly. The Nazi army
developed a highly successful land offense, which they called
*Blitzkrieg,* that is, "lightning-war." We adopted the word to describe the tactic, and promptly made a verb of it: *Rommel blitz-
kriegs Monty.* But the word was too long, so that soon we had
*Monty blitzes Rommel.* The word was handy, too handy to be
left only to military opponents, and soon one prize fighter could
*blitz* another by hitting him on the jaw. The German word for
*lightning* had become an American verb describing any fast,

devastating attack. At this writing the word seems to be dying, but if it had enjoyed more support, critics would now presumably be *blitzing* novels and Senator A. would be *blitzing* Senator B.'s bill. This sort of change in meaning is called *generalization*.

There is an opposite tendency. Since a *tap* was an object to keep liquor in its container, but could also be the means of letting liquor out, the instrument which regulated the flow of liquor by turning a handle became a *tap*. As we have said earlier, this taproom convenience came into great demand with modern plumbing and with the use of flowing liquids in industry. Most taps were threaded into the inside of pipes, and accordingly all instruments for cutting an inside screw were *taps*. Here, by a series of changes, the word for a relatively general concept has become the name of a highly specialized, specific object. The word for the general thing has become the word also for a particular part of the general concept, or for an object used in connection with something already associated with the word. If the word alone cannot be made sufficiently specific it is combined with another, and a *tapper tap* becomes a particular type of tap. Like generalization, this tendency, *specialization*, is always with us. A *shrimp* gets its name from an Anglo-Saxon word meaning "shriveled"—specialization from the concept of being shriveled to an object which looks shriveled. But a shrimp is an insignificant creature and the word sounds insignificant. Thus *shrimp* applied to a human being becomes an insult, specialization of the idea of insignificance. My class in phonetics calls one of the phonetic symbols which troubles them [ɔ] "the little shrimp." Unaware that *shrimp* etymologically means "shriveled," they specialized on the fact that a shrimp is curved.

This long dissertation on the word *tap*, then, illustrates two of the principles we spoke of on page 54: new words and new meanings for words are added to the language both by specialization and by generalization.

In short, words, like amoebas, those amazing one-celled creatures which are constantly pulling themselves in two and swimming off in all directions, are none the worse for the dissection. Our dictionaries are full of amoebas; generalization and specialization are two of the principal means by which they bisect themselves.

*Amoebas*          LET US now check these results against
*and Reverse*      another word, and we may as well choose
*Amoebas*          *pick.* It seems not to have been traced to
                   Indo-European, but it is early, because it
                   exists in languages from Italic, Celtic, and
Proto-Germanic forebears. In English it appears in three forms, presumably descending from Anglo-Saxon and Old French, *pick*, *pike*, and *peak*. It was always associated with sharp-pointed things, or with the use of them. For instance, the form *pike* became associated with a long weapon having a sharp end (specialization); a *pike* was a sharp-pointed fish (further specialization); the young of a pike was a *pickerel,* and in the United States this word is used for a pikelike fish of a smaller species (further specialization); thence the *pickerelweed* (still further specialization); and from that the *pickerelweed family* (generalization). *Pike* became a proper name, attached to *Pike County* (specialization); Pike County folk moved West, and soon almost any Western song could be called a *Pike County ballad* (specialization followed by generalization). Meanwhile, a man named Zebulon Pike climbed a mountain which became *Pike's Peak,* and two of the forms of *pick* have come back together again (specialization associated with a historical event).

The verb *pick* meant, as it still does, "to use a pick to make a hole or series of holes." It meant to remove with a sharp instrument (generalization), or to remove by any means (further generalization), for to *pick* a goose was to pluck it; it could mean to remove, not to get something disposed of, but to acquire it, as in *pick* cotton (further generalization); it meant the thing picked (specialization), as in *this year's pick of cotton;* it meant anything selected, as in *the pick of the crop* (another kind of specialization). At the same time, things were happening to the *pick* which meant "a sharp instrument." All sorts of sharp instruments developed, *toothpicks, gravel picks,* even a *lock pick* (specialization); but since a *lock pick* was used to open a lock, opening a lock by any means, a hairpin or a delicate ear listening to the tumblers, became *picking a lock* (generalization). Meanwhile *pick* as a verb developed a great variety of meanings when used in combination with other words. You can *pick up* some spare change or some excess weight; in neither of these expressions does *pick* mean "to pick," or even "to pick up" in the sense of "to lift." Little Johnny can *pick on* schoolmate Jimmy and his soldier brother may *pick off* an enemy sniper.

This alternation between generalization and specialization is so common that probably no one can imagine how common it is unless he will try it on a dictionary himself. Choose almost any word. For instance, *hackneyed*. The word *Hackney* referred to a gentle-paced horse named from Hackney, England, and the horse was used with a carriage for hire, which became a *hackney coach*. The coach horse was often worn out with use, and *hackneyed* came to mean "worn-out," whether the thing worn-out was a much-used horse or a much-used epigram. A *hack* could be a vehicle drawn by a Hackney, a horse worn out by horse jockeys, or a piece of music worn out by disk jockeys. *Hack writers* engendered *hack writing*, and when carriages gave way to taxis, the taxis, too, became *hacks*, at least colloquially. Since *hack* meant a horse for hire, in slang a woman for hire was also a *hack*. Generalization and specialization, specialization and generalization—they alternate and combine in bewildering variety.

*Self-*
*Determination*
*for Amoebas*

In all this confusion of making new meanings for old words, and in borrowing words from other languages, there are inevitable duplications. Often we find ourselves with two words for a single meaning, *drinkable* and *potable*, *eatable* and *edible*, *naked* and *nude*. Often these words, like the second and third pairs given here, are merely the same word in two different languages; that is, they are the peculiar sort of cognates called *doublets*. Sometimes they live along with very little difference in meaning, though there may be a difference in the way the words are used; a child would be likely to say *eatable*, but a botanist would refer to *edible* varieties of mushrooms. A statue may be *nude*, but it is almost never *naked*; conversely we do not use *nude* as a substitute in the phrase *the naked truth*.

But very frequently words originally identical in meaning, which are the two words for the same object in two languages, or which develop within a language because there are two pronunciations, will diverge and become specialized. For instance, a word spelled something like *skyrte* appears in both Anglo-Saxon and Old Norse, and from those languages both words got into Middle English as synonymous words for a kind of short kirtle. Subsequently, however, the two forms fell apart, the Old Norse form giving us *skirt*, the Anglo-Saxon form *shirt*. Similarly, *tow* and *tug* are the same words, the first from Anglo-Saxon, the second from Old Norse. *Zealous* and *jealous* are the same words from Latin and French, both borrowed, as are *native* and *naïve*. Developing from within English, *unknown* and *uncouth* are merely two past participles of the same Anglo-Saxon verb; *uncouth* apparently developed from the idea that the unknown person comes from the country or from another land, and hence does not know local customs.

Thus there is a strong tendency observable in language—not only in the English language, of course, but in all language—to differentiate words which seem to duplicate each other. And this is another of the principles we are seeking to illustrate: that new words and new meanings for words are added to the language by *differentiation* or *divergence*. By means of this device we have made our language more precise than it could otherwise have been, and we are busy making it still more precise.

Amoebas, once they have themselves well pulled in two, go their ways—they practice divorce, but no remarriage. Not so with words. They also combine to form new words, and in English and its ancestors this combining has been going on for so long that much of the evidence of these marryings is now obscured. Anglo-Saxons, for instance, early acquired the Latin word *campus*, "field," which they reduced to *camp*, "a field of battle." To this word they added a prefix, so that *ge-camp* meant "warfare"; they added a prefix and a suffix, so that *ge-camp-ian* meant "to gain by fighting." With another set of prefixes and suffixes *un-camp-rof*, literally *not-fight-strong*, meant "unwarlike," for *camp-ung* had already come to mean "fighting"—and incidentally, of course, *un-war-like* has been made up in the same way since Anglo-Saxon times. A *homelike* girl is not necessarily *homely*, but the two words are the same. *Homely* is only Anglo-Saxon *ham-lic*, somewhat changed by processes which we shall notice in a subsequent chapter. When *homely* became so much changed as to be unrecognizable to most people, and had developed the meaning "ugly," we started the same word all over again with its original meaning in *homelike*.

Nor did this tendency to combine words and pieces of words— a fourth principle in the making of new words and meanings— begin with Anglo-Saxon. Modern English has inherited prefixes and suffixes from Anglo-Saxon, Latin, and Greek, and in such a horde that we have no use for most of them. Some few have remained free compounding elements, so that we still make new words with them at will. If we wish to say "about six o'clock" we have no hesitation in coining *sixish*. The army has lately devised *reembus* meaning "to get back into a bus." If we develop planes faster than sound we take the root of the Latin word for "sound," and add a suffix indicating "modification," and turn up with *son-ic;* when the plane flies faster than sound it becomes *super-sonic*. If a boat goes under water it is a *submarine*, and when we build a bigger one it becomes a *super-submarine*, however much that may sound like a contradiction in terms. Thus there are free compounding elements which anybody can use, and all of us do. There are others like *met-, meta-*, which are no longer much used except by scientists, and still others which not even scientists use any more.

Old prefixes and suffixes are now often obscured because sounds have so changed that we no longer recognize certain forms of the adhering particle. In a subsequent chapter we shall have to notice that one sound influences another sound. Thus, the Latin prefix *ad-*, meaning "toward, forward," appears in its normal form in *ad-duce*, meaning "to bring forward," because it is followed by a similar sound, but it appears as *ac-* in *accumulate,* "to bring into a pile"; as *af-* in *affirm,* as *ag-* in *aggravate,* and so on through *al-, an-, ap-, ar-, as-,* and *at-.* Sometimes these important little syllables are difficult to distinguish; Latin *in-,* meaning "not," readily becomes confused with Anglo-Saxon *in-,* meaning "into," and the more because we now freely attach Latin prefixes to Anglo-Saxon words and Anglo-Saxon prefixes to Latin or Greek roots. Similarly, the various possible meanings of *di-* and *de-* are so confused that only an expert can unscramble them—and sometimes the expert cannot. Latin *dis-,* meaning "to separate," as in *dis-member,* can appear as *des-, di-, de-,* forms which readily become confused with Latin *de-* —as in *de-spair,* literally "away from hope," and Greek *di-,* meaning "double," as in *di-graph.* These and more can be confused with syllables which look like them but are no prefixes at all; for instance, *despot* comes through French from a Greek word of similar form meaning "lord, master," although it looks as though it is made up with a prefix.

So we go on making words as we need them, tossing in suffixes, prefixes, and infixes, sometimes recognizing them, sometimes quite unaware that old syllables are encysted in words which to us are now just words. *Mac-adam-iz-ation* is made up of Celtic plus Hebrew plus Greek plus Latin, and the Hebrew and Latin syllables may break down into roots involving other prefixes and suffixes. And of course when we need the word we can coin *re-macadamization,* and then politicians can run for office on an *anti-remacadamization* platform, and refer to the good old *ante-remacadamization* era.

*Morals, and the Private Life of the Amoeba*

THESE ARE not the only ways of a man with a word. Recently I was traveling in rugged country with friends of mine from abroad. We had car trouble and camped near an isolated ranch, although the rancher was a bit surly, probably fearing we might be careless with fire. The next day we drove to the neighboring town, without seeing much of our host, who had left early, but later in the day I noticed two women of our party talking to him. They were eminently respectable women, happily married, and consequently I was not unamused when one of them reported their conversation, beginning, "We were talking to that man we slept with last night. I was glad to find out he's a nice man."

The good lady had forgotten for the moment that *sleep* often does not mean "to sleep," if followed by *with*. This sort of colored use of an innocuous word arises frequently. We need delicate ways of referring to matters which local customs have branded indelicate, and accordingly we find innocent, general, vague words, preferably from a foreign language. Words associated with bodily functions, for instance, are likely to go through rapid changes in respectability. What was once delicately called *toilette*—after all, a lady had to make her toilette—and is now with a new delicacy sometimes called a *powder room*, has run through hundreds of words. The Anglo-Saxons called it respectably a *gong*, that is, a place you go to; currently children say they *have to go*. But the word *gong* became crude, and was replaced with the Latin *necessarium*. If Shakespeare wanted to be a bit vulgar, he called the place a *jakes*, that is, a *Jacks*, the literal equivalent of the modern *John* or *Johnny*. Later the establishment became a *water closet*, as it is now a *bathroom*—what could be more innocent than pure water? But not for long. Soon one had to use the letters, *W.C.* Meanwhile, French slang developed the phrase *lieu de l'anglaise*, that is, *place of the English woman*.

Thus words run afoul of our taboos and when they do, several changes are likely to occur. Words shift in respectability and even lose old meanings or acquire new ones under pressure of the taboo. When there is a taboo against speaking a word, we find another way of saying what we mean. We find a noa-word, *noa* meaning "profane" in Polynesian as *taboo* means "sacred." Thus *gosh*, *darn*, and *Codfish Mighty* appear so that we shall not take the name of the Lord or mention His works in vain, and in order that the devil may not appear when he is named we refer to *the Dickens* and *Old Nick*.

Conversely, words with a bad odor sometimes become de-odorized. *Jazz*, for instance, was formerly a crude term for indulging in an action which in polite society is referred to, if at all, only with such vague Latin terms as *intercourse* and *cohabitation*. There was nothing vague about *jazz* in those days. Most good girls never heard the word and if they did, they never used it. Meanwhile the word had enjoyed a respectable if limited use, mostly among Negroes and Creoles apparently, in connection with music. When Negro music became popular, the respectable use of the word crowded out the vulgar use, though for a time bad boys about the age of puberty could be heard to snicker when a nice girl spoke of *jazzing* something.

Sometimes these changes are slow. When I was a child in the rural Middle West, one did not use the word *bull*. If one had to refer to this necessary beast, it was called *the animal, the* making the designation of *animal* specific. My mother labored to keep us children from saying *bull;* it was a short, handy, expressive word for a prominent part of a dairy community, and in spite of our good intentions it would sometimes slip out. Doubtless she would have felt better if she had known that the etymologists of the day assumed that the word meant only "the roarer." Now it is supposed to stem from *\*bhel-*, meaning "to swell up," and *bull* would thus be cognate with *phallus*. Perhaps my mother was a better etymologist than she knew. Meanwhile, the word *ox* was entirely respectable; it was felt to be not quite synonymous with *bull* since most oxen had been, well—fixed. (We did not like to use the word *castrated*—one said *fixed* if he had to, *cut* being reserved for vulgar speech.) But a respectable and cautious woman like my mother might say *ox* to avoid even the somewhat dubious euphemism, *the animal*. Fortunately she did not know that etymologically *ox* means "the inseminator." The idea of insemination she would never have uttered before her small children with any kind of euphemism.

Very delicate subjects are not the only ones in which words become more or less respectable. Everyone now wants to be *nice,* but formerly *nice* meant "foolish." A *villain* formerly was only a crude fellow who had no manners, because he came from the country, that is, from a *villa*. A *churl* was at one time a very humble freeman, but in other languages *Karl*, the same word as *churl*, could be the name of a king.

Or take the word *boy*. It is used now for a male infant from the time the doctor says, "It's a boy," until the youngster grows to some size, but it is used less and less except in special meanings as the youth approaches manhood. It is mainly associated with infancy, childhood, and early youth, and in this context is one of the much-loved words in the language. It was not always so. The origin is obscure, probably from some Low Germanic word— there are a number of similar forms which mean "young man," "knave," "executioner," and the like. The word appears in Middle English in the fourteenth century, where usually it refers to young men or "bigge boyes," mostly with unsavory suggestions. Servants and scamps, along with some young men whose blood was not blue enough, were *boies*. That boys were not necessarily boys in 1360 is apparent in the *Ludus Coventriae*, where we are warned that "the devyl boyes mot breke youre bonys" (the Devil's servants may break your bones), and in the *Morte d'Arthur* of the same century, in which King Arthur refers to the giants he is fighting as "bare-legyd boyes." Though at this time the root meaning seems to have been something like *servant*, and a common simile for promptness was to be as obedient as a boy to his master, the word was associated also with *beggar, leper, bawd,* and *thief*. A pirate was a boy with a black beard. In some such sense as this, apparently, Pilate's wife used the word in the *York Mysteries*. Being a lady of spirit, she lost her temper with the Beadle, and called him a "whoremongering boy," whereat Pilate, who on another occasion interested himself in the nature of truth, had to rebuke her for her insulting tongue. Not just this, perhaps, did Joseph have in mind, but still he was paying Mary no compliment on her supposed lover when, in the *Ludus Coventriae,* he insisted, "sum boy" all gotten up in clean clothes "began this game," and added in effect, "Now you call him an angel."

Often boys were only young men who had the wrong fathers. Laurence Minot thought things had come to a pretty pass when boys were made knights just because they could break a spear, and in *Wynnere and Wastoure* there is warning that the end of the world is near if "boyes of no blode" can "wedde ladyes" just as they please. The word slowly lost its evil connotations, although as late as 1860 William Hancock could write that the term *Bowery Boys* "is understood as implying the personification of vulgarity of manner, showiness of costume, facility in the use of slang, and mental imbecility generally, in their highest development."

The necessity for personal politeness causes curious shifts in the respectability of words. In Japanese, *my home* must be something like *that miserable old pig-sty*, whereas *your home* is *the sumptuous palace. My wife* is *the thing in the house,* but *your wife* is *the honorable thing in the house.* For the same reason of politeness, kings have been addressed in the plural. But a device of this sort does not usually long suffice, for flatterers will use the plural to address those who are less than kings, whereat the king must be referred to in the third person. By the time this has gone on long enough the second person singular falls into disuse, and can be revived again as a polite form. This happened in English, and we now address the Deity in the second person singular, with *Thou,* a term formerly appropriate for servants, which, at the time of the King James translation of the Bible just after 1600, was becoming a term of reverence. There have been similar shifts in French, Spanish, German, and other languages. The conventional polite form in German today is a slight variation upon the third person plural; *Sie sind,* meaning *they are,* is used as though it meant "thou art." Meanwhile to use the singular *du* can be an insult, a sign of long friendship, or a proposal of marriage.

Thus words can alter in respectability as in meaning, for that is another way of a man with a word. We have two fine Latin words for these two principles of language change, *amelioration,* "a getting better," and *pejoration,* "a getting worse."

ANYONE who cares to glance back over the previous examples must be aware that the six tendencies we have identified do not account for everything that has happened in vocabulary. Generalization and specialization unquestionably account for much change of meaning. The great bulk of meanings are either logical enlargements of a meaning already established or they are selections from within the general area of a meaning, with development from within. But not always. Some meanings are radical departures. They appear from some broad jump in logic or relationship.

Notice what happens to parts of the body. Hammers have *heads*, rivers have *mouths*, saws have *teeth*, matched boards have *tongues*, pitchers have *ears*, and books can be *dog-eared*, the sea has *arms*, hills have *shoulders*, boats have *ribs*, sails have *bellies*, tables have *legs*, mountains have *feet*, chairs have *backs*, the earth has *bowels*, and matters have *hearts*. *Skin, bones*, and *flesh* have dozens of uses; in Mexico a small lake is an *ojo*, that is, "an eye," and a hot spring is a *hot eye*. We have invested the world with the familiar parts of our bodies. Conversely, we have described the unfamiliar parts by comparing them to something else; the clavicle is a *key*, and the vermiform appendix *an appendix in the shape of a worm*. The mental processes observable here involve specialization and generalization, but the obvious method of coinage depends upon a comparison, upon a figure of speech. An arm of the sea bears resemblance to a human arm; so does the arm of a chair or the arm of the law, even though the three arms need not resemble each other.

In all these new usages of old words, the mind is more or less at play, giving names by devising figures of speech. *Pike* and *pick* are sharp-pointed implements, but a mountain *peak* is only relatively sharp. Nobody is killed by falling on a mountain peak; he is killed falling off it. We do not know how this usage of *peak* developed, but possibly because somebody, amazed at the abruptness of a mountain, said it was "sharp as a pick." He did not mean it was sharp as a pick, of course. He wanted to say something emphatic, even startling. Similarly, the reporter who wrote that "Kid Rawlings blitzed Henry (Hairy Harry) Scarlatti with a one-two to the jaw" did not literally mean to say that the Kid overran Harry like a wave of tanks hitting Sedan, but he wanted to startle and perhaps delight his readers with a picturesque word. He enjoyed writing *blitzed* and he thought his readers would enjoy reading it. Similarly, whoever thought of "tapping the admiral" enjoyed the phrase and the joke it embodied.

Human minds, at least human minds that are good for much, like to play. They like to play with all sorts of things, and since words are dear to minds, notably with words. The results of the play sometimes become standard speech, and even lose the color they had. Probably few speakers of English now think of the mouth of a river as spewing water into the sea. Other elaborations never gain currency. Once ranch hands had been called *cowboys*, somebody was likely to call them *cowpunchers;* once there were *cowpunchers* there were sure to be *cowpokes, cowprods, cow-* anything else that offered a likely synonym. *Cowpunching* became *cow-walloping.* Soon there were *Pennsylvania cowboys* and *drugstore cowboys*, the latter becoming *lounge lizards* in the evening. And so it goes. "Three cocktails and a chaw of ter-backer" becomes a *Kentucky breakfast* and a dust storm becomes a *Mormon rain.* That is, leaps in semantics take place because people like to play with language, to make similes and concoct epithets, to have fun with the innocent game of juggling words.

Most of these coinages are of brief duration. They are meant to amuse while the blush is on them, and who cares what becomes of them when the blush is off? A joke, to be funny, must be a fresh joke. But some of the jokes attract enough attention to have a short life. They are called *slang.* They may live a few weeks, a few months, a few years. Most of them die, as did *tap the admiral.* It was a good joke, but probably too few people used it—or maybe not enough people could acquire liquor by tapping a keg of alcohol in which a dead admiral was being preserved.

But occasionally a word which has a joking origin fills a need sufficiently so that it lives on. To *bait* someone comes from a figure of speech based upon the ancient sport of bearbaiting, but the word now stands with its own meaning. To *smoke someone out* retains a good bit of its original analogy, but most speakers would probably not hesitate to use the phrase figuratively, and with little thought of its being slang. Not very often, of course, does any semantic joke gain sufficient currency long enough to become part of the recognized body of standard English. But since semantic jokes are legion, only an occasional bit of slang needs to survive in order to provide, over the centuries, a very considerable portion of the language. It may be truly said that slang is never respectable; when it becomes respectable, it is no longer slang.

*Amoebas at Work and Play*

AN AMOEBA is a formless thing which takes many shapes. It moves by thrusting out an arm, and flowing into the arm. It multiplies by pulling itself in two, without permanently diminishing the original. So with words. A meaning may develop on the periphery of the body of meanings associated with a word, and shortly this tentacle-meaning has grown to such proportions that it dwarfs all other meanings. Formerly to say that a writer had a *dry* style was a compliment; the remark meant that the writer had an enviable and difficult type of wit and humor. In the mouths of most young people in the United States today, this is an insult; to these young speakers, *dry* means "dull."

At the same time, however, while one segment of meaning in a word is growing, another meaning-tentacle may wither away. The meaning falls out of use because the object that it implied is also out of use; or because there were two words for the object, and one seemed to be enough; or because the word became vulgar, or became unpopular at the expense of another; or for any combination of all sorts of reasons. As long as human vocabulary rests upon human nature, we must continue ignorant of many of the reasons for the rise or decline of the popularity of certain words—at least until psychologists have learned much more than they know now about why we behave like human beings.

## ❦ 5 ❧

## WHODUNIT? SKELETONS IN THE LINGUISTIC CLOSET

THE LINGUISTIC CHILD, IS HE FATHER TO THE MAN?—MAN,
THE LITTLE MIMIC—TWO CAN BE FUNNIER THAN ONE—THE
GENERATIONS OF ADAM—ETYMOLOGICAL JUST-SO STORIES—
FOLK ETYMOLOGY, OR EVERY MAN A LEXICOGRAPHER

*The Linguistic*    WE HAVE already noted that nobody knows
*Child,*    how language started nor in any final way
*Is He Father*    how it has grown. We know that it filled
*to the Man?*    man's need for communication, and that as
we become more complicated in our lives, it
grows to fill our needs. We have noticed also that the spirit of
play has something to do with our use of language. It may have
had much to do with the early growth of language; some scholars
think it did. It is one of a number of influences at work in the
creation of vocabulary which now seem minor, although they
may not always have been so. These influences still produce occasional picturesque words. They have always produced words, if
we may trust our evidence. Were they always as minor as they
are today? The answer is speculative.

Not always are late purposes early purposes. Looking at language today we must inevitably conclude that the bulk of our
words develop through specialization and generalization, by
combination especially with prefixes and suffixes, that the bulk
of our new words come into being in answer to a semantic need.
We require a name for something, and we find one, usually by
borrowing it or by building it up. But this may not always

71

have been true. In the childhood of the race man had less opportunity to borrow, and he may have been neither so serious nor so logical as he has now become. There are evidences he was not.

If we may consider the problem by an analogy—after all, we have no objectively controlled evidence, and presumably cannot have—there are precedents for hypotheses of this sort. Domesticated animals are now looked upon mainly as part of our economy. They are bred, maintained, and slaughtered for food and raiment. Some few are kept as pets, but even most cats must justify themselves by catching mice; Junior's pup is expected to earn his dog biscuit keeping Junior out of mischief. Cows, sheep, pigs, poultry, and horses, although their masters may look upon them with affection and treat them kindly, are kept and controlled for their utility. It was not always so. Animals were first domesticated, apparently, as pets, with no thought that they were any good to anybody. Doubtless they were "cute." Children loved them. So, to a degree, did adults. Only after the hen had become well established as a pet around the hut did anybody think of stealing her eggs and eating them.

This is no evidence, of course. An analogy of this sort should be used with the greatest caution, for it proves nothing. But it does give us some encouragement to believe in an idea for which we have suggestions anyhow, that purposes other than strict utility may once have played a larger part in the formation of language than they do now. A scientist, entranced with his new discovery, does not babble "ug-ug-ug-ug," and thereafter refer to the device as an "ug-ug." He describes the object in Greek, or his employer names it a *Jadco* (after Jones Aluminum Development Company), and the scientist soberly goes on to the next invention. But in many of our doings with language we can be described only as childlike; we delight in playing with sounds for the fun of it, concocting words like *walkie-talkie* to describe a portable telephone and *creepie-peepie* to describe a portable television camera. In the dawn of the world we may have been more childlike. Wordsworth thought the child was father to the man; in linguistics the child may have been so, more than now appears. Primitive man must have been, as relatively primitive people still are, poetic. The creative qualities of poetry may have entered more largely into early language than they do into the language of a scientific and technical age.

**Man, the
Little Mimic**

WORDSWORTH noted, also, that the child is a little mimic, that he lives

> *As if his whole vocation
> Were endless imitation.*

Certainly in language he loves to imitate. Some children will repeat anything they hear immediately after their elders, with no notion of what it may mean. Most children love to babble—*babble* itself must be an imitative word—and to attach their babblings to their surroundings. It is surely no accident that *mama, papa,* and *baby* (it comes out better in the French *bébé*) are simple repetitions of a simple syllable. Other words are pretty obviously echoes of sounds: *murmur, mutter, bang, ding-dong, cuckoo, whip-poor-will.*

Whether or not an imitative intention created a word, an imitative quality in a word has surely tended to preserve it. We can scarcely doubt that the frequency of words like *squeak, squeal, scream, screech, scrape, scratch,* and *scar* is significant. Surely *hump, dump, jump, slump,* and *bump* have a splendid fitness of sound which must have something to do with their meaning and existence.

Furthermore, there is evidence that we like to repeat sounds; we take especial delight in repeating sounds or parts of sounds which, if they are not clear imitations of another sound, at least suggest by their sound the thing they name. Thus we get *hodge-podge, higgledy-piggledy, harum-scarum, willy-nilly, shilly-shally, heebie-jeebies, hubbub, doodad, hickory dickory dock, best by test, sad sack, mumbo jumbo, nitwit, handy Andy, teensie weensie, honky-tonk, razzle-dazzle, drunk as a skunk*. Currently, rhyme is said to be the basis of Australian gangster argot, as it is of a wave of teen-age slang spoken by the *slick chicks* and *mad lads*. Nor is this tendency peculiar to modern English. German is very fond of the device, particularly in using pairs which are complements or synonyms: *Hulle und Fülle, Schutz und Trutz*. Christ recommended saying *yes, yes*, and *no, no* (Matthew 5:37) as a means of avoiding swearing, and the device of repeating a syllable is common in grammar. Usually the repeated sound is the root (that is, the basic idea) and it may be repeated as a means of suggesting that an action goes on until it achieves a result. Thus Hottentot *go* means "to see," and *go-go* means "to examine," that is, to continue looking until something about the object has been observed. The device was common in Indo-European grammar, and has survived in Latin, Greek, Sanskrit, Gothic, and indirectly in Anglo-Saxon. Gothic had forms like *haithait* and *laiklaik;* similar forms have mostly disappeared from English, although we have words like *goody-goody*, so good as to be too good.

Thus we have at least two tendencies in language which result from an inclination to play with sounds. Naturally, we have fine classical names for them. The making of words by imitating a sound is called *echoism*, or *onomatopeia*, ultimately from two Greek words meaning "to make a name." The inclination to repeat a sound is called *reduplication*, that is, *repetition*. As active agents in the making of modern vocabulary these are certainly minor activities. Whether they played a larger role in earlier aspects of the language is now hard to say; a single syllable in Indo-European can account, through borrowing, development, and descent, for hundreds of words in Modern English. The Indo-European base of *father* (which must have resembled the Latin *pater*) may have been, like *papa*, the result of mimicry, that is, of echoism and reduplication, but it has descendants in many languages, and most of the offspring are no longer recognizable as coming from childish babbling.

*Two Can Be
Funnier
than One*

ANOTHER sort of playing with language which provides us with a modicum of words is the love of sticking words together which have sounds in common. This inclination probably does not account for very much that is basic in the language, but is supposedly prompted by a playful motive. When a modern commentator remarked that the Russians are troubled with an *interferiority complex* he was indulging in an ancient pastime. Lewis Carroll called words like these *portmanteau* words, but the joke has lost some of its force in this country, where the characteristics of collapsible valises are not well known. In the United States words like *slanguage, motel,* and *brunch* are more frequently called *blends.* There has been a recent wave of them, but the urge is nothing new. *Gerrymander* was made up of the name of Governor Eldridge Gerry and the word *salamander;* a juggling of election precincts had produced a map which resembled a griffon-like creature. So we now make words like *alcoholiday, anecdotage, Reno-vate,* and *bumbersoll.* More soberly, we make *autobus* out of *automobile* and *omnibus, dextrose* out of *dextro-glucose, catalo* out of *cattle* and *buffalo.* We even made *futhark* out of the first six letters of the runic alphabet. At this writing there seems to be no limit to the variety of *-burgers* which can be concocted by a blend involving *hamburger.* Perhaps the only impossibility is a *ham-burger,* since a hamburger contains no ham.

*The Generations
of Adam*

"AND ADAM gave names to all the cattle, and to the fowl of the air, and to every beast of the field."

So the Biblical account assures us. The Lord would call forth the beasts and the birds, and presumably the insects and the fish as well, one by one.

And the Lord would say to Adam, "Adam, what do you think that is, the one with the long neck?"

And Adam would say, "Why, Lord, that—that looks to me like a giraffe."

And it was a giraffe, for Adam was a man of very great understanding, not like many of those who came after him in our time, puny of wit.

At least, such seems to have been the Hebraic tradition. Since the time of Adam his children have been less adept at attaching generic names to objects, but the giving of names continues to be a human function. Most of us find that generic names have already been given. We accept the fact that a giraffe is a giraffe, and that Vinylite is Vinylite, even when the name of the object is as fresh as its finish. But we give names to individuals, and sometimes the individual name gets attached to something else.

We eat Boston baked beans, Philadelphia scrapple, and if we can afford it, New York-cut steak. Similarly we have Seneca grass, Johnson grass, Sudan grass, Kentucky bluegrass, Bahama grass, Bermuda grass, French grass, Bengal grass, Spanish grass, Hungarian grass, Grass of the Andes, Grass of Parnassus, grasses without end. Once the Victor Talking Machine Company had popularized its Victrolas, the word went on to become a common noun, and father more common nouns, *victrola records*, *victrola needles*, *victrola cabinets*. The names of important people spread rapidly. *Elizabeth*, *James*, *George*, and *Victoria* are scattered widely because the first two were the names of rulers of England during the explorations of the New World, and the last two during the period of great British colonial expansion. Or consider the strange history of the word *Lincoln*. It comes from something like *Lindum Colum*, the first being an old Celtic word with a Latin ending, the second the Latin name for an outlying place, the same which has given us *colony*. In the Middle Ages Lindum Colum was the name of a town and a shire, and, corrupted to Lincoln, thus could be the name of anybody from those areas. It became the patronymic of a poor settler in Illinois, the name of a great president of the United States, and hence the name of all sorts of places throughout the western part of the country. Having become the name of Lincoln, Nebraska, it is ready to become

part of the names in the city of Lincoln of the Lincoln Ready-
Mix Concrete Company, of the company's product, the Lincoln
Cinder Block, which in turn might become a "Lincoln," or just a
"linc."

This sort of thing has been going on, of course, from the dawn
of time, or at least from the dawn of language, although the evidence is often obscured by linguistic confusions. People need
names for things; the names are given in some sort of logical or
circumstantial way, but even after they are no longer understood
and the logic accordingly obscured, they cling. The map of England writhes with rivers called *Ouse*, because that is an old Celtic
word for *water*. Incoming Germanic people heard the natives
call a river *ouse*, and not knowing that they were just calling it
*the river*, the stream became *Ouse Flood*, literally "river-river."
Thus the name of a stream in Britain can embody two or three
Celtic words for *water*, the syllables left behind by successive
waves of Celts, with an English word added to them.

Similar developments appear in personal names, which in
turn may become place names; and either may become common
nouns. We name boys *John* with no notion that the Hebrew
original of the word meant "the Lord is gracious." If there were
two Johns in a little English community they had to be kept
apart. One would be the *John the Tailor* because of his occupation and the other *John the Black* because of his hair. Or one
might be *John du Field* and the other *John at le Burgh* for *John
from the Country* and *John in Town*, with the English and the
Anglo-Norman all mixed up. Then, when Anglo-Norman
is no longer spoken, and when time has given opportunity
for linguistic changes to obscure the original, the great grand-
sons of the earlier Johns become *John Duffield* and *John At-
tleborough*.

This is not the place for a history of place names. But we
might notice that Adam's propensity for giving names to things
continues, at least in limited ways, and that proper names given
to individual persons and places sometimes go on to become
common parts of the language.

*Etymological*
*Just-So*
*Stories*

UNDOUBTEDLY, some words owe their origin or growth to incidents. During the German occupation of Norway, a little-known person named Vidkun Quisling collaborated with the invaders and was set up as the head of a puppet state. The hardy Norwegians despised him, and *quisling* became a new international word, a common noun for a collaborating traitor. The making of a common noun here involved generalization, of course, but the generalization was occasioned by a historical incident. At this writing Senator Joseph McCarthy, who has gained the reputation of bringing unverified charges against people who may or may not be guilty, seems to be acquiring the questionable honor of bringing the word *McCarthyism* into the language. *Boycott* pretty clearly goes back to an Irish effort to discountenance one Captain Boycott, a land agent. A *locofoco* was a patent match, but it became the name for a non-Tammany Democrat, and eventually the name for any Democrat, after the insurgents had beaten Tammany in a meeting which continued with candles and locofocos after someone had tried to break it up by putting out the other lights. *Mugwump* was Algonquian for *chief*, and had some small currency during the last century as a derogatory slang term for an important person, perhaps because the word sounds impertinent. It was attached as a campaign epithet to those who bolted the Republican Party in 1884, refusing to support James G. Blaine, when Mugwumps were classed with "Pharisees, hypocrites, dudes . . . and transcendentalists." For a time the word was a term for any revolter. Meanwhile a cartoon of the day showing a man-headed bird sitting on a disreputable fence became common as a means of illustrating history books, although the word itself had fallen largely into disuse. Of late, however, it has been revived through a definition attributed to a Congressional wit, that "a mugwump is a bird sitting on the fence with his mug on one side and his wump on the other." Thus a series of incidents has kept the word alive.

Other supposed origins of this sort are less well authenticated. *Buncombe*, later abbreviated to *bunk*, is said to have come from an incident associated with Felix Walker, a representative from North Carolina, sent by a district including Buncombe County. His colleagues, bored by a long speech, tried to stop him, but according to the story he continued, insisting he had to "make a speech for Buncombe," since his constituents in the county would expect him to. This may well have happened, but the story seems to have been unrecorded until some time after the Sixteenth Congress, when the soporific speech is supposed to have been delivered. We know furthermore that stories of this sort spring up with great fertility, sometimes so many stories to account for one word that they cannot all have been true. Lexicographers have become very cautious about accepting these pleasant tales, having learned from a long succession of blunders.

For instance, they continue to enter the word *quiz* in dictionaries as "origin uncertain," or "possibly related to Latin *quis* (what)." And rightly. Not that there are no stories. An Irish actor, for instance, professed to know the origin. According to him a certain producer of plays in Dublin became somewhat intoxicated one night, and wagered that by the next evening, every man, woman, and youth in Dublin would have uttered a word he had never heard before, of which he knew not the meaning, and which indeed had no meaning. The producer roused his billboard plasterers from their beds and sent them out to write four letters, Q-U-I-Z, on every empty space they could find in the town. People asked each other what this scrawled word was, and what it meant. It became the town topic of conversation because it had appeared suddenly, mysteriously, and seemed to mean nothing. Accordingly, the word became a symbol for something unknown, a mystery, and the theatrical producer won his bet—they always win their bets in these stories.

Why not accept an amusing story like this? There are a number of reasons. In the first place, the word seems to show no unusual connection with Ireland; the story is scantily reported and one would expect a good story like this one to have spread rather widely. Furthermore, the word goes back at least to the eighteenth century, a century earlier than the supposed experience of the Irish gentleman. Thus the engaging tale explaining the origin of the mysterious word has its principal use in demonstrating that there are more stories of picturesque etymologies based upon historical incidents than there are etymologies. Most of the tales are part of that charming body of fiction which the human mind has always produced and has always loved. They are folklore.

This, of course, is at variance with the popular impression. Tales like this are pleasant to tell; the few authenticated etymologies of this sort make pleasant reading. Thus books of picturesque etymologies and etymological columns in newspapers are very fond of the words which have come into the language through good stories. And of course more words have started in this way than now appear. Words which had historical origins before historic times may be scattered all through our dictionaries unnoticed. But if so, we have little evidence for them. So far as our evidence allows us to guess, relatively few words grow from single events and those few have attracted disproportionate attention.

*Folk Etymology,* FOLK, OR popular, etymology does not usu-
*or* ally create words, but it provides lore about
*Every Man a* words which is as pleasant as it is unre-
*Lexicographer* liable, and it frequently changes the form
of the words which are its subject. Consider, for instance, the sleepy little limestone village, formerly known as Tete de Mort, which rests in a valley between bluffs on the west side of the Mississippi River. In the early days some Indians killed a French fur trader and thrust his head upon a pole. It was one of the sights on the Upper Mississippi River, and the place was known by the French word for death's-head, *tête de mort*. Many of the early visitors in the area were French, and few wondered at the name. Later came Irish, Germans, and various sorts of Yankees to turn the bluffs into a farming country. What did French mean to these people? Nothing, but here was a name that had to be accounted for. They called the place *Teddymore*,

doubtless assuming that some mythical Teddy Moore had lived there "a long time ago." Similarly, *Mary-la-Bonne* (Mary the Good) becomes *Marylebone* (pronounced as though it were spelled *Marly Bone*), *St. Anne* becomes *Sent Ten*, and *Mean's Well* becomes *Means Well*—after all, to get to the place you take a desert road, which becomes a desert track, which becomes a desert trail, which practically disappears. That the place means well is the most charitable remark one can make.

Foreign words and old words suffer in this way, and since plants, especially domesticated plants, have been great travelers, they suffer accordingly. *Dandelion* represents a stanch British effort to make something of *dent de lion* (lion's tooth). Or consider the way in which the Nahuatl *tomatl* became the English *love apple*. The vegetable was taken from the New World to Spain by Spaniards, and from thence was borrowed into Italian. Since the plant was strange to the Italians, had a fruit something like an apple, and came to them from Spain, they called it *pommo dei Mori* (apple of the Moors). Then the French got the tomato. *Pommo dei Mori* was now mistranslated into *pomme d'amour* (apple of love); when ripe it looks passionate enough, and it was then thought to be poisonous and was used only as a decorative plant anyhow. The English knew enough French to translate the word accurately as *love apple*.

People like to make up, and repeat, stories to account for these fantastic forms, unaware that the forms *are* fantastic, and to account for all sorts of words which seem strange. Take the word *gandy*, which in some areas means any railway track worker. A "long time ago" a Hindu beggar was put off a train out in the West (usually near the home of the storyteller) because he lacked the price of the ticket. He had with him a bear, named for Mohandas Gandhi. Down the track he saw a section crew working, and went with his bear to collect a few pennies. The bear did his act, standing on his hind feet, lumbering in a crude dance, and holding out a cup for coins while the Hindu played a tune. The section crew was replacing some ties, tamping the gravel back around the ties with tamps which they worked up and down with both hands. They looked so much like the clumsy bear that the section boss burst out laughing and called them *Gandhi-dancers*. And that is the way the word got started.

This story is implausible on the face of it, but implausibility never deterred a lover of folk etymologies. There are few Hindu beggars in this country, and they do not transport bears over transcontinental lines—particularly not in passenger coaches, where they find themselves without a ticket for the bear. If the peddler had been a Hindu he would not have pronounced *Gandhi* in any way which to a Western section boss would have sounded like *gandy*. Furthermore, the word *gandy* long antedates the career of the Mahatma. Actually, the explanation is obvious. The tamps used in setting railroad ties were long made by the Gandy Manufacturing Company of Chicago; they had *Gandy* stamped on them. The man who waltzed one of these things about was called a *gandy dancer*, and eventually just a *gandy*. The story about the dancing bear never became very popular; if it had, no doubt the spelling of the word would have tended to become *gandhi*. After all, one must be correct.

People are uncommonly credulous of these tales. Well-educated people, who should know better, will tell you that the Latin-American insult for a *norteamericano*, *gringo*, comes from the following supposed incident. An American sailor in a Latin-American port, joyful at having shore-leave, walked down the gangplank singing "Green Grow the Lilacs." A native, making nothing of the words, thought the song began with the sailor's name for his countrymen, and consequently North Americans were called *gringos*. I have heard educated people defend this etymology with the argument that it seemed very plausible. When I suggested that it was not plausible, they suggested that it was similar to other etymologies—which were, of course, also folk etymologies.

The "gringo" story is anything but convincing. Sailors do traditionally sing songs, but not songs concerning botanical phenomena or the culture of lilacs. Furthermore, South America is a very diverse continent. Is it likely that a random word picked up casually by some wharf rat spread through the jungles of the

Amazon and over the Andes to become the common epithet for a Yankee? And is it likely that this word would then spread north and become so common among Latin-American sections of dwellers in the United States that Audubon's party was "hooted and shouted at . . . and called Gringoes" even before we have the evidence that the song had become popular?

There is no secret about the etymology of the word *gringo*, although it is one of those words about which the public has the vague feeling that nothing is known. It is in all good modern dictionaries. But folk etymologists prefer pleasant fancies to good modern dictionaries. The word is a specialization of Mexican Spanish *gringo*, meaning *gibberish*, and of course to uneducated Mexicans the speech of their nearest neighbors, the *norteamericanos*, is gibberish. Supposedly the word comes from an old form of the Spanish *griego* (a Greek). For very much the reasons that a speaker of English may say, "It's all Greek to me," the Latin Americans must have linked *griego* to *gringo*.

These tales of the *gandy* and the *gringo* represent folk etymology only in a limited sense; the word has presumably given rise to the story, but the story has not in turn influenced the word. Often, folk etymologies do so, as with the barnacle goose. The growth of the word *barnacle* is not quite clear but it stems from a common word for a rather small wild goose, and seems to be the equivalent of "little bare neck," an obvious epithet. The word apparently got into the zoological books in Latin as the name for the goose, where it acquired Latin endings and developed derivative forms in Italian, Portuguese, German, and Danish. Supposedly the word had become attached meanwhile by comparison and specialization to another goose-necked creature which clung to rocks and the bottoms of ships. This marine crustacean was also called a *barnacle*. By this time the name for the goose was no longer recognized, and consequently the *barnacle* which was a goose became the *barnacle goose*. Perhaps because of this reversal from the marine to the ornithological barnacle, folklore began to spring up about the barnacle goose. It came from the barnacle tree which grew on the shores of Ireland. Shellfish clung to this tree as barnacles, and then grew up to be geese. Or the fruits of the tree fell into the water, and became shellfish, and then geese. Or the fruits of the tree just flew away as geese after they had sprouted wings. Thus poor little bare-neck acquired a new name, and became the *tree goose*.

Usually the process is not so elaborate. An archaic or foreign word seems forbidding, and is accordingly changed enough to look and sound familiar. Thus we make the Dutch *pappekak* into *poppycock*, which seems to be composed of English words, and which carries an appropriate air of impertinent banter or patronizing insult. Meanwhile, we are unaware that the Dutch word implied an analogy suggested by its literal meaning, "soft manure."

Such are the linguistic skeletons in the closet of the human race. Many of them can be traced to strange ancestors; others are just there in the closet.

## ⚜ 6 ⚜

## BOTH A BORROWER AND A LENDER BE

BLESSED ARE THE GREEDY FOR WORDS, FOR THEY SHALL HAVE
VOCABULARY—FORGIVE US OUR DEBTS, FOR WE SHALL NOT
PAY THEM—PAY TO THE ORDER OF THE ENGLISH LANGUAGE:
ONE WORD—SHE CALLED HIS NAME GAD: A TROOP COMETH—
AND ALL FROM GRANDMA INDO-EUROPEAN

*Blessed Are*
*the Greedy*
*for Words,*
*for They*
*Shall Have*
*Vocabulary*

"NEITHER a borrower nor a lender be," said Polonius, in one of those triumphs of the folk mind over good sense which have long confused and are likely to continue to confuse modern thinking. Borrowing is and always has been the great fact of civilization. To confess that one has not borrowed other peoples' discoveries is to confess that one knows very little. To say of a people that they have borrowed little is to say that they are barbarians. Dominant cultures everywhere have rested upon borrowing. The great fact of both ethnology and history is that almost everything that any person or any people owns at any one time has been taken from somebody else.

Now, confessedly, I am here using *borrowing* as a sliding middle term, but borrowing is essential to modern life even in the restricted sense in which Polonius presumably used the term, the taking of money on a promise to repay. All modern industry of any size or complexity is based upon borrowed money. In a modern world, most investments must be loans. Without borrowing and lending, automobiles could not be made or sold, airplanes could not be flown. One may disapprove of airplanes and automobiles, but he can scarcely deny that modern society could

85

not exist without borrowing; if one chooses to do without stocks and bonds he must do also without plumbing.

But there are none of the sniveling qualities of Polonius in linguistic borrowing. The linguistic borrower has that fine indifference to distinctions between *meum* and *tuum* lauded by Charles Lamb: "he troubleth you with no receipt." He takes what he wants where he finds it, and assumes that you have served your function in life by being borrowed from. Borrowing in language is almost as important as it is in culture generally, and no language anywhere—or at least none of the great languages now known to us—has borrowed so extensively as has English, nor made such good use of the borrowed products.

*Forgive Us*
*Our Debts,*
*for We Shall*
*Not Pay Them*

IN CHAPTER 3 we noticed that more than half the words as they occur in any passage of ordinary English prose are likely to stem from Anglo-Saxon, and much of Anglo-Saxon comes in direct descent from Indo-European. Now we must notice that if one takes a different approach, and counts the words in an English dictionary, the results are strikingly different. The bulk of the words in the dictionary—almost any dictionary, although of course the results will vary somewhat with the source—do not come from Anglo-Saxon. In one of the large dictionaries like the *New International*, more than half the words are likely to come from Latin, and of these more than half again are likely to come through French. A considerable percentage come directly or indirectly from Greek. A small body of words come from Old Norse, Italian, Spanish, Portuguese, and Dutch; and scattered words come from all over the world, from sources as varied as Algonquian Indian, which through folk etymology gave us *woodchuck*, and African Hottentot, which gave us *gnu*. Depending upon the dictionary, the borrowed element may run as high as eighty or eighty-five per cent of the entries, or, in specialized dictionaries, even more. Thus, although the bulk of the words that most Americans and Britons speak are native Anglo-Saxon words, and more than half the words most of them write are native Anglo-Saxon words, the bulk of the words which comprise the vocabulary of English have been borrowed.

The explanation, of course, stems from observations which appear in a previous chapter. Most of the common words are Anglo-Saxon words. Most of the rare, learned, or highly specialized words are borrowed. Even so, these borrowed words are extremely useful, and they account in large part for the astonishing richness of English vocabulary, for the great variety of synonyms in the language, and thus for our almost unlimited opportunities to use precise terminology. The English language has tremendous debts, debts which there is no immediate prospect of our paying, although English has lately become a great lender of words. Fortunately, we need not pay these debts, for linguistic appropriation presumes no repayment in kind. We have not deprived anyone of anything when we borrowed these words. To parody Shakespeare, Who steals my purse steals trash, but he who filches from me a good word steals that which now enriches him, and leaves me none the poorer.

*Pay to the Order of the English Language: One Word*
How HAS English been able to borrow—appropriate would be a better word—all this tremendous body of nonnative vocabulary? The borrowing started early. When the Angles and Saxons came to the island of Britain they already had with them words which they had picked up here and there. Either they already had the word *street*, or they got it from the Celts. It comes from Latin *strada*, meaning "strewn," supposedly with gravel, and was the Roman word for a prepared road, dating from the time before the Romans had learned paving, when their best roads were graveled. The Saxons may have encountered Roman roads on the Continent. Anyhow, when they got to Britain and found the fine Roman roads there, already designated as *streets* (Watling Street, Ermine Street, Hickenilde Street), the word was retained to describe them, the Germanic words *weg* (way)

and *rad* (road) being used for the humbler Celtic and Anglo-Saxon avenues of transport. The Anglo-Saxons had a few other Latin words also. An Anglo-Saxon *harbor* was any inlet or estuary, but a Latin *port* had some sort of commercial development. Since we have no pre-invasion records it is hard to say whether the Anglo-Saxons acquired these words from Roman traders on the Continent or from Romanized Celts on the island.

The process of appropriation continued. When the Danes and Norwegians moved in, Englishmen borrowed Old Norse words from them. When the Normans became Anglo-Normans, the English borrowed words from these French-speaking Scandinavians. When Christianity became the religion of England as well as the religion of the rest of civilized Europe, the Latin language came with the Latin Church. From all these sources came borrowed words, although not in great numbers during the Anglo-Saxon and early Middle-English periods, that is, speaking roughly, prior to 1250 A.D.

We have had occasion to notice in Chapter 3 that the bulk of the Romance words in English did not come as a direct result of the Norman Conquest. But the great body of borrowed words in English does come from French, or from Latin, the ancestor of French, or from Greek, from which Latin had borrowed extensively. If the Normans did not bring these words, how did they get into English? Before we attempt an answer, let us look at some of the words and at the manner of their borrowing.

Chapter 3 contains a table which suggests roughly the dates at which words were borrowed from French into English. We noticed that the bulk of the words were borrowed after the Anglo-Norman period, long after the Conquest. But during what periods were the words borrowed? Reference to the table will suggest that borrowing from French reached unprecedented proportions during the late thirteenth and fourteenth centuries. Insofar as these statistics are reliable, more words were borrowed in the last half of the thirteenth century (99 as against 46) than in all previous time; more words in the fourteenth century (306 as against 145) than in all previous time; and Englishmen never again borrowed through French with anything like the same abandon. By estimate, some forty per cent of French words now in English came into the language during the period 1250–1400.

We have noticed earlier that these statistics are not entirely reliable. We should now add that the large number of words attributed to the late fourteenth century (198 occurrences, 1351–1400) can be partly explained by the volume of extant fourteenth-century writing. But even when one makes allowances, these figures are still startling enough so that they must be significant. What was happening in England which might account for this flood of French words?

If one were to view anything so complicated as Western European history from a single point of view, then incomparably the best view is something like this: the high civilization of the Golden Circle, that is, the Eastern Mediterranean, moved west to Rome and north across Western Europe. That was the salient fact. The significant fact for the Middle Ages and the Renaissance in England was that the contents of this Mediterranean storehouse of learning, this immense treasure of accumulated human thought and experience, was arriving on the isle of Britain in overwhelming plenty. Some had arrived earlier. The Romans brought a great deal, but the Angles and Saxons, like the semi-barbarians they were, destroyed most of it. As the Anglo-Saxons became exposed to influences from the south, they began to import southern culture, particularly through the medium of the Church. But the trickle was slow, partly because the Anglo-Saxons were not in an advantageous position to receive until they had educated themselves and recovered from the Norse invasions, partly because there were no good channels through which to bring southern culture—France, the natural channel, also was recovering from the Vikings. In the late thirteenth century, southern culture came in an increasing flood which was augmented as a result of the English wars on the Continent, when England occupied considerable sections of France.

In short, when Englishmen imported Continental goods, Continental ideas, and Continental manners, they imported the words for the things along with them. Since the goods came by way of France, they brought French names. This assumption is

supported if we examine the sort of words that were being borrowed at this time. During the fourteenth century, France was
the leader of chivalry, and French armor was standard in England. What form do the words for armor take in English? Except
for a few old general words like *sword* (Anglo-Saxon *swerd* or
*sweord*) they are French. All the words for the new, fashionable
armor were French: *aventail, genouillère, chausses, cuisse, cubi-
tiere, brassart*. Even *armor* itself is French.

And so with other categories of words. Goods and fashions
came from France, and consequently the new stuffs and the new
clothes had French names, even though the words themselves
may have come from the Middle or Far East. *Samite* came from
Medieval Greek *hexamitos* (woven with six threads); *cashmere*
and *shawl* are Persian. But the words arrived in England with
a French form as French words. Similarly, terms for the new
science may have come from an Eastern language, especially
from Arabic, but *alchemy* and *almageste* arrived in England in
a French form. Learning, too, came by way of France, and thus
learned words, particularly theological words, if they do not
remain in Latin, wear a French dress. And of course governmental and legal terms were French, although here the situation
was somewhat different, because Norman French went on being
the language of the law courts long after its use for other purposes
had been abandoned. It got so badly mixed up with English that
it resembled nothing at all but itself, and cases at law could
contain such sentences as the following: "Il jeter un brickbat
que narrowly missed."

This apparently is what happens. Social and commercial intercourse will occasion movement of language, and, in general,
language moves along the current of the goods, not against it.
England was buying French goods, and as a sort of bonus, the
French language or scraps of it came with the goods. Since the
flow of culture was at this time north, not much English flowed
back to France. Meanwhile England was conquering France.
But just as the Normans could not bring the French language to
England by conquering it, the English Black Prince could not

take the English language to France. On the whole the word follows the coin, not the flag.

Movements of this sort have continued. There was another surge of importation of French goods and fashions in the late fifteenth and sixteenth centuries, and again the rise in the body of imported goods, both physical and intellectual, was marked by a rise in the importation of French words. Subsequently Britons have imported French ideas in modest quantities, and French words also in modest quantities. So have the Americans, especially words for cooking and for women's clothes—the more Parisian fashions, the more Parisian words, *couturière, lingerie, ensemble*. We borrow *crêpe de Chine* and do not translate it back into *crape of China;* we borrow *eau de Cologne* (water of Köln) and cut it down to *cologne;* we borrow both the object and the word *brassière;* the object was formerly, in the words of the *Petit Larousse*, "a little camisole to support the bodies of infants," but both the object and the word are now abbreviated to *bra*.

Nor is this phenomenon restricted to importations from France. When Mexican methods in mining and stockbreeding were imported into the southwestern United States, ranching and mining terms came also; *corral, lariat, bonanza, borrasca* were all Spanish words, and when the *vaquero* (buckaroo) or the *barretero* (miner) became *borracho* (drunk), he was thrown into the "hoosegow" (*juzgado*). Japanese have for some time been learning American words, not because of American occupation—for the influx of English into Japan preceded any hostilities between the countries—but because the Japanese were attending American moving pictures, playing American baseball, and imitating American hillbilly songs. When, during the war of the 1940's, American Flying Fortresses were sent to help the Russians, and American mechanics were sent along to teach the Russian mechanics to service the planes, the Americans found that their language difficulties were fewer than had been expected. The Russian mechanics had the names for the parts of the planes; they already knew *spark plug, carburetor, prop*, and so on, having borrowed the American words with the American parts.

*She Called*
*His Name Gad:*
*A Troop*
*Cometh*

WE ARE told on good authority that when Rachel and Leah entered into a jealous contest to produce offspring for Isaac, supplying him with handmaidens when the sources of legitimate offspring proved inadequate, Rachel recovered her poise and her sense of humor, and named one child Gad, which the King James version of the Bible translates, "a troop cometh."

Verily, once borrowing was fairly started into English, a troop came. We have just seen that during the thousand years that speakers of English dialects were in contact with French people and the French tongue, words flooded into English from or through that language. In fact, the English borrowing from the Greek-Latin-French glossarial stream constitutes one of the amazing linguistic phenomena of all time. It will warrant examination, and since the word *glossarial* occurred in the last sentence, we may as well use it as a starting point, though tens of thousands of other starting points would serve as well.

The word goes back to Indo-European, to a base something like *\*glōgh-*, which probably meant "thorn" and became generalized into "a sharp point." With this latter meaning it arrived in Greek as *glōchia*. It arrived, also, in two other forms, Hellenic Greek *glōssa* and Attic Greek *glōtta,* both meaning "tongue," a pointed organ. The witty Greeks had fun with this word; to talk vigorously was to turn your tongue loose and let it go, to gossip was to waggle your tongue until it ached. The idea of "a point" (*\*glōgh-*) became "a tongue" (*glōssa*), "a language" (*glōssa*), "a word in a strange language" (*glōssa*), and the Greeks evolved so many words on the base that the forms occupy more than a column in the fine print of the Liddel-Scott *Greek-English Lexicon.*

The form *glossa* went from Greek into Late Latin in the sense of "a strange word to be explained," became "the explanation of a strange word," and developed a verb *glossare* "to explain a strange word." Soon there was a flood of development. The words may have enjoyed a sparse currency in Anglo-Saxon; they became extremely common in Middle English in forms retaining the Latin meanings, and having meanings also like "explain," "talk nonsense while trying to explain," "try to obscure the truth"—and here the word probably became confused with another word *gloss* from Old Norse, from which we have our word meaning "a superficial finish." Various words based upon Latin *glossa* were popular in Old French, also and probably many of the Middle English "glossa" words either came through Old French or were supplemented from Old French. When Chaucer's Wife of Bath says that learned doctors can "glozen up and down" (by which she meant something like "talk learned nonsense") without being able to prove she should not "wexe and multiplye" even though she indulges in what she calls "octogamye" in the process, she is using *gloze* in a sense which was probably helped along by Old French. But the usage could also have grown directly from Vulgar Latin. Similarly, does our word *glossary*—and hence the word *glossarial* with which we started this spate of words—come from Latin *glossarium* or French *glossarie?* Is *glossator* from Latin *glossator* or French *glossateur?* The usage may be from one and the spelling from the other. The channels of borrowing flow into one another like the bayous of the Mississippi River; and we have no precise way of determining which water is river water and which water bayou water, which words are Latin words influenced by French and which are French words influenced by Latin. There was influence directly from Latin into English, and indirectly from Latin through French. So much we know.

By the end of the Middle Ages, English had a handsome array of words borrowed naturally from Latin *glossa*, either directly or through French. But Latin was the learned language of England, and thus *glossa* became the medical word for *tongue*, and gave rise to dozens of words involved in diseases of the tongue, *glossotomy*, *glossopathy*, *glossoscopy*, and the like. Latin was the language of the life sciences, and thus a bat with a long tongue belongs to the genus *Glossophaga*. Greek, also, was a learned tongue, and Alexander J. Ellis, inventing a system of phonetic spelling, returned to the Hellenic Greek form and called his alphabet *glossic*. Other scientists adopted the Attic Greek form, and the area at the root of the tongue became the *glottis,* with derivatives like *glottal.* Meanwhile still other scientists borrowed the third Greek form, *glŏchis,* with the earlier meaning, "a sharp point," so that anything pointed became *glochidate; glochidium* became the name of a mussel with barbed hair; by generalizing on another characteristic of the glochidium, *glochidial* acquired the meaning "quasi-parasitic." And so on.

Thus for more than two millenniums words have been developing from Indo-European *\*glōgh-*—directly from Greek into English; indirectly from Greek into Latin into English; directly into English from Vulgar Latin or learned Latin; directly from all sorts of French, including various dialects of Old French; and indirectly from Latin and Greek through French and Old French. A chart of this one stream of borrowing would look something like the one on the following page.

The extent and variety of English borrowing from the Classic-Gallic tradition are probably without precedent in the history of language. How has it come about? Many details are obscure and presumably will remain so, but the main outlines are clear enough.

We have already seen that English borrowed from French for centuries, mainly because of close cultural ties. But French itself is a complex language. It grew from Vulgar Latin, but it also borrowed from its cultural creditors, its neighbors, and its classical ancestors on the same principles and in much the same manner as did English. Particularly, French borrowed from Latin and Greek, and from Romance languages like Italian and Spanish, which had both descended from and borrowed from Latin and Greek.

Now, as if this were not enough, English had its own means of borrowing from the classics. We have already noticed that Latin was the language of the Universal Church. Education meant learning Latin, and although most men were not educated, the educated were the eloquent; they were the speakers in public places, the writers of books, the councilors and counselors, and in time they had an effect—the more because, for a time at least, England was a bilingual country, and anybody who knew Anglo-

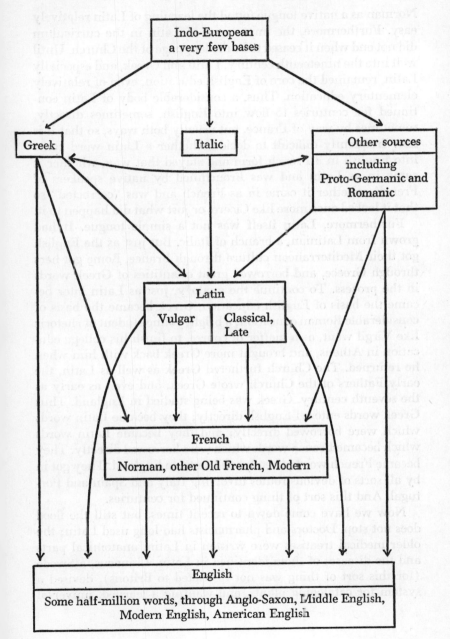

Indo-European
a very few bases

Greek

Italic

Other sources
including
Proto-Germanic and
Romanic

Latin
Vulgar | Classical,
Late

French
Norman, other Old French, Modern

English
Some half-million words, through Anglo-Saxon, Middle English,
Modern English, American English

Norman as a native tongue found the learning of Latin relatively easy. Furthermore, the importance of Latin in the curriculum did not end when it ceased to be the language of the Church. Until well into the nineteenth century, Latin and Greek, and especially Latin, remained the core of English education, even of relatively elementary education. Thus, a considerable body of Latin continued for centuries to flow into English, sometimes directly, sometimes by way of France, but usually both ways, so that it is now frequently difficult to decide whether a Latin word came into English in a French form and stayed that way, whether it came in as Latin and was Frenchified by native speakers of French, whether it came in as French and was "corrected" so that it looked once more like Cicero, or just what did happen to it.

Furthermore, Latin itself was not a simple tongue. It had grown from Latinian, a branch of Italic. But just as the English got their Mediterranean culture through France, Rome got hers through Greece, and borrowed great quantities of Greek words in the process. To continue the analogy, just as Latin later became the basis of English education, Greek became the basis of considerable Roman education; a bright young student of rhetoric like Virgil went, as a matter of course, to finish his college education in Athens, and brought more Greek back with him when he returned. The Church furthered Greek as well as Latin, the early Fathers of the Church wrote Greek, and even as early as the seventh century, Greek was being studied in England. Thus Greek words entered English directly; they became Latin words which were borrowed directly; and they became Latin words which became French words which were borrowed directly. They became French words directly, and came to England. They got in by all sorts of devious routes involving Italy and Spain and Portugal. And this sort of thing continued for centuries.

Now we have come down to recent times, but still the flood does not stop. Doctors and pharmacists had long used Latin; the older medical treatises were written in Latin, anatomical parts and the diseases of them identified in Latin. Linnaeus, a Swede (for this sort of thing was not restricted to Britons), devised a system for cataloging plants, and wanting a learned, universal language in which the words could be given a specific meaning, he gave plants taxonomic descriptions in Latin, which forthwith became their "Latin names," that is, their scientific identifications. This practice became standard in the life sciences, and gave us tens of thousands of Latin words, many of them deliberately coined. Meanwhile, physics and chemistry made great strides, and needing words for new forces and elements, the physical scientists turned to the other great body of unused classical words, the Greek, and used Greek words for new discoveries in the physical world. Thus, if you discover a spruce and your name is Engelmann, the tree becomes *Picea engelmanni*, which is only *Engelmann's spruce* in Latin; if you discover a nonmetallic element and name it *iodine*, you have only called it *looking like a violet*, by giving it a Greek name for the color of its vapor; if you suffer from *pneumonoultramicroscopicsilicovolcanokoniosis*, you may be fatally ill, but your disease is being described in a series of classical syllables.

*And All from
Grandma
Indo-European*

OBVIOUSLY, this sort of thing can become complicated, and not less so because of a curious circumstance. English is an Indo-European language, and has borrowed from its fellow descendants of Proto-Germanic, notably Old Norse, and certain modern descendants like Norwegian, Dutch, and German. It has borrowed extensively from Latin; but Latin descends from Italic, another Indo-European language. It has borrowed from French, Italian, Spanish, and Portuguese, but these are all descendants of Italic through Latin. It has borrowed directly and indirectly from Greek, but Greek, also, descends from Indo-European through Hellenic. In fact, without exception, the languages from which English has borrowed in any quantity are all Indo-European tongues. Even Sanskrit, from which by a political quirk English has borrowed through Anglo-Indian, is an Indo-European language. So are Persian and Russian, from which there have been minor borrowings. And Celtic, of course. By a curious combination of linguistic descent, geographic propinquity, and political hegemony, although most of the English language has been borrowed, it has been borrowed from within the Indo-European language family, the same family from which its native words come.

There are exceptions, of course. A few words like *camel* and many proper names like *Elihu* have come from Hebrew through the Bible and through the long Christian tradition; a few other Hebrew words came through Yiddish, although Yiddish stems from Indo-European through Old High German, and acquired its Hebraic elements by borrowing. Words have come in from various American Indian languages—some, like *potato*, already borrowed through another Indo-European language, not taken directly. There are a number of Arabic words, especially in science (*algebra*) and in music (*lute*). There are a few words from all spots on the earth which have been important culturally—*kimono* from Japan, *taboo* from Polynesia—but the English vocabulary is so overwhelmingly descended from Indo-European that you can check page after page of a dictionary without finding a word which comes from any language outside the great Indo-European family, from the uncles, aunts, and cousins of English.

## 7

# LINGUISTIC ELLIS ISLAND: WHAT CAME IN THE STEERAGE

IMMIGRANTS IN A NEW LAND—THEY SUFFERED A SEA CHANGE
—THE NOBLE REDMAN AS A SORT OF IMMIGRANT

*Immigrants*    IMMIGRANTS are always strangers. And
*in a New*    strange things happen to them, throughout
*Land*    most of the world, and in most of nature.
Words are no exceptions.

    Consider our word *check*. When the Persian game of chess came to the West in the Middle Ages, it brought with it the exclamation of warning and triumph, *Shah mat!*, that is, "the king—he is dead." The term survives in modern *checkmate*. Chess became popular, at least among important people; in the Arthurian romances Gawayne and Launcelot were always at it. The first word of the combination got into common speech, also, meaning "harm, damage, a reverse." It appeared in Old French as *escheque, eschec,* and the like. In Middle English the Old French word was used without the initial syllable, as when, about 1338, Robert Mannyng wrote in his Rhymed Chronicle, "Thou hast broken it alle, & don him many ille check." Meanwhile, words related to *checque* had become names for anything connected with the game of chess. It is said of Sir Tristram that "a checker he fond bi a cheir" (he found a chessboard by a chair), and Guynebands "made with his owne handes a Checker of golde and Ivory." Naturally enough, the checkerboard gave its name to anything having the design of alternate squares, and hence the check pattern in fabrics comes from the dead Persian king. Meanwhile, *check,* meaning "damage," de-

99

veloped the meanings "rebuke" and "control" and Samuel Pepys
records, "I was very angry and . . . did give him a very great
check for it, and so to bed." But if *check* meant "control," it could
also mean "money in control," and accordingly the modern sense
of *exchequer*, probably from French *eschequier* (that with which
one plays chess), had already appeared in Middle English. Langland explains that

Somme seruen the kynge and hus seluer tellen,
In the chekkere and the chauncelrie chalengynge hus dettes.

(*Some serve the king and count his silver, questioning his
debits in the countinghouse and the treasury.*)

Sir Thomas Browne speaks of "Tribute that the swoln floods
render into her chequer." From this meaning a note drawn upon
the funds in check, or control, became itself a *check*, and with the
growth of banking this meaning has now become the dominant
one; the source is the same although the British have reimported
the French spelling *cheque*. Meanwhile another meaning had
started in the Middle Ages, that of a *check-roll*, or *list*. Guild
Records, for instance, require that "euery citezein of the old
checker" (every citizen on the old check-roll) need pay only
seven pence, but that "euery citezein of the newe checker" must
pay thirteen.

Thus the word for *king* in Persian (in modern Persian the king
is still the *shah*) has become the name for a kind of cloth, a piece
of paper worth money, a flick in the margin of a column, the
name of two games (chess, checkers), and dozens of other objects
and activities. Obviously all this has come about in part because,
once the word *eschec* became sufficiently localized so that nobody
thought of it any longer as a foreign word, it developed as any
native word would, by specialization and generalization, by all
the customary growths and changes which are characteristic of
words everywhere. But before this routine development started,
the word went through violent and sudden changes in meaning
and form, presumably because nobody understood the exclama-
tion *Shah mat!* and anybody could interpret it as he pleased.

Nor is this example exceptional, although it is more picturesque than some words. Relatively speaking, a word need not be long in the language to have this sort of thing happen to it. As I am writing this chapter I notice that a candidate for the presidency has remarked that the opposing party "trying to get rid of its Old Guard reminds me of the Australian bushman who got a new boomerang and kept trying to throw the old one away." This was an excellent stroke, but it presumes that the speaker's audience knows the lately borrowed word *boomerang* (from a corruption of a word something like *woo-mur-rang*), and that most of what they think they know about it is erroneous. The boomerang seems mostly to have been used as an erratic missile, hard to dodge. In the hands of an uncommonly skillful thrower it could be made to return. There seems, however, to be no evidence that any bushman so skillful he could make the boomerang return was so gauche as to stick his nose in the way of it. But the idea of a weapon which would return upon the sender has pleased us so much, that the speaker could successfully make his etymologically ill-founded witticism.

What has happened to the Persian *shah mat* and the New South Wales word *woo-mur-rang* is logical enough, but is there any predicting the fate of a semantic immigrant? What, more than another future, is likely to be his? Traditionally a human immigrant to New York was sold the Brooklyn Bridge. What could a linguistic immigrant expect? Since borrowing is still going on, we might look first at what happens to our own emigrants when they become immigrants.

The Mexicans have lately taken up baseball, and you may now read on the sport pages of Mexican newspapers accounts like the following:

El ex-pitcher del Saint Louis tiene enfrente a Ortiz, uno de los lideres jonroneros de la Liga. Tira y el ampayer canta un strike. El manager del Mexico ordena un squeeze-play. Ortiz faulea la segunda bola que lanza hacia el jom Lanier, tratando de bontear, por lo que en el lanzamiento siguiente suelta el palo y saca un lineon que pasa sobre el short. El jardinero izquierdo fildea la bola, . . .

Carl A. Rudisill Library
LENOIR RHYNE COLLEGE

The passage can be translated as follows:

> The ex-pitcher from St. Louis found himself facing Ortiz, one of the leading homerun hitters of the League. He delivered, and the umpire called a strike. The manager of Mexico ordered a squeeze-play. Ortiz fouled the second ball Lanier pitched home, trying to bunt, but with the following pitch he smacked the horsehide and knocked a line drive which passed over short. The left gardener fielded the ball,
>
> . . .

We might notice what the Mexicans seem to have been doing with our words. The words *ex-pitcher, strike, manager, squeeze-play, short,* have been taken over bodily, just as they are spelled in English, although a Mexican would presumably pronounce them differently. *Manager,* for instance, would probably be something like *monna-hair,* and strike, *estree-kay.* It is harder to imagine what a Mexican would make of some of the other words, but doubtless he manages. Some words have been literally translated into Spanish. For instance *jardinero izquierdo* is only a literal translation of the American slang for left fielder, that is, *left gardener.* These words probably represent relatively learned performances which stem either from translated accounts of baseball games in the United States or the inventions of Mexican sport reporters doing their own translating from American newspapers.

Some words seem to have taken a different route. *El jom* and *ampayer* are obvious efforts to spell in Spanish the sounds which were the result of Mexican attempts to imitate the northern sounds which go along with *home* and *umpire.* Words like these may have come through Mexican migratory workers who heard American audiences yell "Kill the umpire" at a ball game, perhaps in towns like El Paso; or they might have come from children or adults who learned to play the game with *norteamericanos* along the border. For some words no such devices were necessary. *Liga* and *bola* are Spanish words, but are here used in special senses borrowed along with the new game; a *bola* is a *ball,* but was not previously used in the sense of a pitched ball which did not pass over *ompleit* between the knees and shoulders of the batter. *Liga* can mean *coalition*, but prior to the advent of *beisbol* (baseball) did not mean an organization of sport teams to promote mutual competition.

Still more interesting are the words which have entered into the language sufficiently to develop native grammatical forms. Such a word is *jonronero;* it is built upon a base *jonron*, which is obviously the result of the ways of a Mexican accent with *home-run*. To this word has been added *-ero*, meaning "one who does so," and *jonronero* thus means "one who hits homeruns." But before this could happen Mexicans had to start thinking of *jonron* as a native word. Similarly, *lineon* has been built up to mean "line drive." *Faulea* is clearly our word *foul*, "to knock a foul ball," with a Mexican spelling and a Spanish verbal ending *-ea*. *Tratando de bontear* is literally "trying to bunt." The word *bunt* has been given an appropriate Spanish spelling, and an infinitive ending *-ear* added to it.

Now, we might notice what is happening here. The Mexicans have borrowed our game of baseball, as we borrowed the game of drafts, which we renamed *chess*, after our mispronunciation of a word we associated with the playing of the game. They have taken words along with the game, and unconsciously altered them in various ways. Some they copied, and kept the spelling; then they pronounced the word in accordance with the spelling and pronunciation practices of their own language. Other words they heard, and they said them, making an approximation of the sounds they heard—though even here spelling may have had an influence, since *ompleit* logically should have been spelled *jompleit* if they followed only American pronunciation. It is a guess, but a justified one, that they were also influenced by the American spelling of *home*. A Mexican would not pronounce the *h* and thus *home* would become *om*. Some words are translated, literally, if possible. Other words, which have recognizable native cognates, are absorbed into the corresponding native words. Finally, these borrowed words, whether based on sound or spelling or both, or translation, or whatever, become familiar enough so that no one any longer thinks of them as the words of *norte-*

*americanos.* They are now Mexican words, and they start growing with Mexican forms, just as though they had come from
either traditional Spanish or native Nahuatl.

Nor are these practices restricted to Mexican borrowers. A
traveler in Japan reports the following incident, which goes back
to the innocent 1920's, when college football was still an amateur
sport. The Ivy League fielded good teams in those days, and the
notion was yet abroad that the best football was played in or
near New England. The University of Iowa had a remarkable
team, and when Iowa beat Yale it was at the time a national,
even an international, event.

The traveler of whom I spoke was asked by a polite Japanese
whence he came.

"Iowa."

The Japanese was puzzled, and asked him to repeat the word.
The traveler did so.

Suddenly the Japanese brightened up, and much pleased with
himself, shouted, "Yah! Ee-wah! Ee-wah! Knock-a-hell out-a
Yale."

Apparently *hell* and *Yale* were familiar enough to him so that
he could approximate an English pronunciation, even though
the sound of *l* is difficult for a Japanese. *Knock the* and *out of*
had either been learned in colloquial form, or the Japanese had
altered them in accordance with familiar linguistic principles.
But *Iowa* was strange, or almost strange, and the sequence of
vowels in the word was too much. The Japanese did well to
produce anything as close as *Ee-wah,* and no doubt he was proud
of himself.

*They Suffered*      QUITE naturally, speakers of English have
*a Sea Change*       done essentially what we have seen speakers of Japanese and speakers of Mexican
Spanish doing. We borrowed words along
with goods, practices, and concepts. If the
words were hard for us, we did the best we could with them.
Sometimes we approximated the foreign pronunciation. Some-

times we took a foreign spelling, and tried to pronounce the spelling as though it represented a native word. Often we did a little of both; sometimes speakers of one sort of English did one, speakers of another English did another. For instance, the British seem generally to have pronounced the borrowed word *Nazi* as though it were English; they produced something that would rhyme approximately with *has he*. In the United States speakers stubbornly tried to approximate the German, saying something like *not see*. There are, of course, examples by the hundreds of thousands.

When the monumental *Century Dictionary* was prepared late in the last century, the editors very properly considered *garage* a French word which had no place in a dictionary of English. Then came the automobile. The French word *garage* meant any kind of place where bicycles, railroad cars, wagons, or anything of the sort could be stored for protection. It came from French *garer*, to protect; Provençal *garer* and Old High German *warer* had roughly the same meaning as their English cognates *guard*, *ward*. In the United States and Britain, as in a number of other countries, the word now designates a building for the storage or repair of automobiles. In a half century the word has become thoroughly acclimated. Most users of it have no notion that it means a place of protection, and they have gone about anglicizing the pronunciation. Some speakers in the United States try to preserve an approximation of the French, and say something like *guh-razh*, but the bulk of the workers in garages, or the patrons of garages do not know French. The growing pronunciation in the United States seems to be that which rhymes with *hodge*. Meanwhile, in England the accent has been shifted to the first syllable, after the conventional English pattern, and the growing pronunciation there seems to be one which about rhymes with *carriage*.

This sort of thing can be doubled and tripled, of course, because many of the words we borrowed had already been borrowed into the language from which we took them. For instance, many French speakers had difficulty opening a word with the sound of *sp* or *sk* or *st*, and preceded the sound with a neutral vowel. We have borrowed the result both with and without the vowel, having accordingly both *state* and *estate*, *squire* and *esquire*, *specially* and *especially*. The Greeks had a word *drama*, which meant "deed" or "action," from which by specialization they developed the meaning of "action in a work of art on the stage." They also had a few relatively rare forms, *dramatikos* (a dramatic work), and *dramatourgia*, for words which we borrowed in turn as *dramatic, dramatics,* and *dramaturgy*. Once the word was at home in English it started to develop; *drama* could be pronounced *drah-mah, drayma, drammer, drammy,* or *dramer,* depending upon one's accent. The derivatives of the word were so handy, furthermore, that we started developing new grammatical forms: *dramatize, dramatism, dramatization, dramaturgical, dramatically*. We tried French *dramatizer,* but preferred another French word *dramatiste,* which the French had apparently borrowed from the Portuguese *dramatista*. Meanwhile we were using the word in new combinations: *dramatic irony, dramatic tenor, dramalogue, closet drama*.

In short, when a word migrates from one language to another, it usually has at first various difficulties in acclimatization, in spelling, in pronunciation, in meanng. But once the word has become at home, once it is thoroughly naturalized—and unless the word is in great demand, as was *garage*, this may take generations—the word has a normal linguistic life like any other native. It develops new meanings and loses old ones; it shifts its spelling and pronunciation with the habits of its new home. It has become a native, and only philologists inquire into its family tree. Other people put it to work.

*The Noble*  THE WORDS we have borrowed from the
*Redman as a*  American Indians have certain quirks of
*Sort of*  their own because of the way they have
*Immigrant*  been recorded. The name of the Navaho
was formerly spelled *Nabajo* because it was recorded by Spaniards; the Iroquois and Algonquin take their spelling from the French; Norwegian and Russian tran-

scriptions have influenced the spelling of the names of Eskimos
(*Esquimaux* in French, of course) in Greenland and Alaska respectively. *Manhattan* is spelled, and to a degree pronounced as
it is, because the Dutch gave us their version of the Indian tribal
name. LaSalle called those Indians *Manhates*, and various other
Frenchmen called them *Mahatones, Manthanes, Manhatesen,
Manhattae, Manhattons,* and *Monhatons.*

Considering that those who recorded Indian names had their
own accents and spellings, that they were often careless and
sometimes drunk, that they usually recorded a name only from
memory and without phonetic symbols or phonetic devices, one
need not be surprised that the same word has become popular
as *Chippewa* and *Ojibway*, or that a list of names like the following appears for one group of Indians: *Meskwaki, Muskwaky,
Musquawkie, Musquakie, Miskwukeeyuk, Mus-quack-ki-uck,
Musquakkink, Musquattaminies, Musquakkink, Messenecqz,
Meskwakiag, Mechecaukis, Mechuquakis,* and many others. The
word apparently meant *Red-Earth People,* supposedly because
the Indians thought they had originally been made from red
clay. But when they first encountered the white men, according
to the story, a Frenchman asked them how they were called.
The particular Indian addressed belonged to the Fox clan of the
Meskwaki, and gave the name of his clan, not of his tribe. The
Frenchman translated *Fox* into *Renard,* and the Indians were
known by that name, and as the *Fox* in English. From some kind
of confusion *Renard* also appears as *Chien,* so that the Indians
were also called *Dogs.* Nor was this phenomenon unique. The
Snake River of the Northwest is named for the Snake Indians.
But none of the Indians living in that area at that time had a
name meaning anything like *Snake.* Apparently a trader asked
some Indians what they were, and one responded with a motion
in sign language, wiggling his hand forward. The trader thought
that looked like a snake, but the Indian seemingly meant to suggest that he was a basket-weaver.

Or to get back to the State of New York, consider the Seneca.
Quite naturally they were not, what their name in modern English would suggest, devotees of late classical drama. Mr. J. N. B.

Hewitt, formerly of the Bureau of American Ethnology, puts the matter succinctly, as follows: "Seneca—place of the stone, the anglicized form of the Dutch enunciation of the Mohegan rendering of the Iroquoian ethnic appellative *Oneida*, or, strictly, *Oneniute a ka*, and with a different ethnic suffix, *Oneniute ron non*, meaning 'people of the standing or projecting rock or stone.'" Most of us unaided would never manage to make *Seneca* out of that, but the fact did not keep our ancestors from selling the crude petroleum which seeped out of shale in the Indian country as a famous Indian remedy, Seneca Oil, which then became even more popular if not more curative as Seneca Rattlesnake Root Oil; nor the State of Virginia from calling the New York Indians *Sinkers;* nor geologists from denominating a subdivision of Devonian strata as *Senecan.* If the French can call Lucius Annaeus Seneca *Sénèque*, why should not we call a tribe of Iroquois *Senecas?* Once a word has been borrowed from language to language, anything is possible.

# 8

# THE GODS WHO TROUBLE THE WATERS OF OUR VOICE STREAM

THE BRIGHT IRONICAL GODS—AIR AND THE GODS OF LAN-GUAGE—HOMO SAXOPHONENSIS—TECHNOLOGY RAISES ITS FOR-BIDDING HEAD—OF BUZZINGS, GRUNTS, AND EXPLOSIONS—THE LITTLE SHRIMP AND HIS FELLOWS

*The Bright Ironical Gods* WHATEVER whimsical gods there be, not the least of their ironies is this, that language, which is often durable as the granite-ribbed hills, is built with air. And this fact must give us pause. In the previous chapters we have dealt with words; we have recognized these words as symbols for meaning, and we have dealt with the words as though they had form, and as though this form were expressed in spelling. This last has not usually been true. Words came into being as sound; during most of their history they existed as sound—early peoples did not have writing—and even of late centuries, when words have enjoyed a spelled existence, their vitality is usually to be sought in their oral form. They are made of air, and in treating them thus far as though they were made from bits of the alphabet, I have done them an injustice, and possibly have led you astray. My only excuse can be that most of us know the alphabet of spelling and do not know the alphabet of hearing; and I could not well discuss everything at once. Let us now rectify this error, and consider language as sound.

We have remarked that language is durable. Few human phenomena can be more so. Skull shapes change, skin color alters, blood types become confused; of all the means by which anthropologists identify peoples, only the cross section of a hair is more permanent than language. And cross sections of hairs do not tell us much about the heads beneath the hairs. Languages, however, even long lost languages, can speak wonders. The face of a language, like Macbeth's face, "is a book where men may read strange matters."

In the mountains along the boundary between Spain and France live a hardy people known as Basques. Racially, we do not know who they are. We may assume they are the survivors of the ancient Iberians who left place names and inscriptions in what are now France and Spain. But did the Iberians descend from some otherwise unknown troglodytes who had been lurking in the mountains for eons? Are they remnants of Asiatics or east Europeans who fought their way west, and so decimated themselves on the way that they could survive only by taking to the hills? We do not know. We know only that the Basques are there, and that they are not closely related to any of their neighbors because they speak a tongue which is not demonstrably related to any other known language. Their speech tells us all we know of them.

Or consider the Hindus. Fifteen centuries or more before Christ, a tough lot of people invaded India, conquered it, and dominated it politically. Who were they? We have some unreliable legends, and the very reliable fact that they spoke Sanskrit. That is, because they spoke Sanskrit, we know they were Indo-Europeans, and had come from central Europe.

Or consider the following evidence, at once like and unlike that provided by the Hindus. To the north of India, across the Himalayas, lies the Gobi Desert, and archaeologists have lately found great cities there, buried in the sands. The inhabitants formed part of Asiatic culture; their artifacts prove that. They came, however, from central Europe; their language, preserved on clay tablets, establishes that they, like the Hindus, spoke a language descended from Indo-European. The natural assumption would be that these people (we call them Tocharians) were an offshoot of the Hindus as those speakers of Sanskrit moved east, or they were Hindus who, after becoming established in

India, moved north. But the natural assumption is wrong, and we know that it is wrong because of the uncommon durability of the spoken word, and because of our knowledge of Indo-European. Indo-European, it will be recalled, broke into two sub-families of languages, one surviving in an eastern division including Sanskrit, another surviving in a western division including languages like Celtic and Latin. Now, the curious fact is that Tocharian resembles Celtic and Latin more closely than it does Sanskrit. That is, the Tocharians were not the northern prong of the Hindu invasion. They were not from any branch of the eastern subfamily of Indo-European. They must represent some portion of the Indo-European family which descended from the western group, but changed their minds and later went east.

In spite of all this evidence of the durability of language, it is not immune to change or decay. Far from it. Whole families of North American Indian languages have left behind them only the silence of the plain and the forest, or are haltingly preserved in scholarly monographs. The remaining Indian languages are fading away. Meanwhile both the African Negro and the American Indian have learned English, and the sons of these races cannot now be distinguished by the languages they speak. Elsewhere in the world uncounted languages have vanished, and surviving tongues have changed. In fact, change is a law of life in language, and all languages change constantly, sometimes slower, sometimes faster. English, for instance, has changed relatively rapidly, so that no speaker of English now or for some hundreds of years past has been able to read or speak Anglo-Saxon without learning it, almost as a foreign language. But across a few miles of water, on the Frisian Islands off the Low Countries, whence Anglo-Saxon came, the islanders can read the Anglo-Saxon epic, *Beowulf*, almost at sight. Frisian, closely related to Anglian, has changed relatively little in fifteen hundred years.

And so, whatever whimsical gods there be, among those which brood over language are stability and change, and the doings of these godlets account for much which at first seems nonsensical in language.

IN ONE sense, language may be made of meaning, but in another, and very important sense, it is made of breath, of the common man's breath, and especially of the breath of the common man's wife and the common child's mother. You and I who read and write books have very little effect upon language. We may think about it, write about it, and read about it, but it goes on without us, or in spite of us.

There was once a copybook maxim, honored in many a reference work, to the effect that Modern English comes from the dialect written by Chaucer, because Chaucer was "the well of English undefiled." There could scarcely be a well of more undefiled piffle than this. No one person ever influences language very much. Certainly nobody influences language much by writing poems in it, more particularly by writing poems which never have been and are likely never to be, more's the pity, very popular. The dialect of London became the ancestor of English because London was the commercial, political, and social center of the country. Chaucer happened to live there, along with a good many other people, some of whom probably influenced the language more than he did, and no one of whom influenced it much. A good case might be made, for instance, that Jack Straw influenced English more than Chaucer did. Jack Straw was a rabble-rouser who led the mob; Chaucer was a learned gentleman who amused the court. Language lived on the garlic-laden breaths of "Jack Straw and his meinie," not on Chaucer's exquisite parchment. While Chaucer was penning a charming bit, accusing his scribe of "rape"—by rape he apparently meant carelessness in copying verses—Jack Straw's mob was shouting more language from more throats into more ears than Chaucer could reach in years, and no doubt enforcing the language with rape of a very different sort.

On the whole, language lives and grows as spoken language—even though parts of a dead language may be preserved in writing—and this principle is true in more ways than may at first appear. In Chapter 2 we noted that we know little about the early history of language except what we can infer. This much, however, we can be pretty sure of. Language was invented as a spoken language, and during the greater portion of its existence, it was only a spoken language. This statement must be true, because only in relatively recent times could anybody read or write. Originally, and therefore basically, language was spoken language.

Furthermore, language has remained mainly spoken language. The great bulk of the human race is still illiterate, except in the most elementary sense. Even in the more sophisticated countries, only a very few people spend any large part of their time reading or writing. A novelist, whose business is writing, does not tell his wife his soft-boiled egg is practically raw by writing notes to her. A college professor, who is presumably producing learned matter, emits hundreds or thousands of spoken words for every one he writes. Most of us read or write very little, and talk altogether too much. Written words have always been relatively rare, and with the advent of radio and television they threaten to become even rarer.

Nor is this all. Not only are the foundations of language oral, the foundation of each person's speech is oral. We learn our languages, all the elementary parts of language, from our mothers, from our brothers and sisters who have learned the language from our mothers, and from the neighbor kids who learned their language from their mothers. Thus it happens that women are the great arbiters of language. Mommy stays home, and Daddy does not—it is as simple as that. Women transmit the language, and they do it by oral means. Some of this transmission is deliberate; the mother tries to teach the child to speak. Most of it is unconscious. The mother has to try to get the child to drink his orange juice, and the child wants to tell his mother that the animal outside the window is a kitty. Then when the child learns that the "kitty" is a dog, that there are two furred animals, both with names, he tries to show off by babbling what he has heard. In the process, language is being transmitted and reborn, preserved and changed.

There is no dearth of evidence that this is what happens. Consider, for instance, the preservation of English during the three hundred years in which it was not an official language. We have already noticed that in 1066 some Frenchified Scandinavians conquered England, and made their Scandinavianized French the official language of the country. Nonetheless, during the following three centuries Norman French influenced the language of Britain so little that the most common classes of English words have come mainly from Anglo-Saxon. They include words which have a grammatical function: *the, a, an, by, in, on, up, are, is, was, that, which, when, he, her, it,* and the like. They include the words of common living: *man, woman, wife, child, husband, daughter, mother, father, house, home, door, roof, pig, dog, cat, plow, road, loaf, corn.* Especially they include the common action words: *eat, live, die, love, hate, fight, kill, work, rest.* That is, Anglo-Saxon gives us the words men live by and with, because for three hundred years men spoke them, even though those same men, or a few of them, were writing French and Latin. The enduring language lives on the breath of men, especially the breath of women; we learn it and we alter it almost as naturally as we breathe.

But if language changes, alters so much that within a few hundred years the speakers of a language cannot understand an earlier form of it, how can language be so durable as we have already seen it to be? The answer is curious and involved, and rests as one would expect upon the breath. Let us turn, then, to what happens to breath to make it language.

Although speech is possible employing a stream of air which goes either in or out, and a few languages make some use of intaken breath, practically, speech relies upon an outward stream. The diaphragm thrusts upward, and the intercostal muscles contract the chest. The lungs, being compressed, expel air, which can escape only through the trachea, or windpipe. Obviously, several things can be done to this stream of air. It can be allowed to flow freely, or it can be disturbed. If disturbed, it can be disturbed in three ways: it can be stopped completely; it can be constricted; it can be made to vibrate as a column. Freely flowing air becomes normal breath; asthma and snoring, from a physical point of view, approach language, because they involve interference with the breath stream. True, snoring has little meaning, but some conversation has little meaning anyhow, so that if one wished to, he might call snoring a sort of subconscious sub-language.

The three means of disturbing the breath stream are the means by which we speak. These three are used in varying combinations, varying degrees, and are contrived by various instruments, but all speech is created by this vocal trinity. A speaker can stop the flow of air completely and then let it go, as in the letter *t*. He can constrict it so that it whistles, as in the letter *s*. He can make it vibrate while he relaxes, as in any pronunciation of the letter *a*; the pronunciation of this letter known as Italian *a* is so beloved of opera singers because it is made by the most uninhibited use of air for language. The singer has only to start his vibrating mechanism, relax, open his mouth, and having thus made himself into a sort of human saxophone, let himself go.

*Homo Saxo-* BUT HOW does one become a human saxo-
*phonensis*   phone? The key organ is the larynx, which
is commonly known as the Adam's apple, just as though, deep in our subconscious, we were aware that the original sin was too much talking. This organ constitutes the upper end of the windpipe, and is made of various pieces of cartilage, elastic tissue, and mucous membrane called vocal cords, all so articulated that the membranes can be relaxed completely during normal breathing, but can be contracted so that they will vibrate in pitch. The result of this vibration we call *voice*, and any sound made with the aid of these vocal cords is said to be *voiced*. You can feel the vibration by putting the tips of your fingers in the hollow of your throat and pronouncing any vowel.

Now to the sounds which we produce in speech. Roughly they may be divided into two sorts, *vowels*, in which the breath is but little constricted, and *consonants*, in which it is more emphatically constricted. Actually, there is no dividing line between the two. Some sounds are restricted so little that they cannot be very confidently called either a vowel or a consonant. For instance, of the various sounds indicated by the letter *r* in *rarer*, which are vowels and which consonants? The answer is not easy, but the distinction between consonants and vowels is traditional and familiar, and has enough reality to be useful in understanding what happens when we speak.

First, then, to the vowels. Since they are made with an almost unrestricted column of air, they must be voiced or somehow disturbed; otherwise we would not hear them. They all are voiced in English and in most other languages. Since the sound of the vowels depends upon a vibrating column of air, the differences in sound must depend upon the various ways in which the air can be made to vibrate. Here we should perhaps think of ourselves not as saxophones, but as instruments resembling a bagpipe, a slide trombone, a cornet, and a cat-tail fiddle. We can vary the stress by varying the pressure of air, as in a bagpipe. We can alter the center of vibration and the character of the vibrating column, as in a slide trombone. We can direct a column of air into different passages, as in the cornet. And we can alter the vibrations by changing the tension of the vibrating instrument, as in the cat-tail fiddle—the cat-tail fiddle being a somewhat legendary device said to have been played by grasping a tomcat by the neck and the tail, and sawing upon it as though it were a violin, increasing the tension on the tail to increase the pitch of the cat.

Of the methods of creating sounds, the most useful for our present discussion is that which permits shifting the point at which the vibration centers. In all true vowels, the vibration takes place in the mouth. If you will now pronounce slowly the words *sleek hawk*, you will notice that the vowel in *sleek* is made far forward and high up, about at the roots of the upper front teeth, and that the vowel in *hawk* is made so far back in the throat that you are almost in danger of swallowing it. Similarly, each of the other vowels has a distinctive place in the mouth at which the vibration centers. The resultant sound can be still further altered by the stress with which breath is expelled and by the shape of the oral cavity. This shape can be altered in many ways, but most noticeably by movements of the tongue, by rounding and unrounding the lips, and by the tenseness or slackness of the tongue and other muscles. Accordingly vowels can be described by the position of the vibration, the degree of stress, the degree of rounding, the degree of tenseness, and the action of the tongue.

*Technology*
*Raises*
*Its Forbidding*
*Head*

AT THIS point, we must become technical. Before we can go further in describing sounds, we must find out, one by one, how they are made. Furthermore, we shall need a vocabulary with which we can talk about sounds, symbols which will permit me to know what I mean to say, and you to guess what I am trying to say. We cannot very well go on with me talking about "the sound of *a* in *aunt*." That is too clumsy, and there are a variety of ways of saying *aunt*. We need symbols for sounds, and then we need an understanding of how the sounds are made which are represented by the symbols.

Both are provided by what is known as IPA, the International Phonetic Alphabet. It runs to hundreds of symbols, and with it one can transcribe phonetically, at least roughly, any language on earth, and it is used by all serious students of language the world over. Fortunately, we shall need only a small part of it. After all, we are not transcribing a tonal language like Chinese or Zapotec. A few dozen symbols will represent most sounds in English, and learning to identify them can be quite a lot of fun.

Besides, doing so is economical. After all, you have been provided with an excellent linguistic laboratory, equipped with all instruments necessary for basic linguistic research, and if you insist on leaving this laboratory locked within you unused, you are guilty of shocking waste. At worst, you ought to run a few simple experiments, just to feel you are getting some return on your anatomical investment.

Seriously, a little attention to the manner in which sounds are made is likely to open vast new understandings of language. In the following discussion, you will do well to try each of the suggestions, using your own vocal laboratory, before you go on to read the discussion of it. For instance, if you are asked to say *cat* slowly, do so, before you find out why.

So now we are ready to begin our experiments. You will recall that a page or two back we pronounced the combination *sleek hawk*, and observed that the first vowel is pronounced just back of the upper teeth. It is tense; it cannot be pronounced without relatively strong tension in the tongue and the oral muscles. Try, for instance, to pronounce *eat* without some tenseness; it will inevitably become *it*, *et*, or *ut*. For this sound in *sleek*, the lips are unrounded. Therefore, we may describe it by calling it a high front tense unround vowel. The IPA symbol for it is [i], and you will find it appropriately placed in the diagram on the following page, which is intended to represent the oral cavity. The vowel in *hawk*, on the other hand, is a low back tense round vowel; the symbol for this sound is [ɔ]—the one my students nicknamed "the little shrimp." (To distinguish phonetic symbols from letters, they are put within brackets.)

Now try a few more sounds on your vocal laboratory. Repeat slowly the following words: *sought, sot, sat, set, sate, sit, seat.* If your pronunciation is roughly normal, you should produce a series of vowels that proceed in an orderly row along the lower side of your oral cavity, from [ɔ] to [i]. As you will observe in the diagram, the second of these vowels, the so-called Italian *a*, is written [ɑ]. The others follow in order, [æ], [ɛ], [e], [ɪ], and [i]. Now pronounce consecutively, *foal, full,* and *fool*. This time you should produce a series of vowels that go forward along the roof of your mouth; you will find them written as [o], [ʊ], and [u] in the diagram. Now say *cutaway*. In this word the first vowel is stressed, the second unstressed. As a result, the stressed sound appears a little higher than the unstressed sound, but the main difference between them is the difference in stress. They are written [ʌ] and [ə]; the latter is often called *schwa*. It is the most common sound in modern American speech, for all American unstresssed vowels tend to become *schwa* or [ɪ].

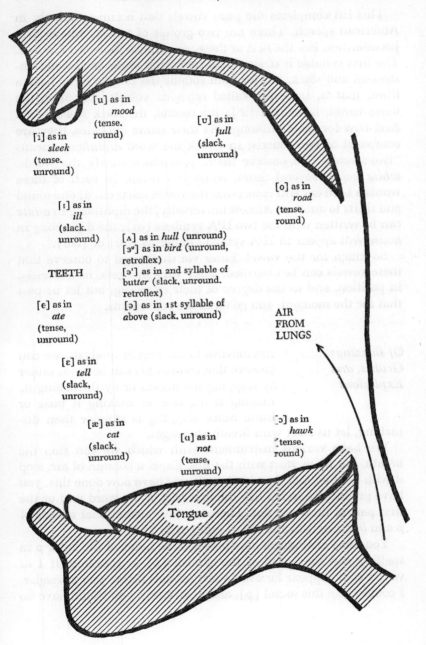

[u] as in
*mood*
(tense.
round)

[ʊ] as in
*full*
(slack,
unround)

[i] as in
*sleek*
(tense.
unround)

[o] as in
*road*
(tense,
round)

[ɪ] as in
*ill*
(slack.
unround)

[ʌ] as in *hull* (unround)
[ɝ] as in *bird* (unround,
retroflex)
[ə'] as in 2nd syllable of
but*ter* (slack, unround.
retroflex)
[ə] as in 1st syllable of
*a*bove (slack, unround)

TEETH

[e] as in
*ate*
(tense,
unround)

AIR
FROM
LUNGS

[ɛ] as in
*tell*
(slack,
unround)

[æ] as in
*cat*
(slack,
unround)

[ɑ] as in
*not*
(tense,
unround)

[ɔ] as in
*hawk*
(tense,
round)

Tongue

This list completes the pure vowels that occur commonly in American speech. There are two groups of vowels which have peculiarities. For the first of these, pronounce the word *Herbert*. The first syllable is stressed and somewhat tense, the second unstressed and slack, but for both sounds the tongue flicks back a little; that is, these are called *retroflex* vowels. The first, the tense vowel, is written [ɜᵘ]; the second, the slack vowel, [ə']. And now for the diphthongs. As their name indicates, they are composed of two sounds; in Greek the word *diphthong* means "two-sounds." To observe them, pronounce slowly the words, *white house*, several times, while you listen. In each of these words a keen ear will detect that the vowel starts out as one sound and shifts to another. Almost universally, the diphthong in *white* can be written with the two IPA symbols [ɑɪ]; the diphthong in *house* will appear in IPA symbols either as [ɑʊ] or [æʊ].

So much for the vowel. Later we shall need to observe that these vowels can be classified. They vary in stress, in tenseness, in position, and in the degree of their rounding, but let us pass that for the moment, and go on to the consonants.


*Of Buzzings,*   RETURNING to our earlier analysis, we can
*Grunts, and*    observe that consonants can be made either
*Explosions*     by stopping the breath or by disturbing it,
                 making it explode, or making it buzz or
                 hum. Since stopping is simpler than disturbing, let us start with breath stoppages.

We have various instruments with which we can stop the breath, but let us start with the lips. Expel a column of air, stop it with the lips, and then let it go. If you have now done this, you have produced a sound like the first part of the word *putt* or the first part of the word *but*. These are the conventional sounds of *p* and *b* in English, and of [p] and [b] in IPA.

You must distinguish here between the name of the letter *p* in spelling and the sound of the symbol [p] in speaking. If I as writer could appear for even a few seconds before you as reader, I could make this sound [p], and thenceforth you would have no difficulty understanding what is meant by a phonetic symbol. But since obviously I cannot, you will have to make the sound. It is not anything I can describe, except that I can tell you how to make it. Purse your lips as though you were to say *put;* let some air pressure build up behind the lips. Then let the air go with a slight puff, but do not say any more of the word *put* except so much as is involved in the explosion when you suddenly open your lips. This much, and no more, is embodied in [p]. It is the transcription of a sound; it is not the name of a letter in spelling.

Now for the next sound, place your tongue against the roof of your mouth, just back of the upper teeth, stop the breath column with your tongue, and let the air go in a small explosion. You should have produced either the first part of the word *tub* or the first part of *dub*, that is, the sounds [t] or [d]. Now try raising your tongue in the back part of your mouth, stopping the air, and then releasing it. You will produce either [k] as in *kick,* or [g] as in *gig.* A little girl of my acquaintance would understand this explanation. She brought home the first report card on which she had received grades more explicit than *S* for *Satisfactory* and *U* for its opposite. Her mother praised her for her good grades, saying, "I know that reading is hard for you, but I see you got *G* in it."

"Oh, Mother," the little girl replied impatiently, "that's not *gee,* that's [g]."

Here we might pause to notice a curious detail. Is it not surprising that all of these stops occur in pairs, that wherever and however you make the stop, you get two? It is curious. It is more: it is significant, and if you will use your vocal laboratory you can find out why. Put the tips of your fingers on the hollow of your throat and make consecutively the sounds represented by the IPA symbols [p] and [b]. You ought to feel a vibration in your throat with [b] that you do not feel with [p]; if you feel this vibration with [p], it means that you are not pronouncing [p] only, but are following it with a vowel. Now try the same thing with the other stops, the sounds associated with [t] and [d], with [k] and [g]. You should have vibrations with [d] and [g], very little with [t] and [k]. Now pronounce any of the vowels, several of them. You should feel vibration similar to that in [b], [d], and [g]. But the vowels, you will remember, are all voiced. Now you will suspect—if you have not suspected it already— that certain of the consonants are voiced and others are unvoiced, and this causes the difference between them. A stoppage of the air by the lips produces [p] if the sound is voiceless, [b] if the sound is voiced; a stoppage of air with the tongue at the roots of the teeth produces [t] if the sound is voiceless, [d] if the sound is voiced; farther back in the oral cavity [k] is voiceless, [g] is voiced.

Those are the stops in English, all the sounds that are made by a complete and simple stoppage of the air. Now for the sounds made by obstructing the air; since they are made by friction of air, we may call them *fricatives*. First, direct a column of air straight at your middle upper front teeth. Your mouth should be nearly closed, and the air should be channeled through your tongue, but your tongue will probably take care of itself if you just try to make the air hit your two upper central front teeth. Let the air whistle past them. You have produced either the sound of *s* or the sound of *z*, in IPA [s] and [z] respectively. You will not need to be told why these sounds appear in a pair; [s] is voiceless, [z] is voiced. Now direct a column of air at the roof of your mouth just back of the upper teeth. You have produced the central sound in either *fresher* or *measure*, the first voiceless, the second voiced. Since these sounds are not well represented in European languages by one letter, we have special symbols in IPA for them, [ʃ] for the sound of *sh*, [ʒ] for the corresponding voiced sound. Now, barely touch your upper teeth to your lower lip, and constrict air as it passes through. You have produced either the sound associated with *f* or the sound associated with *v*, the first voiceless, the second voiced, and written [f] and [v]. Now, put your tongue against your upper teeth, and constrict the air. You have produced the first consonant in either *thing* or *this*, the first voiceless and written in IPA with the Greek theta [θ], the second voiced and written with the Anglo-

Saxon crossed *d* [đ]. And these are all of the fricatives common in English.

There are, however, a few more consonants. Repeat the sentence, "The *judge* went to *church*." A keen ear will detect that the consonants in *church* are neither exclusively stops nor fricatives. A very keen ear will detect that they are both, that the sounds begin with a [t], which shifts into a [ʃ]. That is, the word *church* sounds as though it should be written in English *tshurtsh*, and is written in IPA [tʃɜᵘtʃ]. And as you will imagine, or find out by trying it on your vocal cords, the consonants in *judge* are only these same sounds voiced; that is, they sound like *dzh*, and are written [dʒ]. These sounds, which begin with a stop and continue with a fricative, are called *affricates*.

In the next set of consonants, you use your abilities as a cornet; that is, you stop your oral passage, and let the air out through your nose. Close your mouth completely, and make a sound through your nose. It was *m*, written [m]. Now stop the air by putting the forward part of your tongue against the roof of your mouth, and as before, make a sound in your nose. It was *n*, written [n]. Now stop the air farther back in your mouth, and again make a sound. It was the final consonant in *sing*, in IPA, [ɜ]. These are the common nasals in English. In French, there are more, but we manage with the three. All are made as a matter of course by voicing, and the sound you hear is the vibrating of the voiced column of air as it passes slowly through the nasal passages. This passage of air is so slow as to be almost imperceptible, but if you doubt that the air is moving, hold your nose, and then try to make the sound. If you tried it, you made no sound. This is, of course, the basis of the old joke about the man who delights in spring by saying, "Sprig is cub." His nose is stopped up, so that he cannot pronounce nasal sounds, and he makes the corresponding stops. These consonants are called *nasals*, or *nasal continuants*, or just *continuants*.

A few consonants will not be pinned down. For instance, say slowly the words *your*, *year*, and *loyal*. All the consonants here are said with so little restriction, that you may not be quite sure whether to call them vowels or consonants. You will probably notice, also, that they do not stay in one place in the mouth. There are many ways of pronouncing the sounds we indicate by the letter *y*, and perhaps even more ways of pronouncing the sounds indicated by *r* and *l*, but you will probably notice that they slip around, that they glide from one vowel to another, and, accordingly, they are called *glides*. They are sometimes called semivowels, also, because they resemble vowels. The sound of *y* is written [j]; *r* and *l*, [r] and [l]; the semivowel *w*, [w], is little more than a rounded vowel. The sound of *h*, [h], is a voiceless breath—it is sometimes called an *aspirate*, Greek for *breath* —with enough friction far back in the mouth to make it audible. This sound is combined with [w] in words like *when*, which are spelled *wh*, but in prevailing usage pronounced (hw). In IPA this combination is often represented by the letter *w* inverted [ʍ]. The simplified pronunciation [w] is now heard in increasing frequency.

We have now examined the commonest sounds in English and noticed roughly how each is made. We have found that they can be classified on the basis of their production. Since we shall need names for these sounds, we had best name them, also, from the manner in which they are produced. To do so, we shall need a few terms, not many, but if you do not know them you had better fix them in mind now. We have already used the word *vowel*, and have defined *voice, stop, fricative, affricate, nasal*, and *glide*. Now we need to define a few points in the oral cavity. The ridge just back of the upper teeth is called the *alveolar ridge*. Back of this, the roof of the mouth is called the *hard palate*, referred to in the adjective *palatal*. Back of the hard palate is the soft palate, or *velum*, referred to by the adjective *velar*. Back toward the throat is the *glottis*, and this area is identified as *glottal*. These words can be combined; for instance, *alveolopalatal* would mean that the sound could be made in the vicinity of either the alveolar ridge or the hard palate. *Lateral* refers to sounds which are spread out across the width of the tongue. Other words are more familiar; *labial* refers to the lips, and *bilabial* to both lips; *dental* to the teeth, *lingual* to the tongue, and *nasal* to the nose. *Retroflex* means turned back.

*The Little Shrimp and His Fellows*

WITH THESE definitions we are ready to name sounds by describing the manner in which they are made. The following list is intended for reference.

### VOWELS

| | | |
|---|---|---|
| [i] | as in *sleek* | High-front unround tense |
| [ɪ] | as in *ill* | Lower high-front unround slack |
| [e] | as in *ate* | Mid-front unround tense |
| [ɛ] | as in *tell* | Lower mid-front unround slack |
| [æ] | as in *cat* | Low-front unround slack |
| [ɑ] | as in *not* | Low-back unround tense |
| [ɔ] | as in *hawk* | Higher low-back round tense |
| [o] | as in *road* | Mid-back round tense |
| [ʊ] | as in *full* | Lower high-back round slack, lowered and retracted |
| [u] | as in *mood* | High-back round tense |
| [ʌ] | as in *hull* | Lower mid-back unround |
| [ɜʋ] | as in *bird* | Mid-central unround retroflex |
| [ɚ] | as in 2nd syl-lable of Al*bert* | Mid-central unround retroflex slack |
| [ə] | as in 1st syl-lable of *a*bove | Mid-central unround slack |

### CONSONANTS

| | | |
|---|---|---|
| [p] | as in *papa* | Voiceless bilabial stop |
| [b] | as in *baby* | Voiced bilabial stop |
| [t] | as in *tat* | Voiceless alveolar stop |
| [d] | as in *did* | Voiced alveolar stop |
| [k] | as in *kick* | Voiceless palatal or velar stop |
| [g] | as in *gag* | Voiced palatal or velar stop |
| [f] | as in *fife* | Voiceless labiodental fricative |

| | | |
|---|---|---|
| [v] | as in *vivid* | Voiced labiodental fricative |
| [s] | as in *sissy* | Voiceless alveolar fricative |
| [z] | as in *dizzy* | Voiced alveolar fricative |
| [θ] | as in *think* | Voiceless interdental fricative |
| [đ] | as in *this* | Voiced interdental fricative |
| [ʃ] | as in *she* | Voiceless alveolopalatal fricative |
| [ʒ] | as in *pleasure* | Voiced alveolopalatal fricative |
| [h] | as in *how* | Voiceless glottal fricative (also called aspirate) |
| [ʍ] | as in *when* | Voiceless glottal fricative followed by voiced labiovelar glide |
| [tʃ] | as in *church* | Voiceless alveolopalatal affricate |
| [dʒ] | as in *judge* | Voiced alveolopalatal affricate |
| [m] | as in *mama* | Voiced bilabial nasal continuant |
| [n] | as in *nanny* | Voiced alveolar nasal continuant |
| [ŋ] | as in *song* | Voiced velar nasal continuant |
| [l] | as in *lull* | Voiced alveolar lateral continuant |
| [w] | as in *water* | Voiced labiovelar glide |
| [r] | as in *roar* | Voiced retroflex tongue glide |
| [j] | as in *youth* | Voiced linguopalatal glide |

Admittedly, the preceding discussion and this table are vastly simplified. (For more detailed statements, see the Bibliography.) None of the characteristics mentioned here is a simple thing, and the characteristics are interreliant. Tenseness, for instance, is not one thing in all vowels which we have called tense; [i] is certainly more tense than [ɔ]. Tenseness itself is not a single thing. There is more tenseness in the tongue in [i], but perhaps more in some of the other muscles in [ɔ]. Similarly, tenseness tends to increase with stress. It tends to increase when the vowel is adjacent to certain consonants, before terminal stops, for instance. Note the difference between the vowels in *heat* and *stream*. Even the consonants are not so simple as we have made them seem. There is more than one sound for *t*, for instance, as you will see if you will say carefully, "take a step." The sound associated with the second *t* is made closer to the teeth than is the first; it uses a part of the tongue farther from the tip than does the first, and it has a little of the quality of a fricative. Even so, we should have to transcribe both sounds [t]. Similarly, the [z] in *freeze* is not identical with the [z] in *needs*. But for our purposes, the description here should be sufficiently detailed.

# 9

## THE WAY OF A MAN WITH A NOISE

### THE MORE IT CHANGES, THE MORE IT REMAINS THE SAME— LINGUISTIC LEMMINGS TO THE SEA—HERE WE GO ROUND THE MULBERRY BUSH

*The More It Changes, the More It Remains the Same*

HAVING described the way man makes the noise from which he makes his language, we are ready to use this information.

Some pages back we asked the question, how is it that language is durable if it is always changing? Part of the answer is this: it always changes in accordance with linguistic principles. The principles are knowable and durable, for they are rooted in human nature and the organs of speech. Anyone who knows the railroad system outside New York City will know that a train which travels south and west from New Haven will likely land in New York, and that it will pass through New Rochelle on the way. Similarly, if we have a little information and know the principles of linguistic change, we can tell where a language came from, where it has been in the meantime, and we can even guess where it is likely to go.

To see how this works, we might look at an earlier form of the language. A famous passage in *Beowulf*, here written as prose, begins as follows:

Gewat    pa   ofer waegholm            winde gefysed
*Departed  then over the billowing sea, driven by the wind,*
flota famiheals                        fugle gelicost
*the floating one, foamy-necked, most like to a bird.*

Clearly, this passage differs strikingly from Modern English. It differs in many ways, including words, grammar, and sound, but since we are here interested in sound, let us restrict ourselves to that subject, and for brevity, to one word, the next to the last, *fugle*, which has become modern *fowl*. In the nominative the word would be *fugol*. It came to us from Proto-Germanic, from an Indo-European base *\*pou-*. Now, we know that a sound like [g] in the middle of a word regularly disappeared from Anglo-Saxon, and thus we are not surprised to find that Chaucer pronounced the word like the modern word *fool*, dropping the consonant and combining the two vowels into one. But we know also that words which Chaucer pronounced with the phonetic long *u* [u] are now pronounced with the diphthong heard in *house, mouse, our*, that is, [ɑu]. Thus Anglo-Saxon *fugol*, if it changed as a student of language would expect, should have become *fowl*, and it did.

Nor is this unusual. Just this sort of thing, and more, can be known about millions of words in languages all over the world. What we know of the changes which have taken place in the sounds of languages, are still taking place, and will probably continue to take place, is no less than appalling. Can any order be brought out of it?

Perhaps a few principles may help:

1. Indolence is native to the human animal, even to *Homo Saxophonensis.*
2. Sounds influence adjacent sounds.
3. Any shift in stress (accent) is likely to lead to shifts in sound.
4. Occasionally great sound shifts sweep through a language, changing it in particular but regular ways.

We might look at these in order. For the first, we like to drop pieces out of words. We whack their tails off, we chop their middles out, we even occasionally behead them. We have whacked endings off most of the words in the language, partly because the endings were no longer any good to us, but partly because, linguistically, we like to amputate. We have reduced *homelike* to *homely*, *everich* to *every*. We are now in process of reducing *examination* to *exam*, and *telephone* to *phone*. We also like to operate internally. The Anglo-Saxon word for a general director was *stigweard*, the *sty-ward*, the man who looked after the pig-pen, for an Anglo-Saxon capitalist was likely to have his stocks and bonds mostly in the form of razorbacks. We have reduced the word to *steward*. The boss himself was a *hlafweard*, a *loaf-ward*, the man who looked after the bread. We have cut that word down to *lord*, and we are in process of reducing *government* to *guvmnt*.

Similarly, we like to slur sounds, substituting an easy sound for one we find difficult. Englishmen used to pronounce *substitution* so that it ended with a sound like *you-see-on*, but now Americans end it with a sound like *oo-shun*. That is, in IPA [jɪusɪəŋ] has become [uʃəŋ]. The nasal sound for *ng* [ŋ] is a more pronounced and prolonged sound than the nasal for *n* [n], so that many speakers reduce *going* to *goin'*—in IPA, [goɪŋ] becomes [goɪn] or [goən]—*joists* becomes *jois*, *old* becomes *ole*, *when* becomes *wen*.

And now for the second principle, that sounds affect adjacent sounds. In *houses* the sounds indicated by an *s* have the sound of *z*. They did not always do so, but the adjacent vowels are voiced, and accordingly the voiceless [s]'s have become the corresponding voiced sounds, [z]'s. The preterit and past participle of the verb *wrap* ends with the sound of *t*, and the corresponding forms of *club* with the sound of *d*. Why? In Middle English they were the same, but *p* is voiceless, and the following sound has become unvoiced, whereas *b* is voiced and the voiced *d* has remained. These changes entail through our nouns and verbs, and elsewhere. The adjacent nasals in *chimney* force the speaker to stop between the *m* and the *n*. Careless speakers will stop the nasal [m] with the corresponding stop, [b]. But making an [n] after [b] is even harder than making an [n] after [m]; accordingly the [n] becomes the glide, [l], and the whole word *chimbley*. Similarly, the two fricatives in the middle of *diphthong* [dɪfθɔŋ] require a break, so that careless speakers will pronounce the word

as though it were spelled *dipthong*. Consonants within words tend
to become fricatives as the voice carries on, and thus Anglo-
Saxon *faeder* becomes Modern English *father*, with the voiced
stop [d] becoming the corresponding voiced fricative [đ]. On
the other hand, fricatives at the ends of words tend to become
stops, and to stop with the voice. Thus Anglo-Saxon *drugath* (to
use a modernized spelling) tends now to be pronounced as though
it were spelled *drout*, with the fricative [θ] becoming the corresponding stop, [t]. *Could* was formerly pronounced as though it
were spelled *cuth*, ending in [đ], which has become the corresponding voiced stop [d]. Changes of this sort can be found scattered widely through our language, and through all languages.
In Chapter 4 we noticed that the Latin prefixes which are spelled
*ad-* and *at-* are historically the same. The syllable appears as
*ad-* before a voiced sound, because [d] is a voiced stop, as *at-*
before voiceless sounds because [t] is voiceless. We see the difference in *adequate attack;* both words once began with *ad-*.

Now for our third principle, that any shift in stress is likely
to result in a shift in the quality of sounds. The word for *heaven*
in Anglo-Saxon was something like *heafon*, with the accent on
the *hea-* and with moderately strong secondary stress on the second syllable, *-fon*. But Anglo-Saxon had endings on most nouns,
so that *to heaven* was spelled *heafonum*, with a dative ending.
The word in this form is three syllables, and accordingly the
secondary stress was reduced and the word became something
like *heafnum*. The *-um* is an ending, and endings mostly fell off
during the Middle Ages. Thus we have now a word which might
well be written *hevn*, in IPA [hɛvn̩] or [hɛvən]. (The dot under
a symbol, as in [n̩] implies slight vocalization.)

Changes like this took place, sometimes in elaborate series, in
Anglo-Saxon, but we need not go back to Anglo-Saxon to observe
the phenomenon. We have already noticed that more than a
quarter of our vocabulary comes to us from French. Old French
had a moderately strong stress far along in the word, descended
from the Latin accent of the penult or antepenult. This is strongly
opposed to the speech rhythm characteristic of English speakers,
who prefer stress on or near the first syllable. Thus, the stress

in French words borrowed into English has tended to move forward toward the beginning of the word, knocking vowels in every direction as it came—or rather, one should probably say, dumping vowels in a heap in the middle of our mouths, for the vowels made by these shifts tend to be the unstressed schwa [ə] made in the central position. Thus Chaucer could rhyme *piteous* with *saw a mouse* (to modernize the spelling), because *mouse* was then pronounced like our word *moose*, and *pitous*, being a word lately borrowed from French, was accented on the final syllable, and also had the sound of *oo*, [u]. In IPA they were [mus], [pɪtus]. Similarly, with Chaucer, *to pour* and *labor* rhymed because the two words were pronounced as though we were to spell them *toe poor* and *lay-boor*.

Furthermore, in Modern English, and especially in Modern American, any vowel which becomes unstressed is likely to become schwa [ə] or [ɪ], or to disappear. Thus *restaurant*, which was borrowed with a sound which might be suggested by *restau-raunt*, with a considerable stress on the last syllable, has become something like *restrunt*, or in IPA either [rɛstə'ənt] or [rɛstrɑnt]. This change is so common in Modern American speech that it is happening to one or more of the vowels in most of the longer words in the language, and in the shorter words when they are used in positions which are unstressed. For instance, the vowel in *her* would probably be preserved in the sentence, "That freak? I wouldn't have a date with her," but would be reduced to schwa in, "My dear, will you look at the size of her rear!"

*Linguistic Lemmings to the Sea*     AND NOW we come to the last of our four general principles, and by all odds the most curious, that there are occasional great shifts in human sound. The first three principles are sensible enough. Granted that we make sounds the way we do, granted that we are human beings with human foibles, then the first three principles are merely a statement of what it means to be a human being and to have vocal organs. But the fourth principle is baffling. It makes too much sense to be nonsense, and not enough sense to be reasonable.

A limited group of sounds which have remained stable for long periods will inexplicably change in accordance with some common tendency. They will do this for a certain length of time, in a certain place among certain peoples. Then they will stop, and change no more. It is as though we were all lemmings in our speech. Those curious polar rodents have occasionally gone on long migrations, starting no one knows why, and going they apparently know not where. The older legend is that they rush down to the sea and plunge into it, but certainly they have not always done so. They move, however, in masses, in relatively orderly masses, though to no apparent purpose. Impelled by a mysterious urge, they start in countless numbers, devastating fields as they go, decimated by birds and beasts of prey, marching over hills and valleys. Then, for years, or decades, or generations, no more lemmings feel the need to move. Something like the migrations of the lemmings, having an explained order, but an unexplained impulse, are these great shifts in human sound.

Stated as simply as possible, the principle would be about as follows: Sounds tend to remain relatively fixed; but within stable areas of sound, certain sounds may at any time become unstable and shift. If they do so, they perform this shift within a limited time and space, and in accordance with directions which can be described linguistically.

Most English sounds today are very near to what they were more than a thousand years ago. When Hengist and Horsa stormed ashore on the island of Britain—if they did—seizing a hill and demanding land, they said the words *hill* and *land* very much as we say them. But certain other words that these estimable gentlemen must have used during the course of their robber-baronage have changed so much that they are now unrecognizable, and part of this change is a change in vowel sounds. Furthermore, this shift has come about with an orderly progression that seems nothing less than planned and deliberate. The whole thing suggests the march of the lemmings.

For instance, the word which is now *she* was pronounced like our word *shay*, *boat* something like our word *bought*, *cat* like our word *cot*, *meat* like our word *mat*, *hate* like our word *hat*, *mood* like our word *mode*, and the like. Now, if anyone has the curiosity to sound these words out, and check them against the phonetic symbols in the chart of vowel sounds on page 119, he is likely to make an amazing discovery. These sound changes may seem as idiotic as the antics of a wild goose eating hashish, but they are orderly to the point of being pedestrian. The sounds are moving forward and upward in the mouth. The amazing fact is that, in general, Anglo-Saxon tense sounds have moved forward about one jump. Sounds like [i] and [u], which were as far forward as they could go, have turned back and become diphthongs. *Ride* was pronounced like our word *reed*, and *louse* like our word *loose*. Furthermore, this shift occurred only among the tense vowels. Anglo-Saxon [ε] remained unchanged, as in *hell, tell, well;* Anglo-Saxon [ɪ] remained unchanged, as in *hill, till, will*. Nor did the change occur all at once. A word pronounced like our *hay* acquired its pronunciation as *he* before a word pronounced like *heed* became our word *hide*. That is, [e] became [i] before [i] became [ɑɪ]. And this difference seems to be part of a pattern.

Why? Similar sounds did not undergo similar changes in Old Norse, which was a sister language to Anglo-Saxon. They did not so change in related dialects in Low German. Why did the Germanic peoples who came to the island of Britain, just after they had got nicely inured to the British fogs, start shoving all their tense vowels away from their glottises? Why did they not shift any of their slack vowels? Why, having started this process, did they not continue it? Since the highest, most frontal vowel possible is [i], why did not all vowels move forward until they all became [i]? Why, in our progressive age, can we not make vowels go onward and upward as could Chaucer and the Venerable Bede? Nobody knows. Nobody has even a good guess. For some reason Englishmen started shoving tense vowels forward in their mouths. Then they stopped. And they have remained stopped. Nobody knows why they started or why they stopped.

Of course there have been theories. There are always some people who try to explain everything by climate, who will even try to explain language by climate. Language, however, pretty clearly rests on human nature and human vocal organs, not upon fog and sunshine. The Eskimos, for instance, make sounds very similar to those made by the Ubanga. But let us have a look at the climatic theory, since it seems to be one of those hardy perennials that the frosts of scholarship do not much discourage.

The thesis is something like this. The tough Teutons, full of vitamins and the scent of the health-giving balsam, came out of the woods of northern Europe and settled the fog-girt island of Britain. Naturally, the poor things all got colds. They could not pronounce low back vowels any more, and their vowels moved forward to something they could pronounce. Unfortunately, this same theory works in just the opposite way—it is a good theory which can be made to prove diametric statements.

For consider, the believers in climate would say that the vowels moved away from the glottis because the English had colds. But they would also say that the Germans and Scandinavians have many back vowels and consonants in their languages because these peoples lived in rigorous climates, had colds, and therefore husky voices. Why do colds prevent low back sounds among Englishmen, and cause them among Swedes? Similarly, the believers in climate would say that the Italic peoples expanded under the warm suns of Italy, threw out their chests, breathed deeply through their nonasthmatic windpipes, and emitted broad Italian $a$'s. But if the warm sun makes [ɑ] sounds, how does it happen that the poor Paiute, shivering on his bleak plateaus between the Rocky Mountains and the Sierra Nevadas, has a laudable collection of broad $a$ sounds, a variety of them that Verdi might well have coveted for his arias. In short, if we accept the climatic explanation of linguistic change. we must be prepared to assume that similar conditions will bring about opposite results.

But let us get back to England, and to Hengist and Horsa, who have conquered Britain, and have found that the paths of glory lead but to a cold in the head. Since, according to the climatic theory, English noses were stopped up, the English would have been incapable of pronouncing nasal continuants, and all nasals should have disappeared. But they did not. Quite the contrary. They increased. For instance, it was during this time that we acquired the present participle ending in *-ing*, that is, ending with the nasal [ŋ]. The Anglo-Saxon present participle had ended in *-nd*, and there was nothing wrong with it at all, but for some reason the sons of Hengist and Horsa preferred to add another nasal to their list of unpronounceable sounds. And where did they get it? They probably got it from the Scandinavians, who lived among even colder fogs than the British fogs, and should have had worse head colds than Hengist and Horsa did.

In short, the whole thesis makes no sense. Nobody has ever been able to prove that climate determined language, except by deciding first what he wanted to prove, and then looking about in the Lord's plenty of linguistic evidence and selecting only those bits which would seem to prove his thesis. We know that the tense vowels in Anglo-Saxon moved forward and upward in the mouth, and although we suppose and even hope that there must have been some reason for this, we do not know the reason. The lemmings marched, whether to the sea or somewhere else, and the stressed vowels marched forward in the mouth. The lemmings stopped marching; so did the vowels. For all we know, the behavior of the British vowels is no more logical than the behavior of a Norwegian rodent.

There is a curious footnote to this. Although most English consonants are very much what they were when Hengist and Horsa bargained with Vortigern, one consonant has disappeared, leaving traces of itself in a few vowels, and an occasional glottal or voiceless labiodental fricative. In Anglo-Saxon the sound was written with an *h*, and it sounded much like the Modern German *hackle*. It is formed by starting as though you expect to make the sound [k], and then going on to clear your throat. The phonetic symbol for it is [χ]. It was used, for instance, in the Anglo-Saxon word for an enclosed place, which was spelled *burh*, and was pronounced about as an American would try to pronounce *boorkh*. This sound dropped out and left others in its place. It could become the sound of hard *g*, as in *burg*. It could become a vowel, the final sound of *Canterbury* and *Salisbury*. It could become a different vowel, as in *borough* and *Edinburgh*. It could acquire the sound of *f*, as in *Brough-under-Stainmore* (pronounced *Bruff*).

Again, why? Nobody knows. Frequently in language we can tell what happened; we can even see order in what happened. But often we cannot tell why changes occurred as they did. But here, at least, is an interesting guess, for what it may be worth.

Let us first examine the palatal and velar stops mentioned in the list on page 125. Try pronouncing consecutively the words *gawk* and *geek*. You will surely notice that in *gawk* the sounds indicated by *g* and *k* are pronounced far back in the mouth, and that the sounds indicated by the same letters in *geek* are pronounced far forward in the mouth. Why? This time the answer is obvious. The vowel in *gawk* [ɔ] is a back vowel and the vowel in *geek* [i] is a front vowel, and [g] and [k] move with the vowel. Other consonants do not move in the same manner. The sound [d] must be made at the base of the teeth no matter what the preceding vowel, and [s] can be made only with the teeth. But the velar stop becomes a palatal stop as the adjacent vowel moves forward, and if the vowel moves forward far enough, the stop is likely to disappear. If you doubt it, try saying a syllable like *awkh*, and move this forward.

Did the guttural *h* in Anglo-Saxon disappear because it tried to move forward when the Anglo-Saxon tense vowel moved forward, and did it then get lost in the confusion? Perhaps. At least this is a tolerably plausible guess, and the *h*-sound did disappear, leaving behind it the spelling *gh*, which has become one sound in *enough*, and has disappeared into other sounds in *though*, *through*, and *thought*.

*Here We Go*
*Round the*
*Mulberry*
*Bush*

THIS, then, is the movement in sound which is called the Great Vowel Shift in English. An even more spectacular shift had occurred prior to Anglo-Saxon times, described in what is known as Grimm's Law, or the Progression of Mutes, a sound change named for the same Brothers Grimm who collected the fairy tales, Jacob Grimm having popularized a statement which seems to have been worked out mainly by the Danish philologist, Rasmus Rask.

Grimm's Law concerns a shift in consonants which can be observed if we examine a few words in Latin and English. *Fish* in English is *pisces* in Latin; *father* in English is *pater* in Latin; *foot* in English is *pedes* in Latin. Is it not remarkable that in these three words where *f* occurs in English *p* occurs in Latin? It is; and it is more remarkable that these are only three common words of which there are hundreds having similar characteristics. Furthermore, whereas *father* in English is *pater* in Latin, *mother* in English is *mater* in Latin, and *brother* in English is *frater* in Latin. That is, where *f* occurs in English you may expect to find *p* in Latin, and where *th* occurs in English you may expect to find *t* in Latin.

That is startling enough, but we should now consider that [f] is the fricative which corresponds to the stop [p], and that *th* is the spelling for the fricatives, [đ] and [θ], which correspond to the stop [t]. This is altogether too consistent to sound like a series of accidents, and the whole becomes even more amazing when we realize that *hundred* in English and *centum* in Latin are the same word, and that [h] represents the fricative of which [k] is the stop.

This can become complicated, too complicated to go into here. But any careful examination of the consonants in Indo-European languages will reveal an amazing system of linguistic musical chairs. The consonants have moved about in an orderly way, taking each other's places in accordance with linguistic principles. When Grimm's statement is supplemented with another known as Verner's Law, a simplified diagram of the movement of Indo-European consonants looks something like this:

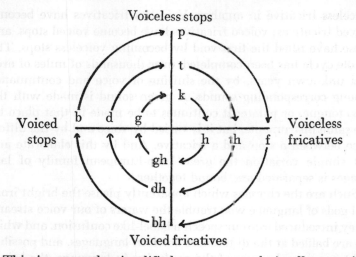

This is a greatly simplified statement, admittedly too simplified. To call Grimm's and Verner's statements "laws" is to seem to give them an authority they do not have. They are not laws even in the sense that the law of gravity is a law; the changes described did happen once, but they need not happen again. Furthermore, the diagram should be at least three-dimensional, so as to suggest that the sounds changed phonetically as they progressed chronologically. Nor is our information so accurate and detailed as we could wish; the sounds of the Indo-European consonants can only be inferred, not with entire confidence. And of course there are exceptions, limitations, and aberrant tendencies, but even these exceptions can often be described linguistically. The voiceless fricatives mentioned in Verner's Law, for instance, were voiced only when a preceding voiced sound did not carry the principal stress in the word.

But if the orderliness of the progression of Indo-European consonants can readily be exaggerated, it can also be unduly belittled. After exceptions and variations are allowed for, the central fact remains. And this fact is relatively simple, considering the detail it involves, and astounding. Whatever the sound in the parent Indo-European, a given Indo-European consonant has become a voiceless stop in one language and the corresponding voiceless fricative in another. Voiceless fricatives have become voiced fricatives; voiced fricatives have become voiced stops, and these have filled the first void by becoming voiceless stops. The whole cycle has been completed, over thousands of miles of area and unknown years, by the shifting of voice and continuance among corresponding sounds. A given sound is made with the lips, tongue, or palate; it continues to be made in that place by the same instruments, but it is varied by voice and by the difference between a stop and a fricative. And by this elaborate and yet simple variation the great Indo-European family of languages is separated and bound together.

Such are the changes which apparently please the bright ironical gods of language who trouble the waters of our voice stream. They introduced into our speech a babel-like confusion, and while we are baffled at the differences between languages, and possibly fight our wars because of the confusion in language, the bright gods know that beneath all this complexity and confusion is the simplicity of the gods themselves. But only occasionally, and imperfectly, can we glimpse divine simplicity.

# ❧ 10 ❧

## WHOM LINGUISTICS HATH JOINED TOGETHER LET NO MAN PUT ASUNDER

UNITED IN HOLY WORDLOCK—GIVING AND TAKING IN LINGUISTIC MARRIAGE—COME SIT BY ME AND BE MY LOVE—THE SONS OF HENGIST AND HORSA GET EMBARRASSED ABOUT GRAMMAR—CRUSADER FROM CONNECTICUT—COMMON LAW MARRIAGE IN GRAMMAR—CAN WE MAKE HONEST WOMEN OF OUR WORDS?

*United in*
*Holy Wordlock*

LANGUAGE, too, finds itself in an honorable estate, and if the holy bond within which it lives and breathes and has its offspring is at times sinned against, the cohabitation is usually fruitful. And like human matrimony, the state of language results from a mating of complementary opposites.

With one of the high contracting parties, whether bride or groom—sex in language is as difficult to determine as sex in kittens, but she resembles a bride—we have become acquainted in the previous chapters. This is meaning, meaning which can be embodied in symbols, that is, in words. But words are seldom pregnant of precise or extensive meaning, not without some help. To become so pregnant they must be married with an activating agent which will prompt them to generate new meaning, meaning not quite of the words but growing out of the words. In language, this new meaning is conceived by the assistance of some device which shows relationships between words, so that meanings can grow into new meanings, larger meanings, more exact meanings. This device, this system, this bridegroom of the word, we call grammar. Without both symbols for meaning and devices for grammar no linguistic agglomeration can be more than a language in name only.

The study of grammar has been honored in accordance with its importance. For instance, Shakespeare, to discredit Jack Cade as a rebel, has him burn the laws and abolish representative government, and then go on to murder Lord Say for being guilty as follows:

> *Thou hast most traitorously corrupted the youth of the realm in erecting a grammar-school. . . . It will be proved to thy face that thou hast men about thee that usually talk of a noun and a verb, and such abominable words as no Christian ear can endure to hear.*

Conversely, with men of nobler stamp there has always been opprobrium attached to ignorance of grammar. After an honorable fellow in righteous wrath has told a blackguard what he is, to wit, a murderer, a blasphemer, and a rapist, what more is there to say than that he is an utterer of solecisms?

The study of grammar has been uncommonly applauded among most civilized peoples, and particularly in our own tradition, where for centuries the basis of all formal education was Latin grammar. Today there is a furtive notion about in some English-speaking countries, based upon the success of the self-made and sometimes apologetically nongrammatical man, that perhaps the rules of grammar are not so important after all. But these are the exceptions. The United States armed forces believe in the rules. Important businessmen believe in the rules. The more literate senators believe in the rules. And the poor freshman who fails his English is likely to assume that the trouble was he "just never could learn grammar." Meanwhile, generations of thwarted teachers of the traditional grammar, seeing their years flee from them and leave behind neither wealth nor honor, have felt they had some reward if they could honestly face their Maker and say, "I taught the difference between the gerund and the gerundive."

Theirs is a bitter irony, and it is well that many of them have
gone to their reward without learning the truth. For the truth
seems to be that they were victims of a mighty hoax, one of those
truly belly-rumbling impostures which a workaday world can
but seldom afford. They were good men and true, those teachers,
and good women as well: spinsters hunting for a way to be useful
in the world, young people crammed as full of ideals as syntax,
devoted students who would gladly learn and gladly teach. And
yet the study to which they devoted their lives almost did not
exist, at least not in the form in which they were trying to teach
it. Or, more exactly, the grammar which these good people re-
spected and professed was not the grammar of English at all; it
was at best a pallid reflection of Latin grammar, an insignificant
part of English grammar. Usually the dullest dolt in school
learned more English grammar playing with his fellows than
was printed in his grammar book.

In short, if English grammar were only what is codified in
most books of grammar and taught in most classes in grammar,
then there never could have been a marriage of words and relationships in English. For the bridegroom which most of us have
been calling "grammar" most of our lives is no bridegroom at all,
but a clotheshorse draped in somewhat skimpy morning clothes.
With only him to show relationships, no man living could use
the English language in any way to be understood. Fortunately
the bridegroom did arrive for his marriage with meaning, even
though he has not been recognized by all of his well-wishers. Our
vocabulary is not living in shame. Far from it. But the background of the bridegroom is curious and will bear investigating.

Before we do so, however, we shall need to define our terms,
for the word *grammar* is used variously, and unless we are careful, I shall be endeavoring to say one thing and you will think
I mean something else. Popularly, grammar is concerned at least
in part with deciding such questions as whether or not *ain't I*
and *he don't* are correct. These are more properly questions of
*usage,* an important field to which we must eventually turn, but
of secondary importance for an understanding of grammar.

Grammar, in the sense in which I use the word in this book,

comprises whatever the users of a language do with symbols of meaning (in English, words) in order to express extensive and complicated meanings. That is, grammar is not a set of rules; it is something inherent in the language, and language cannot exist without it. It can be discovered, but not invented. Presumably grammar in this sense should be described in the statements about language which are included in the grammar books in common use. But is it? To this question we should address ourselves. In doing so I shall try to refer to the grammar which is commonly taught today as *conventional* or *traditional grammar*. When I refer to grammar without qualification I mean to imply grammar as a phenomenon of language, or the grammar of English, whether it is or is not well reflected in the conventionally accepted grammatical statement.

*Giving and Taking in Linguistic Marriage*

WORDS AND grammar can become one in meaning in accordance with various bodies of linguistic law and custom, which can be reduced to two. We can change the form or composition of the symbols for meaning (in English, words), or we can leave the units of meaning untouched but change their arrangement. Both principles can be illustrated in English.

Consider the words *sing* and *song*. By changing the form of the words many effects become possible, but here are a few:

sings songs — the addition of an *-s*, meaningless in itself, makes one word a verb with a particular use, the other word a plural noun

sang songs — an internal change alters the time of the action

singable song— the addition of *-able*, which has a known meaning but which cannot be used alone in this sense, makes one word a modifier

singsong — stuck together, the words become one modifier

To suggest the second grammatical principle, that which relies upon a change of order, consider the words *harvest* and *apples,* and leaving them unchanged in form, alter their relative positions.

| | |
|---|---|
| harvest apples | —the words suggest a juicy fruit which will not keep |
| harvest the apples | — the words are now part of a command |
| apples harvest | — the words are now nonsense; they have lost their grammar |
| apple harvest | — the words make sense again, but not without a change of form which accompanies the change of position |

That is, there are two fundamental principles in grammar, and English makes at least some use of both of them.

What is true of English is true very widely. The grammars of most languages make use, in one way or another, both of change in the form of a word and arrangement of words, principles which are useful in understanding grammar, but not exact as a basis for classifying grammars or languages. The late Professor Edward Sapir made a learned attempt to classify languages; his performance was brilliant and the results complicated, but he was prompt to insist that the resulting classification was very rough. The results may be found in his excellent book, *Language* (New York, 1921), pp. 59–156, and especially pp. 150–51. No such classification will be attempted here. I shall be concerned only with comprehending enough of the essential nature of grammar so that we can have some basis upon which to examine English grammar.

Let us consider the two principles in more detail, noticing first that which employs changes of form. Man is ingenious at meddling with things—not without significance is the fact that we are related biologically to the monkeys—and he has devised a variety of means of altering the forms and composition of words. For instance, some languages, notably Chinese and many languages of the Sudan, make extensive use of pitch as a grammatical device, and pitch is a change in spoken form. A South

Alaskan speaker of Tlingit, for example, uses a low tone for the past, a high tone for the future. We make some use of the device; *That's right?* is quite different from *That's right!* Similarly, reduplication, noticed in Chapter 5 as a device in vocabulary, can be used also in grammar. In Bantoc Igorot *anak* means *child*, but *ananak* means *children*, that is, "child-child-child-child," or "child keep coming one after another." The three most commonly recognized devices for changing the form and composition of words, all of which appear in English, are called *inflection*, *agglutination*, and *polysynthesis*. They are closely related, and not always distinguishable, but a rough distinction may be useful.

The first of these, inflection, is familiar to anyone who knows conventional grammar; it commonly includes the following: *declension*, that is, changes in the endings of nouns and adjectives; *conjugation*, changes in the endings of verbs; *ablaut*, changes within words. To observe the working of inflection as a device of grammar, consider the following words: *Canem devorabat scriptor.* The three Latin words are forms of *dog, to eat*, and *copyist*, and the whole might be translated very freely, *The newspaperman ate the dog.* They mean this because the endings for *canis* and *scriptor* indicate that the newspaperman did the eating and that the dog was eaten. The subject need not come first in a Latin sentence, since its form, determined by its ending—that is, by its inflection—indicates that it is the subject. In fact, in classical Latin no word had to occur in any particular place in the sentence; position, however handy it may have been for rhetoric, had practically no grammatical use. Latin, at least the classical Latin of Cicero and Virgil, was so extensively inflected that, speaking roughly, we may refer to it as an inflected language.

Less exactly, we may call Anglo-Saxon, the ancestor of English, an inflected language. *Beowulf* begins, after a flourish, "We gardena." This means "We of the people of the Spear Danes," and the ideas which we must translate with phrases are involved in the fact that *gardena* is a genitive plural, as is indicated by its ending. After all, Anglo-Saxon came from Proto-Germanic, which was an Indo-European language, and presumably inherited an inflectional system much like that preserved in Latin and Greek.

Now for agglutination and polysynthesis. They resemble each other, since agglutination refers to the joining of symbols which can serve also as separate words, synthesis to the joining of symbols, one or more of which cannot serve as words. These devices have but limited use in English. Accordingly, let us turn to an American Indian language, since most aboriginal American tongues use them heavily. I am here relying upon the work, as yet unpublished, of my good friend Dr. Sven Liljeblad, who has long been engaged in a monumental study of several northern Shoshone dialects.

Let us take the casual remark of an old Bannock, who wanted to say, "I am going to the place where the junipers grow." To write the old man's sentence we need symbols not included in Chapter 8, but since we shall not need to sound the sentence out to understand it, pass over the following collection of symbols if they look repulsive. (They constitute, incidentally, the first Bannock sentence ever printed.)

nə:   ìwáwá:písəakwaitù   míaukwə̀

Of the three sections of this sentence separated by spaces, the first is the subject, and might be called a word. The other two are clusters of stems, suffixes, and the like, which cannot be used as words except in combination. A literal translation of the sentence would read something like the following:

I   many-juniper(the kind of)grow-at-to   go-instantly-shall

With the diacritical marks omitted for simplicity, this statement would break down into something like this:

nə   —the equivalent of *I*
iwa- —*many;* in this usage it cannot stand alone
wa:- —*juniper,* a noun stem
-pi  —a classification suffix
səa- —*grow,* a verb stem
-kwai—*place where,* an indication of a noun

-tu   —*to,* another indication of a noun

mia-  —*go,* a verb stem

-u   —verb suffix, indicating that the action is to be brief

kwə  —verb suffix, indicating that the action will occur in the immediate future

That is, the sentence is made up of the following elements:

1) a particle, phonetically a word
2) a particle, plus a noun stem, plus a suffix, plus a verb stem, plus two suffixes, all of which function as a noun
3) a verb stem plus two suffixes, all serving as a verb

The order of these three could be changed without affecting the sense much, just as the order in a Latin sentence can be changed.

To see how agglutination and synthesis work, we might look in a bit more detail at one part of the sentence. The noun stem *wa:-* with its suffix *pi* could be either singular or plural, but could be designated plural by one of several additions. In this sentence plurality is provided by *iwa,* a particle which in this form can occur only within a compound with a noun or a verb stem, forming together one construction, so that the two could be said to be agglutinated. Synthesis can be observed in the suffix. The stem *wa:-* relates the noun cluster to the juniper sort, and the suffix *-pi* indicates a tree of the juniper sort. A suffix *-púi* would indicate berries of the juniper sort, and *-pu? a* bark of the juniper sort. In Bannock, every noun stem must be followed by suffixes similar to these.

All of these devices have some use in English. Nouns are usually inflected to form plurals and possessives, and many verbs have inflectional endings. In the example above, the words in *sings songs* are inflected. Synthesis has some currency in English. In the example above, *singable* has an affix; many others could be mentioned, *songster, singer, unsingable,* and the like. Most of these prefixes and suffixes have some grammatical function, since they alter the function of the word. Of the three, agglutination is used the least as a grammatical device, although we employ it in vocabulary. That is, we stick words together to make new words, but not mainly to provide new grammar. A blackboard was once a black board, although now it can be made of gray slate or green plastic, so long as it serves as a surface upon which to write with chalk. Blackboard is a new word, although it is grammatically comparable to a black board. But we cannot say *outhouse* when we mean *out of the house*—an *outhouse* is something quite different. Even more emphatically we cannot say *outIhouse,* meaning *I am about to go out of the house.* Our speech might be terser if we could use such devices; American Indian languages are often very terse. But we cannot. For better or for worse, our grammar has never made much use of agglutination.

*Come Sit*　　　AND NOW for the second principle in gram-
*by Me and*　　mar, changing the arrangement of the units
*Be My Love*　　of meaning, variously known as distribu-
　　　　　　　tion, analysis, and isolation. The distribu-
tive principle is very simple, at least in larger aspects, so simple that in general it consists of stringing one word after another, and allowing the words to acquire their relationships from the fact of their sitting side by side. Now, consider the sentence which I have just written and you have just read. There is some declension in it. *Their* is a declined form, as is *larger.* The nouns are singular or plural depending upon whether or not they end in *s. Consists, stringing, allowing,* and *sitting* have endings. Without these endings we would feel that the grammar is "wrong." Curiously enough, however, we would understand the sentence if these words were not declined. *From the fact of they sit side by side* would raise a titter, but it would be understandable. Inflection, apparently, is not of primary importance in understanding the sentence. Agglutination does not occur. Synthesis appears in suffixes like *-ship,* but the suffix has become so much a part of the word that its occurrence is not very important for grammar. *Relations* would have served almost as well as *relationships.*

Next we need to notice another grammatical device. In classical Latin, as in other declined languages, a speaker could indicate the differences between *in the town* and *to the town* by a case ending, but even in classical Latin times the ordinary people were talking an extensively distributive speech which we call Vulgar Latin. Vulgar Latin was likely to precede the words *town* with *in* or *ad*, the one meaning *in* and the other *to*, and not worry much about the ending. For similar purposes, Anglo-Saxon had declensions, but we now use all sorts of words, commonly called prepositions, conjunctions, and relatives, to indicate the relationships of certain words if the relationship would not be clear by setting the words side by side. In the sentence under discussion words like *at, in, so, of, after,* and several more are mainly concerned with showing relationships, not with exhibiting meaning. *General it consists stringing* makes no sense; *in general it consists of stringing* is clear as far as it goes. We might notice one of these little words, for example, *of,* one of the commonest words in the language. Can you define it? Probably not. You will do very well if you do. Practically, it has very little meaning— *dozens of answers, I have heard of him, of little use, a bad habit of my father's.* But if *of* has little meaning, it has a great deal of use in showing relationships. It is only one of many English words which are mainly or partly concerned with establishing the interreliance of English symbols for meaning.

But these relationship words are the mark of a distributive language. They help to determine the meaning of the sentence, along with the much more important device of the words "sitting side by side."

Let us repeat the sentence we are discussing, since it occurred so many sentences back.

"The distributive principle is very simple, at least in larger aspects, so simple that in general it consists of stringing one word after another, and allowing the words to acquire their relationships from the fact of their sitting side by side."

Now try to swap any one of these words with its neighbor. You are likely to find that the result is nonsense. For instance, "Distributive the is principle simple very." In fact, from end to end, from *distributive the* to *side side by* you cannot change the position of one word so much as one position without either changing the meaning of the sentence or rendering the words into gibberish. A few changes are possible; the sentence could have been started, "At least in larger aspects," or "In larger aspects, at least," but the possible changes are very few, and can be executed only within narrow and rigid limits. Nor is this sentence unusual. Try this test on any Modern English sentence of any complexity at all and you will get very much the same result.

We are now ready to enunciate a principle. We have the evidence before us. We have seen that English words have meaning in a sentence because of their position in the sentence, that English words have one meaning in a certain order, another meaning or no meaning in another order. Since this is true, what is the basis of English grammar? Obviously the order of the words. The root fact of English grammar is that English words have precise meaning in a certain position, and are gibberish in another position. This fact, however one wishes to phrase it, embodies the most important grammatical truth that can be enunciated about English: *Order in the sentence is the basis of English grammar*. And yet, barring a few students of Modern English, the chances are that not one in a hundred readers of this page will ever have heard anything like this statement before. That is the simple, the almost unbelievable truth.

*The Sons of Hengist and Horsa Get Embarrassed About Grammar*   ENGLISH grammar, like other phenomena of this world, must have grown through some prolonged, almost infinitely complex evolution. That, we would probably all assume. But if modern notions of English grammar are so new that most users of the language have never heard them whispered, the changes in our thinking about grammar must have been so violent as to be described as nothing short of revolution. They are revolutionary, not to say, in some quarters, pyrotechnic. Let us try to find out how this revolution came about. Or rather, let us first try to find out how we acquired a grammatical statement, which we accepted as English grammar, and which was so remote from English that it did not contain some of the most elementary principles. When we know that, we should know why we had to have a twentieth-century revolution in English grammar. Let us start with English in the earliest forms we have it, with Anglo-Saxon.

Hengist and Horsa, and their sons after them, were intelligent and somewhat subtle people. They knew how to kill their enemies, and even how to kill each other; they knew how to steal land, cattle, and other people's wives; they knew how to keep the faith even though they lost their heads as the penalty; and they knew also how to do what they had promised not to do and yet do it so cleverly that they could not be accused of breaking their word. We know these facts about them, because these are among the facts which interest many people, and they were recorded. The sons of Hengist and Horsa must have known, also, how to use grammar. Otherwise they could not have made themselves understood. But if they had any abstract curiosity about the nature of grammar, when it was right or wrong, good or bad, precise or slovenly, their chroniclers did not record the fact. As far as we know, the Anglo-Saxons just talked their grammar, and did not talk much about it. And why should they? Latin grammar was theirs to study—the few, that is, who supported learned pretensions—but nothing learned was written in Anglo-Saxon. Not until Alfred's time, just before A.D. 900, was there much practical writing in the native tongue, and then only as a war emergency. Then, before Englishmen had developed enough leisure to become self-conscious about their grammar, the Normans arrived, made French the official language, and reduced English to a vulgar speech. Only among very sophisticated people is the language of swineherds and wood-choppers a subject for serious study, and the descendants of Hengist and Horsa were some time becoming sophisticated.

But the time came. In the fifteenth century, and especially in the sixteenth century, Englishmen became self-conscious about their language. They recognized that their native tongue was an obscure dialect, not much removed from the speech of barbarians, nothing to be compared with Latin. Latin was not only the speech of the Holy Roman Empire, but assuredly the language of the Lord God, of Christ, of the Holy Ghost, of all the angels and devils, and of the Virgin Mary, even though the Virgin, being a woman, presumably could not read and might therefore get her declensions wrong. Nor was Anglo-Saxon—and later Middle English—anything to be compared with French or Italian, which had many words like Latin, and in any event were the languages of relatively sophisticated peoples. But by the fifteenth century all this was changing, at least somewhat.

Chaucer had lived and died, and had left behind him a body of poetry of very high order, and a school of imitators who were trying to be little Chaucers. Chaucer, if he was not quite a national poet, had become a national hero. He had proved that the English language was a good language, good enough to write great poetry in. Accordingly, Englishmen began worrying and started to do something about grammar. If English was to be an important language, it surely needed a grammar. But where were they to get one? Not even Chaucer seemed to have any grammar, at least nothing that was much like what was taught in the Latin grammar schools. If Chaucer wanted to rhyme the past participle of *find* with *bounden*, he spelled it *y-founden*, and if he did not want the extra syllable, he left off the *y-*. If he wanted to rhyme it with *hounde*, he spelled it *founde*, but if he wanted to rhyme it with *ground*, he spelled it *found*. Was this inflection? And he would make plurals with either *n* or *s*. What kind of a grammar was that?

Very well, if Englishmen needed a grammar, they would get one. By the sixteenth century the revival of classical studies, which we know both as the Renaissance and as Humanism, was in full cry. Everybody who was anybody at all knew how to get information—one went to the classics after it. Especially, everybody knew that the Greeks had been famous students of grammar. The Romans had made use of this excellent Greek grammar, and had elaborated it with Latin. Furthermore, this grammar was taught to every schoolboy. Quite naturally, scholars assumed that Latin grammar was not merely Latin grammar, but that it was grammar itself. They borrowed it and made the most of it.

Not that they could make much, since Latin grammar was the grammar of an inflected language, and English had by now become mainly a distributive language. That is, the two languages were radically different in the etymological sense of that word, different down to the roots. But the scholars did not consider such problems, and as a matter of course they did not go to the English language itself, study a piece of ordinary prose, and ask themselves, what is it that gives the prose meaning? No. The world was as yet too young in science for that, and the study of grammar is a science. They went to Aristotle and Pliny for their physical and biological science, and even more they went to Greek and Latin grammar books for their syntax. For which, after all, there was good reason. Pliny may have been bad zoology, but the Roman grammars, as grammars of classical Latin, were excellent. Apparently no one stopped to ask whether or not the principles embodied in these grammars applied to a language descended from Anglo-Saxon. That, they assumed.

Accordingly, the Humanist grammarians took out their Latin textbooks, and searched in them for rules which would apply to English. They found some, made up examples in English to fit the rules, and these became the basis of what has become our traditional grammar. They did not find as much as they might have liked. Obviously, there were many splendid agreements which could be expressed in Latin endings for which there were no English equivalents. That was a pity. But what should one expect? Latin was the great language of all time—unless Greek, being more elaborately declined than Latin, had this honor— and should one expect to find English, a tongue but lately derived from barbarism, possessed of all the grammar that Latin had? Of course not. But the grammarians were happy to find that some of the rules applied, and no doubt they hoped that in time the language would become purified so that more would apply. Meanwhile, anything which came to their attention and which was not accounted for by a Latin rule, they assumed was either bad grammar or no grammar at all. Most English grammar never came to their attention.

WITH variations, this veneration and repetition of Latin rules continued. The Humanist grammar books were modest works, but their descendants did not remain modest. They grew, they elaborated, they became even more authoritarian, and they continued to be written on the basis that grammar was Latin grammar. Grammarians, disputing the rules of English grammar lost their tempers but not their love of Latin. Thus Noah Webster, publishing a new grammar book in 1807, could write, "Since the days of Wallis, who published a Grammar of the English Language, in Latin, in the reign of Charles II, from which Johnson and Lowth borrowed most of their rules, little improvement has been made in English Grammar." He goes on to say that many of Lowth's criticisms were "extremely erroneous"—Lowth's was long the standard grammar book. When the Lowth work was superseded, it was replaced by Murray's *English Grammar*. Lindley Murray, "the father of English Grammar," Webster dismisses as follows: "Murray, not having mounted to the original sources of information, and professing only to select and arrange the rules and criticisms of preceding writers, has furnished little or nothing new."

Noah Webster was a very downright sort of Yankee, given to dismissing people who disagreed with him, and few men have been able to commit and print so many errors in solemn places as he did. Yet Noah Webster, in spite of his bad temper and his occasional bad judgment, was a very great man. He often had the wit to recognize a good suggestion when he saw it; he had the courage to think with his own head; and he had the stubbornness to fight for his beliefs in the face of ridicule, indifference, and poverty. He was a born crusader and his love was language. He managed to live, in considerable part, on the returns from his spelling book; he gained fame from his dictionary. Meanwhile, but little attention has been given his *A Philosophical and Practical Grammar of the English Language*, in many ways a more original book than either of the others.

For Webster was original. His detractors sometimes mentioned his monumental conceit, and even seemed to feel that his peculiarities were not restricted to the bounds of sanity, but none of them, so far as now appears, ever accused him of being conventional. And in grammar he had good reason to believe that he was the mouthpiece of the new truth, for he had happened upon a remarkable and neglected volume, by one Horne Tooke, and he apparently conceived that in his crusade for truth in language the line of battle formed where Noah Webster and Horne Tooke defied the world.

Horne Tooke was the assumed name of John Horne, vicar by profession, politician by practice, and philologist by avocation. He was the author of *Epea Pteroenta, or Diversions of Purley*, perhaps the most original and suggestive statement by an Englishman on the whole subject of language prior to the nineteenth century. It did not come to the attention of many people. Had not Tooke been tried for high treason and changed his cognomen for shame? Had he not been convicted of libel? Had he not been excluded from Parliament? And was it not extremely improbable that any such person, a liberal, a believer in the Bill of Rights, and a supporter of the American Revolution, would have anything important to say about philology, even though he had been only accused, not convicted, of high treason? No doubt many British students of language reasoned in this way, and in any event, if they looked into the *Diversions of Purley* they would have found there no adequate respect for the importance of Latin. For whatever reason, they pretty much ignored the book.

Not so, Webster. The *Diversions* was republished in Philadelphia, and Webster saw it in 1787, shortly after he had published a conventional grammar as Part II of his *Grammatical Institute*. In Tooke he discovered that the accepted parts of speech were all wrong, that the accepted verbs were not the verbs of the English language, that the rules in the grammar books were not the rules of English at all. He discovered further that to understand English grammar the scholar should not go to Latin, but to Anglo-Saxon (which Webster called Saxon), and devise the grammar of English from the English language. He set himself to learn Anglo-Saxon, and twenty years later he produced his grammar book.

In the preface, he gives credit for his ideas to Horne Tooke, and goes on to explain why he had written the book, as follows:

> *I have long expected that some English scholar would attempt to reduce these [Tooke's] discoveries to practical use, by framing a system of rules to illustrate the construction of sentences, upon the genuine principles of the language. Being hitherto disappointed, and seeing nothing issue from the press but new compilations of old rules, and fresh editions of the same errors, I have at length undertaken to construct a Grammar, upon what my own researches into the ancient English, or Saxon language, with various extensive reading in modern books, have proved, to my full satisfaction, to be its only legitimate principles, and established usages.*

Nor was Tooke's influence restricted to Webster's grammar. It is all over Webster's dictionary; Tooke may have altered the whole course of Webster's life, but that is another story, not to be told here.

Tooke had not been immune to error. Webster was not immune to adopting Tooke's errors, or augmenting them with errors of his own. For instance, he thought the article *the* developed from an Anglo-Saxon relative, and that the relative *since* grew from the verb *see*. The resulting grammatical statement was what he himself would probably have called "extremely erroneous" if it had been written by somebody else. Yet Webster's *Grammar* was a remarkable work. If we know what English grammar is, then Webster did not, but he made great strides in the direction in which English grammar and our understanding of English grammar have recently gone.

Lately there have been important changes which presage more changes, but the fact remains that almost a century and a half after Webster wrote his grammar, most books in use and most courses being taught in schools are still founded upon a grammar very much like that in the books by Lowth and Murray. And if Webster was not always right when he described our grammar, he was certainly right when he said that Lowth and Murray were wrong. If he did not appreciate the importance of a shift from an inflected to a distributive language, he did have an inkling of this shift and of its import. Most American textbooks on the subject do not betray an inkling.

*Common Law Marriage in Grammar*

Now WE might ask ourselves a question. Latin and English both stem from Indo-European; their ancestors must have had a common grammar. How does it happen that the grammars of Latin and English are essentially different? The whole story is not preserved in extant Anglo-Saxon, because we have no written scrap of our language much earlier than A.D. 700, but we do know that Proto-Germanic, from which Anglo-Saxon descended, was a highly declined language. Even in Anglo-Saxon there are some seven classes of strong verbs with a number of subclasses, three classes of weak verbs, six or more classes of nouns with a variety of case endings, two declensions for adjectives, various declined pronouns, and the like. These endings are so important that reading early Anglo-Saxon without them becomes extremely difficult. For instance, in *Beowulf,* composed soon after 700, the King of the Danes speaks to the hero as follows: (the interlinear translation gives the basic meaning of the words, but not the grammar provided by the inflection)

Hafa      nu   ond geheald      husa   selest
*To take now and to preserve house good*

gemyne        maertho maegenellen cyth
*to remember glory      battlemight   know*

waca with        wrathum
*guard against fierce*

Clearly, the position of the words has here some importance for grammar, enough so that the meaning of this passage can probably be guessed, at least roughly, but to translate it with confidence and accuracy the reader must know declensions. With them the passage can be seen to mean something like the following:

> *Receive now and preserve this best of buildings;*
> *bear in mind your reputation, your well-known might in*
> *    battle,*
> *and protect all this well against the terrible one.*

Now let us look at a piece of Anglo-Saxon written something more than two centuries later in the *Anglo-Saxon Chronicle*.

> Ond thaes ymb  ii   monath gefeaht Aethered cyning ond
> *And that  about two month  to fight  Ethered  king  and*
>
> Aelfred his brothor with    thone here    aet Meretune ond
> *Alfred  he  brother against the    pirate  at Merton    and*
>
> hie    waerun on tuaem gefylcum ond hie   butu gefliemdon
> *they to be   in two     band     and they both to defeat*
>
> ond longe on daeg sige    ahton
> *and late  in day  victory to control*

Inflection appears here, but is much less needed, because the order of the words makes most of the grammar clear. Anyone is likely to guess that the passage means something like the following:

> *And about two months from then, Ethered the King and*
> *Alfred his brother fought against the pirates at Merton, who*
> *were in two bands, and they defeated both, and late in the*
> *day, gained the victory.*

Now let us drop down a few hundred years more, when we find Chaucer writing this:

*So hote he lovede, that by nightertale*
*He sleep namore than dooth a nightengale.*
*Curteys he was, lowly, and servisable,*
*And carf beforn his fader atte table.*

This still looks a little strange, mostly because the spelling is unfamiliar—in Middle English nobody bothered much about how
he spelled anyway, and partly this spelling represents sounds
which have changed since Chaucer's day. But the grammar has
become so nearly distributive that this passage, although it is
poetry, can be left in its present order if we wish to modernize it.

*So hot he loved that by night time*
*He slept no more than does a nightingale.*
*Courteous he was, lowly, and helpful,*
*And carved before his father at the table.*

In short, from *Beowulf* to Chaucer, the language had gone from
one which still retained an elaborate inflectional system to a
language which used a distributive grammar, had lost most of
its declensions, and did not have much use for those it kept. Iron-
ically, soon after this, well-meaning grammarians started trying
to explain this language by applying to it a grammar based upon
classical Latin, a highly inflected language.

Nor is this irony made less by a strong suspicion that classical
grammar was not the grammar of any living language, even in
classical times. Classical Latin grammar was certainly studied,
and classical Latin was used for all sorts of formal purposes.
Cicero composed orations in it; Caesar wrote official accounts of
his campaigns in it; Virgil built it into rolling, sonorous verse.
But many scholars doubt that anybody spoke it in conversation,
even in Virgil's time. The question is uncertain, for we have
little written conversation from which to judge. If a gossip-
monger like Suetonius had possessed a tape recorder we might
have some genuine daily speech, but even approximations of
colloquial conversation are but sparsely preserved in the plays
of the day. Certainly Latin had started to become a distributive
language in prehistoric times. It became even more so. Vulgar

Latin, the speech of ordinary people in Rome and the Latin
which has become the ancestor of Italian, French, Spanish, and
Portuguese, was a strongly distributive language. Did ordinary
workmen find it impossible to learn, remember, and use the
elaborate declensions? Probably not; even ignorant people can
remember quantities of detail if the detail is significant. Did
inflection break down because so many foreigners tried to learn
Latin? Perhaps, though there are chronological difficulties. Was
there some deep change moving over western Europe that made
people—Roman as well as Londoner—become impatient of
elaborate declensions and prefer order and relationship words?
Sounds fantastic, if intriguing. Did Italic grammar suffer with
the wanderings and wars of Italic people? Possibly, although
Sanskrit grammar seems not to have suffered from Aryan wanderings.

In short, we do not know the answer, but we do know that
classical Latin had become somewhat rare even in Cicero's time,
even when elaborate grammars of it were prepared, which books
later became the basis for grammars all over western Europe. But
let us look at a bit of this Vulgar Latin. Here is a sentence written
about A.D. 535, by a clubwomanish sort of person who took a
trip to the Holy Land. It is not conversation, and thus probably
less distributive than the same woman's speech would have been,
but it is obviously colloquial.

Haec est autem vallis ingense et planissima in qua
*There is next a valley large and very flat in which*

filii Israhel commorati sunt his diebus quod
*the children of Israel camped were those days when*

sanctus Moyses ascendit in Montem Domini et
*saint Moses climbed into the mountain of God and*

fuit ibi quadraginta diebus et quadraginta noctibus.
*was there forty days and forty nights.*

There is still some inflection here, and where it helps the grammar I have made use of it, but with slight changes, this passage

can be read as Modern English. In short, the grammar of this sentence is mainly determined by the position of words in the sentence, and by relationship words. If Lowth and Murray and their predecessors had based their grammar books on the spoken, not the classical language of Rome, their rules might have provided a description of something at least resembling English grammar.

*Can We Make* WHAT IS this grammar which has been
*Honest* growing for two thousand years or so with-
*Women of* out our having even an elementarily sound
*Our Words?* notion of what it is? That we could be so
deaf seems now preposterous. How could we fail to know how we talk?

One might answer by asking, how could we fail to know how we think? But the world blundered along for millenniums before it hit upon the scientific method. How could we fail to see how we grew? But the world of evolution was all about us from the dawn of time, and even a Buffon could insist that abrupt and miraculous creation was the obvious fact of the universe. How could we fail to know how we feel? We waited a long time for Freud.

Anyhow, we did fail. There was enough in classical Latin grammar which made sense in English so that we could cling to it, and we clung. Even now a number of my readers will feel that this chapter is the rankest sort of heresy, although there has not been a reputable student of grammar for a long time who believed the grammar books which are in common use. But we, the people, are loyal to our supposed grammar. Having labored to learn it, we now cherish it in accordance with the labor we have invested to acquire it. Like a problem child, it is the dearer for all it has cost us, or perhaps its inadequacy enlists our sympathy. Problem child or no, it is our own, or at least we feel that it is, being unwilling to admit that it is a problem child just because it is not our own, and deep in our hearts we never loved the adopted brat.

What is our grammar? If it is not what is published in the conventional books on the subject, what is it? Does anybody know?

In detail, no. If anyone has worked out a satisfactory statement of the various types of verbs and their uses in modern American speech, I have not seen it. If anyone has devised a satisfactory paradigm of the verb—that is, a list of classified verb forms—I have not seen it. If anyone has prepared an adequate catalog of the various sorts of complements in English, I have not seen it. The best grammarians do not agree as to exactly how our grammar works, and what makes it work that way. They have not even agreed as to whether it is best understood through an analysis starting from meaning or from speech rhythm. But there is very general agreement as to many of the most important things to be said about our language, and there have been startling observations of the way it develops.

This book is not a grammar book, nor will it endeavor any close examination of the structure of English, but we might note some broad tendencies, and some strange and significant changes. Enough of those are known so that we should be able to glance at them, and hope we are not making too many blunders. And if we make blunders about English grammar, we shall do so in good company.

# THE SPEECH THAT BLOOMS ON THE TONGUE, TRA-LA, HAS LITTLE TO DO WITH CASE

## GRAMMAR IS NOT A PIGEONHOLE DESK—THE GRAMMATICAL SYSTEM WE DO NOT HAVE—GRAMMAR IS SLIPPERY STUFF— THE NEW LOOK IN LANGUAGE

*Grammar Is Not a Pigeonhole Desk*

THE PREVIOUS chapter has suggested that our traditional grammar and our actual grammar bear little resemblance to each other. Many people to whom this statement may be unwelcome would reply, however, that whatever the theory may be, the practice of modern grammar is sound. They will say that although applying grammatical rules may be a little difficult, because grammar is a difficult and complicated subject, grammatical rules do explain the language. These people are likely to feel that they themselves can explain most of the language, and would be able to explain the remainder if they knew their grammar a little better.

This I have not found to be true. For years I have taught a college course in the nature of language through which have passed a considerable number of persons who were sure that the grammatical rules had been worked out and that they knew these rules. During this time I have maintained a standing challenge to anybody to make the following simple experiment. Pick up a book at random, open to a page at random, and put your finger on a sentence. Then explain the meaning of the sentence by conventional grammar. I have never found anyone who could do so. Some day I will. Some day I will lose because somebody will be lucky enough to put his finger on *Ouch!* He will say

"Interjection," and I shall have lost, at least by his rules of the game. In reality, to explain the grammar of *Ouch!* we should need to examine adjacent sentences, but the conventional grammarian would never concede I was being fair in expecting that of him, and accordingly I should lose. As yet, however, this has not happened, and nobody has explained a sentence for me on the basis of Latin grammar.

People who think the conventional grammar makes sense usually do so because they are not examining the grammar at all. They are doing one, and usually all, of the following:

(1) They restrict their examination of language to sentences made up to fit rules, and they do not examine these sentences further than to notice that they do fit. This of course is nonsense. If grammar will not explain ordinary prose—to say nothing of sentences made up *not* to fit the rules—there is something wrong with the grammatical rules.

(2) They expect to save any rule which gets into trouble by assuming, in any example which will not fit it, that additional words or a different order is "understood." The sentence is accordingly changed so that it does fit. Let us see how this works. Since I have recommended taking a sentence at random from a book, I will take one from a book which happens to be lying open on the table. It is Josephine Tey's *The Daughter of Time* (New York; Macmillan, 1952), opened to page 80. Running my eye down the page—since I am now looking for an example, not trying to explain any piece of prose—I find that one character says "Oh!" unexpectedly, and the hero asks, "What was the 'Oh' for?" Let us endeavor to parse this last sentence. *What* is an interrogative pronoun, subject of the sentence. *Was* is the verb. *Oh* is the complement. What is *for?* The *New International Dictionary*, second edition, which embodies a good compendium of conventional but relatively liberal grammatical opinion, gives *for* as a conjunction or a preposition. (Lest I be accused of treating dictionaries unkindly—and I am very far from wishing to do so—let me say once for all that I am citing dictionaries partly for my own convenience, and partly because the makers of widely used dictionaries have generally been more liberal than

the makers of widely used grammars.) But *for* in this sentence cannot be a conjunction; it has nothing to join. It cannot be a preposition; it has no object.

Obviously, *for* must be something. Accordingly a conventional grammarian would be likely to start by changing the sentence to another which is "understood." He might substitute "What was the 'Oh' intended for?" *Intended* can modify *oh*, and if *for* can be an adverb, it can modify the past participle *intended*. This is possible, for although the *New International* does not enter *for* as an adverb, doubtless some other authority does so. Or the grammarian could change the sentence to "For what was the 'Oh' intended?" *For* has now become a preposition. Other additions are possible, for instance, "For what remark which you suppressed was the 'Oh' intended to substitute?" and "What does the 'Oh' stand for?" The conventional grammarian also changes the order, although, if order is the basis of English grammar, one wonders what right he has to change it. He might say that the sentence is understood to be "For what was the 'Oh'?" No one would talk such nonsense, but let us pass that. Is *for what* the subject? Obviously not, for whatever a *for what* is, it is not and was not an *Oh*. Nor does the sentence improve if we try to make *for what* the complement and *Oh* the subject. Can *for what* be a modifier of *is*? Surely not; it does not qualify the is-ness of *is*. Unless *is* means *serves*, *substitutes*, or something else it does not mean, *for what* can scarcely modify it.

This sort of grammatical juggling might warrant several comments, but here are two obvious ones. First, these additions of words and changes of structure are not "understood." If they are understood, how are we to know which of the various possibilities we are to understand? I suspect that Miss Tey would have been outraged were we to suggest that she had meant any of these words or structures to be understood in place of the words and structure she used.

Now for a second comment. If we are to discuss the grammar of this sentence, we must discuss the sentence as it is. Obviously it has grammar. It was written by a reputable writer; it is put into the mouth of a presumably well-educated man and one who is highly intelligent; the man is at the moment discussing a subject seriously. Certainly Miss Tey thought the sentence had grammar when she wrote it. Any competent reader of English would know at once what the sentence was intended to mean. Therefore, Miss Tey is right; the sentence has grammar, and any grammatical statement which will not account for "What was the 'Oh' for?" without changing it in any particular is an inadequate statement. Our grammatical rules, not Miss Tey's grammar, are at fault.

(3) The people who defend conventional grammar are not concerned with understanding the grammar, but with putting words into pigeonholes. This is a harmless diversion, but it has little to do with English grammar, particularly since there are no pigeonholes into which grammatical concepts in English can be assorted so as to form anything like a classification. On what basis does the conventionally accepted grammar classify words? Not on form. Most of the so-called parts of speech have no connection with form, and those which do have some have not much. Adverbs end in *-ly,* but *fast* and *well* are adverbs (unless you call them verbs, modifiers, or adjectives, which of course they can be) and *homely* and *family* are supposedly not adverbs, although they end in *-ly.* Neither does traditional grammar classify words on meaning. Supposedly nouns are determined on meaning, and within limits the division is valid, but the presence of nouns determined by meaning among other pigeonholed objects determined on other bases only confuses the classification. And last, the conventional grammarians do not use function as a means of classification, although this is the most commonly supposed basis. Most of the supposed functions do not exist, and those that do, do not fit the categories.

For instance, where does the verb in the following sentence begin and end?

*You'd better start doing something about getting the tire blown up. You* is the subject. *Had* (contracted to *'d*) is part of the verb, but part of what verb: *had start, had doing, had start doing?* None of these makes any sense. Unless the verb includes *better* the sentence has no meaning, and yet no conventional grammarian can admit, and no conventional authority I have consulted does admit, that *better* in this sense can be part of a verb. (Just in case anyone should suggest that this sentence is not "good grammar," notice E. B. White's "I better get them today" [*One Man's Meat*, p. 261]. I assume that most modern writers would agree that if *better* as a verb is good enough for White it is good enough for them.) Is the verb *better start doing?* This still has no meaning. *Had better start doing something* has meaning, but not the meaning of the sentence. Clearly the verb must include *doing something about;* it must also include *getting,* and *blown up* if the words in the sentence are to have their meanings. *The tire,* by all conventional statements, is a noun with its article and presumably is a complement. But observe what happens if we remove it: *You'd better start doing something about getting blown up.* Can we say that even a noun is not somehow involved in the verb if the entire meaning of the verb changes when the noun is removed? Pretty clearly we have one idea which develops all the way from *had* to *blown up;* it cannot be broken up into little chunks which can be filed in pigeonholes unless we are willing to ignore the meanings of words and the whole meaning of the sentence.

But perhaps this sentence is exceptional. Suppose we try *Grandma was peeling apples by the window.* This is certainly a simple, ordinary sentence which should fit conventional rules if any sentence will. The conventional statement would be as follows: *Grandma* is a noun, subject of the verb; *was peeling* is a verb made up of present participle *peeling* and auxiliary *was; apples* is a noun, direct object of *peeling; by the window* is an adverbial prepositional phrase, made up of the preposition *by,* which introduces the object of the preposition, *window,* modified by the article *the,* and the whole prepositional phrase modifies the verb, *was peeling.* This sounds objective, learned, even final. But does it make much sense? *By the window* is said to modify *was peeling,* but it must also modify *grandma* and *apples.* They must all have been by the window or grandma could not have been peeling the apples. But to say this is heresy, for *grandma* and *apples* are both nouns, and modifiers of nouns are adjectives, not adverbs. That is, it is completely impossible to decide whether *by the window* is an adjective or an adverb. It is a modifier, but pretty clearly it modifies the whole sentence. Now for *apples;* it is said to be the direct object, because it receives the action of the verb. But it also determines the action of the verb. Remove it, and the action becomes quite different: *Grandma was peeling by the window.* Grandma has now become scrofulitic, or perhaps, like Gypsy Rose Lee, ecdysiastic.

And these, of course, are not the difficult grammatical categories. They are the common ones. Even a concept like *pronoun* will stand no analysis. "A pronoun is a word used in place of a noun." Consider the following:

Johnny is my nephew.
He is a brat.

Conventional grammarians would say something like this of the pair of sentences: *He* in the second sentence is a pronoun because it is used in the place of the noun *Johnny*. To simplify:

*Johnny = he* ∴ *he* is a pronoun because it is used in place of *Johnny*, a noun.

Now substitute another word for *he* in the second sentence.

Johnny is my nephew.
The boy is a brat.

Follow the same procedure with this pair of sentences.

*Johnny = he* ∴ *he* is a pronoun because it is used in place place of *Johnny*, a noun.

If *boy* is a pronoun, and it must be, by the logic of conventional grammar, then what has become of the concept of nouns and pronouns? Why cannot all nouns be pronouns?

*For* is called a co-ordinating conjunction and *because* a subordinating conjunction, but are they not identical in use in *I honor Brutus, for he is an honorable man; I honor Brutus because he is an honorable man?*

And so it goes. Any careful examination of the conventional

categories of the parts of speech will reveal that they mean very little; they do not include what they should include, they do not exclude all words outside their category, and they do not reveal the functioning of Modern English. Usually they are unworkable, and when they can be made to include the words we use, most of them tell very little about what gives the words meaning. In short, the conventional grammar is not much more revealing of the actual grammar of Modern English than one would expect it to be when we consider what has happened: The grammar of an inflected language, Latin, has been forced upon a distributive language, English, which has been wrenched in an attempt to make it fit the alien grammar. A large number of intelligent people have labored for generations to make sense of this forced wrenching, this set of rules which is fundamentally wrong. That the conventional grammar makes as much sense as it does is a high tribute to the patience and intelligence of our grammarians.

*The Grammatical System We Do Not Have*

ACCORDING to the traditionalists, the core of our grammar is nouns which have gender, number, and case, and verbs which occur in certain tenses and moods. Let us examine these assumptions. Most nouns have number, expressed in form; except for certain borrowed words and some words which retain archaic characteristics, the plural is formed by adding *-s,* or *-es.* We have developed other plurals by distributive means *(many a man, person after person),* but on the whole, declension provides number in the noun.

Of gender there remain scraps, such fragmentary scraps that most Americans do not know what gender is. With us it has become a synonym for sex, which it is not, because distinction on the basis of sex is the only bit of gender we have left, and that appears only in the third person singular pronoun *(he, she, it),* unless one excepts forms like *comedian, comedienne, actor, actress.* Gender is a much broader concept, which can include any sort of classification of objects, and in Indo-European must have included a considerable number, distinguished by different sets of case endings. So in other languages. Certain North American Indian languages have gender which requires with any noun the use of syllables which indicate one of the following: that the object mentioned is in the immediate possession of the speaker; that it is not in his possession, but can be reached by sight, sound, smell, or touch; that it is not within reach of his senses, but is supposedly not far away; that it is at a remote or unknown place.

Of case, also, almost nothing remains. Of the seven cases in Indo-European, only one, the so-called possessive, can now be recognized. It is steadily being replaced by forms with *of*, and of course it often does not indicate possession. Consider the following:

> Please keep *your* seats while I introduce *your* candidate for sheriff. From *his* earliest childhood he has been a staunch supporter of *our* party; he has been a noble servant of *his* constituents in *his* previous offices, promoting *their* best interests in *our* county as, prior to *his* entry into public life, he promoted the interests of *his* company, distributing *their* products in *your* community.

The italicized words are all "possessives," although most of them do not show possession in the capitalistic sense. *Your seats* are yours only because you are sitting in them; they belong to whoever owns the hall. *Your candidate* is yours only in the sense that you are expected to vote for him. *His childhood* is his only in the sense that he experienced it. *Our party* is ours not because it belongs to us but because we belong to it. The candidate did not own *his offices, his constituents,* or *his company;* and the company, although it owns its products, would still call them *their* products after they have sold them.

Such are the remnants of declension in the noun. Most of the relationships within a sentence which involve names for things are now made clear by order or by relationship words. Anybody who tries to talk about nouns on the conventional basis is not talking about much.

With verbs the situation is no better. The following are the commonly recognized tenses:

| | |
|---|---|
| *Present:* | I drive |
| *Past:* | I drove |
| *Perfect:* | I have driven |
| *Pluperfect:* | I had driven |
| *Future:* | I shall (will) drive |
| *Future* | |
| *Perfect:* | I shall (will) have driven |

But these are not the tenses they profess to be. *I drive* is not simple present. No one would say, "I drive an automobile," meaning that he is now at this moment in process of operating a vehicle. If he wishes to say that he would probably say "I'm driving an automobile," which is supposedly a progressive form. One says, "I drive to work every morning," thereby implying a past, a present, and a probable future. Similarly, the past is not usually the past, and the perfect is not usually the perfect since it does not represent a "perfected" or completed action. The past is most commonly used for the perfect (I *drove* into the yard and *stopped* at the front door), and the perfect is commonly used for the past (I *have driven* all my life; I *have been driving* all my life). Curiously enough, the pluperfect is actually used for the pluperfect. The future can be the future, but the approved form *I shall drive* is certainly less common than *I'm going to drive*. The future perfect also exists, but is a rare form which might well be removed from a simplified paradigm in favor of some of the common uses of the verb which we do not recognize.

The supposed uses of the verb, then, are not the uses they are supposed to be. But do these forms give us any notion of the English verb, even though the uses are misnamed? They do not. Consider, for instance, the following list, which by no means exhausts the forms which we use constantly as futures:

> I shall (will) drive (I'll drive)
> I am going to drive (I'm going to drive)
> I drive tomorrow

I am just about to drive
I am just going to drive
I am off to drive
I am on the verge of driving
I am now in a position to drive
I expect to drive
I am considering driving
I am scheduled to drive
I am determined (have decided) to drive
This requires me to drive
It would seem best to drive
I am bound to drive
There will be the drive
And then there is the drive
I have to plan on driving

This is only a beginning. One might notice that although the simple present *I drive* is not a simple present, it can be a future. One might notice, also, something about the nature of the future tense. The future is always uncertain, and Modern English, since it builds its verbs mainly by distributive means, is uncommonly rich in devices for expressing degrees of future uncertainty. The list above includes futures which allow for doubt in the speaker's mind and for the unpredictability of events. The following forms provide for a still wider latitude of uncertainty:

If I am able to drive
If I could drive
If I were able to drive
If only I were able to drive
Could I drive
Were I in a position to drive
If I could manage to drive
If it were possible to drive
If the road were drivable
I should like to drive
I should like to be able to drive
I wish I could drive

If I were in a position to drive
If the driving conditions were other than they are

The list omits many of the strongly subjunctive forms, expressing a wish, like *Oh, that I could drive;* the passive forms like *I'm going to be driven, I am about to be driven,* and the imperative and interrogative forms.

Furthermore, we have ignored the concept of aspect, one of the most important qualities of a verb, but one so neglected that until recently it did not even appear in dictionaries as a grammatical term, and it still does not occur in many grammars. It might be called the attitude of the speaker toward time. For instance, *I keep falling into mudholes; I am forever getting into debt* are iterative; they imply a repeated action. *I walk to work whenever it is not raining* and *Rain usually accompanies a moist front of air* imply habitual or routine actions. *I am just going to start making payments* is inceptive, implying beginning, and *I have only now finished the inventory* is conclusive, implying ending. By combining aspect with tense and mood, and by combining the resulting verbs with modifiers and complements, verb forms can be devised which permit extremely exact expression: *We used to go to the beach every Sunday, but this summer we haven't felt like bothering except now and then.*

The English verb, and especially the American verb, can become extremely complicated. Early in this chapter we observed a verb which seemed to be so amorphous that it was taking unto itself various supposed nouns, pronouns, and modifiers. But let us not complicate the situation so much. Let us now use a verb which is made of nothing but recognizable verb forms:

I should like to go
I should like to be able to go
I should have liked to be able to go

These are acceptable forms. Furthermore, they represent slight variations in meaning, so that the writer of English can vary his statement with extreme exactitude if he wishes. But what are the names of these forms? Do we have paradigms for them?

On the whole, no. No book which has gained any currency contains anything like a description of the Modern American verb. If anyone has as yet made a genuinely serious effort to collect and classify the forms of the American verb I have not heard of it—although I admit that this may be going on and I do not know about it. There is a good beginning in Harold White-hall's *The Structural Essentials of Written English* (Indiana University, 1951), and Professor Whitehall would be the first to point out that his paradigms provide only a beginning. Margaret Bryant's *A Functional English Grammar* (Boston, 1945) contains a sound survey of verbs. I say with admiration that much excellent work in the study of modern language, including grammar, is now going forward in this country. The fact remains, however, that as yet nothing like a full description of Modern English has been published; and only recently have we begun to become aware of the fantastic depths of our ignorance.

*Grammar Is*  GRAMMAR is somewhat like a freshly caught
*Slippery*  fish. Take it in your hand to wash it in the
*Stuff*  stream; two wriggles, and it is gone. So
with grammar, and I speak as one who
has gone through the chastening experience of asking himself quite soberly what our grammar is. I have tried to divest myself of old grammatical prejudices beaten into me at an early age, and acquired later with the profligate expenditure of midnight electricity. I have at times thought I had drawn from the deceptive grammatical waters a fine, trim, grammatical fact. I grasped him firmly by the tail, and meant only to clean him up a bit. Two flips, and he was gone.

And thus it is in all humility that I point out that we have not as yet described our grammar. Grammatical concepts are not easy to deal with. Grammatical phenomena are extremely numerous, extremely varied, and bafflingly shifty. Part of our trouble is that we have no precedent. Except English, Chinese is the only great distributive language, and the Chinese have apparently done no more than we to understand their grammar. At least, if there is any adequate Chinese analysis of language it has gained no currency in this country to provide students of English with anything like a pilot job. Apparently, if we are to understand our language we shall have to think, and observe, and argue our way through the exploration ourselves.

We have a start. In fact, we have an excellent start. All grammarians now concede—even those who still think as though Latin grammar is the basis of grammar—that the grammar of any language must be derived from the language itself. All grammarians now concede that the source of English grammar is to be sought in Anglo-Saxon, and in the changes which the English language has undergone since Anglo-Saxon days. They all concede that in studying language we must take account of both written and oral language, and that of the two, oral language is probably the more significant, although the more difficult to deal with.

It is hard to see how this new understanding of the revealing ways to work with language can be wrong. It is also hard to see how any work on the old basis, a basis that is fundamentally wrong, could produce entirely valid conclusions. But we have now changed our approach to one which seems basically right. We now think we know how to work with English grammar and we are working.

We have acquired this new approach neither easily nor quickly. Apparently the new attitudes grew out of the study of Anglo-Saxon and Middle English. It is interesting to observe that linguistic truth came as a sort of handmaiden of literary love. Early English was not much studied before the last century; *Beowulf* was not known, and nobody knew how to pronounce Chaucer's English. Only a smattering of early writing had been printed, and that smattering mostly in poor editions. Even universities did not teach the study of early English languages; Latin, Greek, and Hebrew were either the marks of a gentleman or the tools of a divine, but relatively few scholars bothered with Anglo-Saxon or Middle English. Partly the change came about through the Romantic Movement, which made old things, especially bizarre, primitive, and "Gothic" things popular. Partly the change is due to German philologists who started studying language, especially all dialects of Germanic language, with patience, competence, and objectivity.

Then love took a hand. Scholars discovered that the ancient and medieval Germanic writings constituted an entrancing body of literature. *Beowulf*, for instance, appeared no longer as the crude product of a barbarous time, but as a highly wrought, powerful, and in some ways sophisticated poem. Chaucer was obviously a literary craftsman of very high order, as well as one of the most engaging human beings who ever harbored a sly smile. Since *Beowulf* and the *Canterbury Tales* had become works of art, their grammar became subjects of scholarly study. Gradually, students who had gone to the older literatures for love of the literatures saw in these works evidence that English grammar was a native thing, that it existed before Anglo-Saxons knew anything about Latin, and that English seemed quite capable of living on its own resources, using a grammar that differed sharply from Latin.

While all this was going on, a philosophical background was growing for a new linguistic approach. Brilliant grammatical thinkers, mostly German and Scandinavian, had broken loose from traditional limitations. The whole concept of language families, which appeared with the knowledge of the relationships of languages like Sanskrit, Gothic, Greek, and Anglo-Saxon, suggested that grammatical notions needed revision, that linguistic truths might be much broader, deeper, and more significant than the older writers upon language had been aware. Men like Bopp and Rask, Max Müller and the Grimm brothers produced most fruitful researches and most pregnant thought, although, as a matter of course, these men were wrong much of the time. Their conclusions have required revision. Nevertheless, they shook Western linguistic study loose from its old classic complacency, and in a general way they laid out the lines which modern thinking about language has followed.

*The New*     THIS IS not the place for a history of mod-
*Look in*     ern linguistic thought. Among the results
*Language*    of this growth, however, are bodies of care-
               ful linguistic study, and in this century
               several efforts to approach Modern English
grammar objectively. The Danish grammarian, Otto Jespersen,
endeavored to salvage the terminology of conventional grammar
while superimposing upon it a system of ranks in words. He
started with the noun as the name of an object, and a use as
subject or complement; this noun became primary, its modifiers
secondary, and the modifiers of modifiers tertiary. Thus in the
combination, *slightly aching head, head* is primary, *aching* is
secondary, and *slightly* is tertiary. This ranking he maintained
in the face of the older conceptions; *father* would normally be
considered a noun, but in the combination *father's aching head,
father's* would become tertiary. There is much to be said for this
system; it certainly has some logic behind it. But it provides us
with two schemes of grammar, where one is baffling us already,
and it has never received the subsequent careful working over
which would be required in a satisfactory grammatical statement—assuming that a statement could be worked out with this
system.

Some grammarians, recognizing that speakers of English make
themselves understood by naming a subject and then modifying
this subject, have tried to reduce the parts of speech to two, subjects and modifiers. This would seem to be simplicity itself, and
certainly as far as it goes it is hard to find out what is wrong
with it. In the sentence *John runs, runs,* although it is commonly
called a verb, certainly modifies our conception of John. Or
expand the sentence as follows: *John, being as stubborn as a mule
and as conceited as a peacock, runs every four years for President of the United States, having himself nominated by the No-
Cigarettes-for-Women Party.* We still have *John,* the subject,
modified in our minds by all that comes after it. But assuming
that this description is valid, does it help much? In effect, this
approach provides us with a new term for the old grammatical
tenet that a sentence is made up of a subject and a predicate.

If we accept this statement, the fact remains that the modifier (or predicate) can be an extremely complicated agglomeration, which would seem to need some breaking down before we can hope to grasp it very well.

I. A. Richards suggested that the study of grammar be based entirely upon meaning, but understandably did not care to spend the remainder of his life trying to do so. No systematic study of English grammar has been founded exclusively upon meaning, but since grammarians have usually assumed that the "use" of a word—that is, its function in composition—was to reveal meaning, the whole idea of function rests upon meaning. Other grammarians have forsaken both meaning and function as a starting point for the study of English grammar, and have tried to study it upon the basis of speech rhythm, upon word patterns, or upon something which can be approached with relative objectivity. Studying meaning objectively has proved very difficult, because meaning is highly varied and shifting.

The most elaborate recent attempt is embodied in *The Structure of English* by Professor Charles Carpenter Fries of the University of Michigan. Professor Fries has long been an independent thinker and indefatigable worker in language. During the late war he was able to acquire some fifty hours of transcribed conversation. By studying the conversation he constructed a theory of grammar which makes but limited use of meaning. He relies upon sentence patterns and accepts as a part of speech any word which can fall into a certain position within the pattern. The results are extremely interesting, and they will certainly be worked over carefully by other grammarians. Obviously Professor Fries is right about many things, and his book will deeply affect our thinking about Modern English grammar. Whether the book will be accepted as the standard statement no one can as yet safely predict—it was published while this manuscript was being written—but it suggests the degree to which modern grammar is at last being studied, in and for itself.

Another interesting recent treatment appears in *The Structural Essentials of Written English* mentioned above. Professor Whitehall employs sentence pattern, as indeed anyone must, for if modern grammar has demonstrated one fact it is that a distributive grammar relies upon patterns of words as an inflected language relies upon forms of words. He also makes use of the phoneme, a relatively recent concept in language, which may be defined as all the sound within a spread of sound which hearers would recognize as part of the same word. For instance, the vowel sound in *roof* is usually either [ʊ] or [u]. These two sounds, then, constitute one phoneme, because they occur in pronunciations of the same word. But when these two same sounds occur in other circumstances they may be two phonemes. For instance, in *could* [cʊd] and *cooed* [cud] they are two phonemes, because [cud] cannot mean *could* and [cʊd] cannot mean *cooed*. In his use of pattern and the phoneme Professor Whitehall is modern, although not startlingly new; but in resting grammar and grammatical analysis mainly upon the rising and falling tone of the spoken voice, he is pioneering. He asserts (the italics are his): "Remember that *English sentences are not sentences merely by virtue of the kind of constructions they represent or the kind of words they contain; they are sentences because they possess one or other of the final tone patterns characteristic of English.*"

At this writing Modern English grammar is a lively if confusing subject. We do not understand our grammar, but apparently it has become something distinctive enough to intrigue our interest and warrant our understanding. And we may yet solve its mystery.

## 🌿 12 🌿

# ENGLISH'S SHRINKING GRAMMATICAL PANTS

WHAT WILL THE WELL-DRESSSED GRAMMAR WEAR?—WINNIE
AND THE NAUGHTY PREPOSITION—VERBS WITHOUT END—
WHEN IS A COMPLEMENT NOT A COMPLEMENT?—WHILE DOC-
TORS DISAGREE—GRAMMATICAL PEACE IN OUR TIME?

*What Will the
Well-Dressed
Grammar Wear?*

In the previous chapter we have noticed
that the familiar grammatical concepts are
inadequate to our grammar because our
grammar has shifted from an inflectional
to a distributive basis. We should now add,
what has been implied but perhaps not insisted upon, that our
grammar is still changing. It is growing at a rate perhaps unprecedented since the Middle Ages. I say "perhaps" because
knowing what happens in contemporary language is extremely
difficult. Speakers of a language take it as they use it, and do not
think much about its past or future. They think of it as "right"
or "wrong," but they are not much aware that the *wrongs* may
become *rights* and the *rights* become *obsoletes*. Even the careful
student of language can observe only what has happened, and
guess at what may happen. Such is the subtle nature of language
that even careful students may miss important developments
until after they have been developing for a long time. Knowing
when a movement stops is equally difficult; once a new trend
has been discovered, investigators find new evidence for this
trend, and thereafter for a time new discoveries of old developments are confused with supposed new developments.

181

But perhaps we should turn to cases. Consider the following: *The bomber blew up.* What is the meaning of *up* in this sentence? Obviously not *up* as the direction opposed to the pull of gravity. The pieces flew in all directions and eventually came down. Nor does *blew* have the meaning we normally associate with the word. *Blow up* has become a new verb, which means "explode." Similarly, *slip* and *on* have meanings in *slip on a dress,* which are different from the meanings of these words in *slip on the ice.* A gunman who *holds up a bank* is not using his biceps for the job, and the boy who *calls up a girl* does not expect her to start climbing a flight of stairs. You can *get over* a disease by lying in bed, and you can *get up* in the morning, if you occupy an upper berth, by getting down. In short, our language is now seeded with complex verbs which mean something that their parts do not mean, and we are so fond of these verbs that we are turning them out (*to turn out* is such a verb) with great industry. Many of them are still colloquial; but the fact that expressions like these are common orally suggests that we are fond of them, and are making them as fast as we can.

These verbal combinations have sometimes been called *verb-adverb combinations,* sometimes *merged verbs. Verbs with separable suffixes* might be a better term; the second elements of these verbs, although they probably were once modifiers, have now become parts of new verbs. *Blow up* means "explode"; *get over,* in the sense employed above, means "recover," or more exactly, "recover from." This is by no means a unique phenomenon in language. German, for instance, has a separable prefix. The verb *to see* in German is *sehen,* the verb *to look* is *ansehen.* The prefix, *an-,* however, must usually appear at the end of the sentence or clause. For instance, *I look at them* becomes *Ich sehe ihnen an,* and *he does not look his age* becomes *Man sieht ihm sein Alter nicht an.*

*Winnie and
the Naughty
Preposition*

IT IS perhaps time to notice that the little words, *at, by, in, off, out, up,* and the like, which make these combinations possible, are not prepositions, whatever they are. Well-meaning schoolteachers have long tried to enforce the so-called rule that words of this sort must not be put at the end of a sentence. There are few more striking evidences than this of the lengths to which we will go in our subservience to verbal dicta—not that I am blaming the schoolteachers. They read the rule in reputable books. But this is what happened. We called words like *at, by, in,* and *on* prepositions, supposedly because we noticed that they often appeared before nouns in what were called phrases. *Pre-position* means *a position in front,* and since we did not want to have to decide what these words were doing, we covered our ignorance by naming them from their place. Next we confused the form *up* in a sentence like *If you do not know the word, look it up* with the same form in *He climbed up the waterspout.* But this, said the makers-of-rules (they were scarcely grammarians), must be wrong. *Up* is a preposition. A preposition by its name must stand before something. A word at the end of a sentence cannot possibly stand before anything. Therefore, *up* must not stand at the end of the sentence.

This would not be very good logic even if we were to ignore that it was the maker-of-rules who had called the poor little word a preposition in the first place. Winston Churchill is said to have given the retort fitting to this sort of nonsense. According to the story, a clerk had penned a comment in the margin of one of the prime minister's manuscript speeches, pointing out that here was a preposition indiscreetly allowed to remain at the end of a sentence. Mr. Churchill is said to have commented upon the comment as follows: "This is errant pedantry, up with which I shall not put." He had neatly demonstrated that there are sentences which can be appropriately ended only with *up with.* To notice how many seeming prepositions can pile up at the end of a respectable sentence, one might recall the tale of the small boy whose father had contracted the onerous habit of reading him to sleep. The boy, after the manner of youth, wanted to hear the same story out of the same book over and over again. The father, after the manner of parents, was bored with the book. Accordingly, when the father went to his son's bedroom, smuggling in a new book, the child objected as follows: "What did you bring that book I don't want to be read to out of up for?" There is nothing wrong with the child's grammar, or with Morris Bishop's in *The New Yorker:*

### The Naughty Preposition*
#### BY MORRIS BISHOP

*I lately lost a preposition;*
*It hid, I thought, beneath my chair;*
*And angrily I cried, "Perdition!*
*Up from out of in under there!"*

*Correctness is my vade mecum,*
*And straggling phrases I abhor,*
*And yet I wonder, "What should he come*
*Up from out of in under for?"*

Winston Churchill's remark emphasizes another curiosity observable in these verbs with separable suffixes. The suffix must sometimes appear at the end of the clause, or at least after the complement; it must sometimes remain beside the verb; it must sometimes appear within the verb; it must sometimes assume another position in relation to the complement; and it can sometimes wander almost wherever it pleases. For instance, in *As for the cloth, they were busy turning it out*, the *out* must come at the end, but in the sentence *They were busy turning out cloth*, the *out* more properly comes before *cloth*. In *put the cat out* and *put the light out* the *out* can appear at the end or immediately after the verb, but if considerable other matter follows either *cat* or *light*, the *out* usually follows the verb immediately, as in *Put out any cat that has been misbehaving himself behind the sofa*. And notice what happens to the meaning of the verb *call to* as the position of the *to* is shifted in the following sentences: *She*

---

* Copyright 1947 by The New Yorker Magazine, Inc. Reprinted by permission.

*called to him; She called him to her.* In the sentence *I'll think about it,* the *about* cannot come at the end of the sentence; in *I'll think it over* the *over* must come at the end. Both sentences become nonsense otherwise. Sometimes the meaning shifts with the movement of the suffix. Consider the man who is recounting the fact that he drove his car past a vehicle driven by the wife of an acquaintance. He says, "I pulled around his wife." The meaning would become quite different if he were to say, "I pulled his wife around." Or notice the following:

> *She overlooked the table.*
> *She looked over the table.*
> *She looked the table over.*

Notice that, in these sentences, if *look* plus *over* is to mean *examine, over* must come at the end. *Over* need not come at the end, however, if the complement is anything which cannot be looked over physically, as in the following:

> *She looked over the table of figures.*

Such are bits of the evidence that English grammar is rapidly outgrowing its linguistic trousers. There is more evidence, as much as anyone could want. In an earlier chapter we noticed that the English verb is growing in such strange ways that it is difficult to decide where a verb begins and where it ends. To appreciate the delicacy of this situation, we should look a little more at the associates of verbs, especially complements.

*Verbs*
*Without*
*End*

THE MOST commonly recognized complements are the so-called direct objects. But these objects are very far from being a single thing. Consider the role of the direct object, *goldfish,* in the following sentences:

> *God made a goldfish.*
> *Jimmy saw the goldfish.*
> *Jimmy considered the goldfish.*

> *Jimmy wanted the goldfish.*
> *Jimmy grabbed the goldfish.*
> *Jimmy weighed the goldfish.*
> *Jimmy swallowed the goldfish.*
> *Thereafter, Jimmy disliked goldfish.*

Presumably a direct object "receives the action" of the verb, but if all of these objects are to be described as "receiving action," then we shall need highly flexible definitions for *receive* and *action*. In *God made a goldfish* the object receives the action so essentially that the object does not exist without the action. In *Jimmy grabbed the goldfish* and *Jimmy swallowed the goldfish* the object receives the action, in the sense that the object is moved, and even its fate determined by the action. But in the second sentence, *Jimmy saw the goldfish*, "receives the action" implies rather too much. The body of the goldfish reflects certain light rays, which register on Jimmy's retina, so that Jimmy is aware of the goldfish, but the goldfish is probably swimming happily in the aquarium, unaware of Jimmy, or at least unaware that he is being seen. In the next sentence, also, although the goldfish is the object of consideration, and eventually of being wanted, the goldfish now has so little to do with the action that he is not even necessarily reflecting light rays which impinge on Jimmy's retina. Possibly Jimmy has now gone off and has thought about the goldfish for a long time. In *Jimmy weighed the goldfish*, the goldfish is, in a way, receiving action; but in another sense Jimmy is finding out what the goldfish weighs. Or suppose we make the sentence, *The goldfish weighed an ounce*. Does the *ounce* receive any action? In the last sentence, *Thereafter Jimmy disliked goldfish*, the goldfish is so far from receiving any action that Jimmy would presumably dislike goldfish even if there were no goldfish on the face of the earth, if they had all been removed by a goldfish plague.

Now notice the following sentences:

> *God made up a goldfish.*
> *Jimmy looked at the goldfish.*
> *Jimmy thought about the goldfish.*

> *Jimmy had a desire for the goldfish.*
> *Jimmy made a grab for the goldfish.*
> *Jimmy determined the weight of the goldfish.*
> *Jimmy gulped down the goldfish.*
> *Thereafter, Jimmy had an aversion for goldfish.*

Anyone who wishes to compare these sentences with those above will observe that the meanings are the same, or similar, but that for each supposed direct object in the first list of sentences there is now a construction involving what in conventional grammar would be called an adverbial prepositional phrase. But obviously these so-called phrases still retain the direct object, or if they do not, they are somehow associated very closely with the relationship between the verb and that which completes the verb. Some of these *goldfish* are clearly the complements of what we have just called verbs with separable suffixes, but some seem to be even more complicated. Consider the following:

| | | |
|---|---|---|
| *Jimmy* | *wanted* | *the goldfish.* |
| *Jimmy* | *had a desire for* | *the goldfish.* |
| | | |
| *Jimmy* | *grabbed* | *the goldfish.* |
| *Jimmy* | *made a grab for* | *the goldfish.* |

When the sentences are put in this form it becomes hard to escape the suggestion that the combinations of words *had a desire for* and *made a grab for* are verbs, although they are made up of what would usually be called a verb (*had, made*) plus a modifier (*a*) plus a noun (*desire, grab*) plus a preposition (*for*).

*When Is a Complement Not a Complement?*

THIS, of course, is what we noticed in the previous sentence concerning the blowing up of a tire, that all sorts of things seemed to become inextricably involved in verbs and their complements. Now let us look at the beginning of two of these sentences:

> *God made* . . . .
> *Jimmy made* . . . .

Not until we know that *a goldfish* is to be used as the complement of the first sentence, and that the second sentence is to be continued *a grab for the goldfish* do we know what the verb *made* means. That is, if *goldfish* receives something from *made*, *made* also receives something from *goldfish*. In fact, it receives so much that we do not know which *made* this *made* is until we know what comes after it.

To observe the manner in which other words become involved in the meaning of the verb, let us take this same subject and the same word *made*, and change in various ways the words which follow it.

> *Jimmy made a mud pie.*
> *Jimmy made up a mud pie.*
> *Jimmy made the mud into a pie.*
> *Jimmy made up his mind about the pie.*
> *Jimmy made a face on the mud pie.*
> *Jimmy made a face at the mud pie.*
> *Jimmy made a face when he ate the mud pie.*
> *Jimmy made a mess of the mud pie.*
> *Jimmy made a mess with the mud pie.*
> *Jimmy made a fuss over the mud pie.*
> *Jimmy made trouble among the neighbors.*
> *Jimmy made trouble for his mother.*
> *Jimmy made his mother angry.*
> *Jimmy made the place a shambles.*
> *Jimmy made a mistake.*
> *Jimmy made up with his mother.*

We have almost as many meanings of *made* here as we have occurrences of *made*, and these differences arise out of the various words and combinations of words which follow the verb, and which, whatever technical words we use to name them, certainly "complete" it. Obviously, any satisfactory statement about Modern English grammar will require some quite elaborate explanation of what happens when we complete a simple verb.

Let us look at the following sentences:

> *The boys lie down.*
> *The boys lie there.*
> *The boys lie on the beach.*
> *The boys lie where they can be seen from the*
> *    kitchen window.*
> *The boys lie for hours on the beach.*
> *The boys lie for hours.*
> *The boys lie.*

Now, one should notice that in these sentences, none of the words which come after the word *lie* would normally be considered a complement. They would be considered adverbs or adverbial modifiers of some sort. But they are not modifiers. In the sentences *He runs* and *He runs swiftly*, *swiftly* can be considered a modifier because it modifies our conception of the running. But the words which follow *lie* do not—at least not most of them— modify the lying. They determine it. *The boys lie* would usually be felt to mean that the boys are at the moment telling lies, or are habitual liars. But as soon as the word *there* (supposedly an adverb) follows the word *lie* the word means that the boys are continuing in a horizontal position in a certain place. If *down* replaces *there*, *lie* means *assume a horizontal position*. One might notice, also, that all of the other sets of words which follow *lie*, except one, make the word mean "continue in or assume a horizontal position." When the only words following *lie* are *for hours*, *lie* means "to tell lies." That is, *for hours* is a modifier; but *down*, *there*, and *on the beach* are complements, without which *lie* would normally be interpreted as having a different meaning.

Nor is this situation unusual. Even superficial thinking about English will reveal that the language is full of verbs which have no meaning, a different meaning, or a choice of meanings, and that the verb cannot be determined without some sort of complement. Consider the varieties of meanings which appear from *will catch* as the words which follow it shift:

$$\textit{You will catch}\begin{cases}\textit{the bus.}\\ \textit{a cold.}\\ \textit{it.}\end{cases}$$

English verbs, as far as we can determine what verbs are, seem to fall into three classes:

Linking verb:　*He is a boy*
　　　　　　　(*Boy* and *he* are identical)

Complete verb:　*He lives*
　　　　　　　(Often called intransitive)

Transitive verb: He lives his life
　　　　　　　He lives at 42 Water Street
　　　　　　　(Must have a complement to have its
　　　　　　　　meaning)

Obviously, the great bulk of our verbs fall into the third category. Linking verbs are very few in number, although some of them are frequently used; the verb *to be*, and a few verbs like *seem, appear, look, smell,* and *sound* can be linking verbs. They link the subject to a noun or a modifier in the predicate which must be closely related to the subject. The verbs which are complete without a complement are also few: *jump* in the sense of *spring up*, but not *jump* in *jump over the fence, jump twenty-five feet; live* in the sense of continuing in a state not interrupted by death, but not in *live for her children, live life fully, live in Mexico,* or any of dozens of others. The great bulk of verbs in Modern English are so intimately related with some kind of complement that they cannot have their meaning, cannot function in their sentences, without a complement.

This, apparently, is part of being a distributive language. Our verbs have become so numerous in their forms that we have no adequate paradigms of them. They have become so interrelated with their complements that we do not know where they begin or end. The complements have become so varied and intricate that we do not understand them, and find them cutting across the conventional lines of grammar in multitudinous ways. At the same time, our verb has become so varied and precise that, without wishing to conjure forth unwonted superlatives, one can plausibly wonder whether there is now, or ever has been, so admirable and extensive a linguistic instrument since the dawn of time as the Modern English verb and its complement.

*While Doctors Disagree*    PERHAPS it is time we take leave of our distributive grammar and its puzzling ways. We could dwell longer with it. There are other prominent evidences of grammatical shifts in Modern English. Particularly in Modern American speech, one of the best known is what is called *conversion*. Given a word which has a use in one part of speech, we are inclined to convert it into another. If we invent a helicopter we immediately start helicoptering with it; we make helicopter flights and repair the machine with helicopter parts. Meanwhile we have become fond enough of conversion so that we have started converting old words, even though we do not need the new word which we acquire by conversion. *Suspicion* is supposedly a noun, and we have a suitable corresponding verb, *suspect*, but many Americans want to use *suspicion* as a verb, also. A change of this sort may be natural to a distributive language in which parts of speech seem not to be very important as parts of speech, and in which relationships between words are intricate and flexible. I suspect that conversion is actually no change in parts of speech at all, that we are here confusing ourselves by our shifting use of terms. But of that, more later. Conversion does represent something, and it is characteristic of our grammar.

The shifts in Modern English grammar are so many and so far-reaching that they could not be described adequately here, even if they had been described in scholarly works. As yet most of them have not been, at least not fully. Some day they will be. Of that we may be sure, but meanwhile can we make any working guess at the nature of Modern English grammar? No grammatical statement is worth much unless it is right, or at least contains enough truth so that it seems to be going in the right direction. If we were confident of the basis of our grammar, an interim report might be in order. But since the doctors do not yet agree as to whether the grammatical statement should be based upon function, rhythm, or pattern, where are we?

Perhaps nowhere that we can be sure of, but some things we think we know. Presumably all languages—certainly English—work by a subject and some modification of the subject. Furthermore, English is mainly a distributive language, and its grammar is largely recognizable by pattern, enhanced by speech rhythm and by a sense of this rhythm as we write or read. But the main purpose of language is to express and communicate meaning. Thus, meaning is the end of grammar, and it is hard to see how any grammar which refuses to take account of meaning can be entirely satisfactory. Of course we may find, as Professor Fries apparently believes, that whatever the purpose of grammar, it can best be studied by some other criterion than its purpose. (One should perhaps notice in passing that Professor Fries, as he rightly insists, does not ignore meaning; he considers himself as occupying the middle ground between those who rely upon and those who reject meaning as a basis of grammar.) But as yet these new approaches to grammar have not been worked over sufficiently from various points of view to permit their being accepted on a popular level. If we are, at this state of our knowledge, to have any sort of working understanding of grammar while we are waiting for the report of the experts, clearly that understanding must be based upon function. As yet no other approach to grammar has been pursued with sufficient persistence to permit its use as the basis of a popular statement.

For what it may be worth, then, and in all modesty, here is an effort to devise a statement which proposes to do no more than suggest a basis for grammatical peace in our time. It may be wrong. It is certainly inadequate. But since so many of the illustrious learned have found themselves in error, why should one hesitate to add his name to the list of those who have been wrong about grammar? Besides, as the late Professor Sapir remarked— and who should know better than he?—"all grammars leak."

*Grammatical*
*Peace in*
*Our Time?*

THE BASIC tenets would be these:

(1) The grammatical statement must account for the language as it is used, not as it might be used.

(2) The primary purpose of language is to communicate meaning, and our grammatical statement should describe the way words are handled so that they communicate meaning.

(3) Since English is mainly a distributive language, we must not expect that there will be consistently tight relationships between words or groups of words; we must expect that words will lean upon each other to produce a total meaning, which meaning cannot be broken up into parts, and the meanings and functions divided precisely among the various words involved.

These may not be sound assumptions. Grammatical notions have a protean way of becoming wrong just when their propounder supposes he has them pinned down as right. Right or wrong, let us see where these tenets would lead us.

## ANOTHER LEAKY GRAMMAR

GRAMMATICAL FOUNDATION GARMENTS—THE NEXUS WE
THINK WITH—LINGUISTIC CAST-OFF CLOTHING—THE PUD-
DING, CAN IT BE EATEN?

*Grammatical*
*Foundation*
*Garments*

WHAT ARE the basic observations to be made about our grammar? Professor Sapir thought that the basic grammatical facts are sequence and stress. For English, surely the following is among the important statements: words placed in patterned relationship combine to complete a predication. For this phenomenon we may best use the word coined by Jespersen, *nexus,* that is, tying together. Jespersen used the word to describe the manner in which subject and predicate combine, but I shall endeavor to show that a very similar sort of nexus works within the predicate, combining verb and complement. The second observation is this: English uses subordination. In the sentence, *The man who was shrouded in an old black suit looked like a gloomy scarecrow, shrouded in an old black suit* is subordinate to *man,* or subordinate to the basic nexus of the sentence, and *gloomy* is subordinate to *scarecrow.* Subordination is essential, but it functions within nexus. The third observation is this: English uses co-ordination. In the sentence, *The man who was shrouded in an old black suit and the woman in her tattered dress both looked like gloomy scarecrows, man* and all that goes along with him and *woman* and all that goes with her are co-ordinated, although there is subordination within this co-ordinated pair, and the co-ordinated matter functions within nexus.

194

These three observations, as far as I can detect, include all of the grammar of an English sentence. Let me emphasize, an English *sentence*. There is grammar of non-sentences, which is certainly somewhat different. There is grammar between sentences, and that we shall have to examine, though briefly. This discussion I shall endeavor to restrict to sentences, in the conviction that if we can make any sense of the grammar of a sentence we shall have done enough.

We start, then, with nexus, subordination, and co-ordination— in that order of importance—as the basis of the grammar of an English sentence. This is almost simplicity itself, at worst a linguistic three-in-one, particularly since each of these three can work within either or both of the other two. For instance, in the examples above, *who was shrouded in an old black suit* illustrates either subordination or co-ordination, but contains nexus. But this statement, like all simple statements, lacks detail. Let us try to provide some.

Looked at more intimately, the grammar of a sentence seems to comprise certain functions. In the sentence, *Girls run,* we conventionally say that *girls* is the subject and *run* the verb. I do not see how this can be denied, and yet I believe that just at this point much grammatical thinking has gone wrong. Notice what happens if we complicate this sentence a bit so that it reads, *Irresponsible girls may run up outrageous bills getting themselves frizzed up at the hairdresser's.* That *girls* is now the subject is by no means certain; all girls do not do this, only irresponsible girls. And surely *run* is not now the verb in the same sense that it was the verb in *Girls run.* The trouble arises, I believe, from the fact that although a function may be comprised by a word, as it is in the childish sentence *Girls run,* function is usually complicated in any complicated sentence. And most sentences are complicated. We should not expect a function to be limited to a word and usually it is not. If we are to think clearly about language we must start with function, and we must refuse the enticing error of confusing a function with a word which may serve within the function.

Perhaps the distinction will be clear if I suggest that we should not think of words as subjects or verbs. We should think of the function of being a subject within nexus, the function of being a verb within nexus. A word may serve within this function. It may be one of many words which serve within the function. And it may serve within more than one function. Clearly, this statement leaves no room for parts of speech, in the conventional sense. We have already noted that the accepted parts of speech make no sense. We have already guessed that they make no sense because we have inherited them from an inflected language; we may now guess further that they make no sense because there are no parts of speech in English in the sense that a word can be a part of speech. In English—and perhaps in distributive languages rather generally—the "parts of speech" are not words but functions.

What, then, are these functions? Functions are slippery things; they merge into each other. I am by no means certain that the following classification is the best one, but it has considerable support, and at the moment it seems to me at least plausible. I propose the following five sorts of function within the sentence: *being a subject, being a verb, complementing, modifying,* and *expressing relationship.* These are cumbersome terms. For convenience I shall use the more familiar *subject, verb, complement, modifier,* and *relationship term,* but I shall try to use these names to designate functions. It is to be understood that if I say that a given word functions in or as a verb, I am not precluding other words from functioning in the verb, nor am I assuming that the word can function only as a verb. All verbs, for instance, modify subjects.

Functions work through *sentences* and *non-sentences,* many of which can be broken into clauses. Other grammatical concepts within the sentence are subdivisions or properties of these five functions. Many supposed concepts have no real existence; the so-called prepositional phrase, for example, breaks down into a number of functions, and has no real existence as an entity. As for words, we shall probably find great difficulty calling them anything, but we might make the attempt. Obviously, many words combine with other words to perform a function; the degree to which any word does this may be so nebulous that a classification cannot mean much, but if a name for words of this sort will help, we might call them *phrasal words*. Conversely, words may serve several functions, and we may then call them *multiple-purpose words, Jack-of-all-trades words, Pooh-Bah words*, or whatever takes our fancy. In the Gilbert and Sullivan operetta, *The Mikado*, Pooh-Bah is Lord High Everything Else, comprising in his portly figure all functions of government. He can combine his functions whenever he finds it personally profitable to do so. Similarly, some words seem able to combine within themselves most functions of grammar, to serve, perhaps, as complement, modifier, verb, and expression of relationship, all at the same time.

*The Nexus*
*We Think*
*With*

LET US consider the functions in order. The basis of communication is the actor-action-complement means of thinking, which we have called nexus, and this complex finds expression in the subject-verb-complement sentence pattern. Normally the subject comes first in the sentence and is the subject not only grammatically but semantically, since it names the subject under discussion (*Mary ran; The President spoke at a whistle stop*). There are variations upon this pattern. Reversed, the pattern suggests a question (*Are you off to Florida? Did you or did you not get married?*). Sometimes the effectual subject is postponed and a meaningless word like *there* put in its place, just to maintain the pattern and remind us that the subject will be along in due time (*There is no nonsense about her*). Sometimes for emphasis the pattern is varied, but the variations are rigid, so that the reader or hearer still recognizes the subject (*He said he would go, and go he did; but not, except in exceptional circumstances, went he*). Sometimes the subject is unknown, or the writer does not wish to use the subject, or prefers to subordinate it; these variations can be managed with a pattern, with the complement moved into the position of the subject, and with a verb in the passive voice (*That matter was taken care of by the superintendent; The man had been clubbed to death).* That is, although somebody as actor clubbed the man, in the passive the man who received the clubbing becomes the subject. By various devices certain parts of the predicate can trade places with the subject; in the following the central word in the grammatical subject is italicized:

> If you want to save your marriage, *you* should watch your husband's stenographer.

> If you want to save your marriage, your husband's *stenographer* is the one to watch.

> If you want to save your marriage—well, your *husband* has a stenographer you should watch.

There are other minor patterns which can not be introduced into a hasty summary like this one, but on the whole the subject can be readily and certainly identified either by the actor-action-complement pattern or by standardized variations upon it.

Predication, which is the basis of serious communication, requires a subject and a verb, and, if necessary, a complement. Most verbs are of such nature that they do require complements, and usually the functioning of the verb cannot be understood except in conjunction with the complement. This characteristic of English verbs need not be labored here, since it is discussed in the preceding chapter. A verb like *lie* has one meaning if it has no complement, another meaning if it has a complement, even if the complement is a word that according to the conventional grammatical statement is an adverb (*It lies there; she is lying on the sofa*). A verb like *talk* is affected less by its interreliance with the complement than is *lie*, but its meaning shifts as its relation with a complement changes. *Talk* without a complement means "to emit speech" (*He talked and talked*). With a complement *talk* may mean "to give expression to" (*He talked nonsense*). *Talk* with a separable suffix has other meanings, which usually are determined in connection with a complement. *Talk about* is roughly a synonym for "to discuss" (*He talked about the wage scale*), but *talk of* is often roughly the equivalent of "to consider, to propose a given action" (*He talks of firing his troupe of insubordinate midgets*). The linking verbs or copulas, also, are so reliant upon complements that complete verbs have meanings which differ from linking verbs having the same form (*He is; He is dead; Johnny looked; Johnny looked sick*).

Verbs and complements, then, combine to form the core of the predication, to complete with the subject the framework of the sentence pattern. Neither can be considered successfully without the other. We have noticed above the main classes of verbs: *complete, linking,* and *transitive,* the latter being much the most numerous. The second and third of these verbs require complements. These complements can be varied and intricate, and have not, as far as I know, been successfully analyzed. Often a verb has several complements; in the sentence *I told him they ought to elect Jim dog catcher,* conventional grammar would say that *him* is an indirect object, *they ought to elect Jim* a direct object, and *dog catcher* an objective complement. Of these, the supposed direct object is not the only one which affects the verb. In this sentence the verb has no meaning without the supposed indirect object, *him,* although *told* can have a meaning without an indirect object in the sense of "to narrate" (*She told a story*). Nor are these three—direct object, indirect object, objective complement—the only kinds of complements. We have already seen that indications of time, place, nature, and the like can be complements. We have noticed that verbs and complements blend into each other so that they are sometimes hard to distinguish, as in the sentence about blowing up the tire. Or notice sentences like the following:

> *I took a train to Bear Mountain to look at the bridge.*
> *I took a pill to get rid of a cold in the head.*

Which of the words which come after *took* are complements, and just which kind of complement is each? The answer would need to be elaborate, but for the present we might notice at least this much. Complicated complements usually break down into functions which themselves comprise the actor-action-complement pattern, sometimes repeated and interlocking. That is, there is nexus within many complements, and this nexus so overlaps that we might appropriately call it *interlocking nexus*. In these examples, which are relatively simple, the complements break down as follows:

| Complement with *took* and subject within new actor-action-complement pattern | Verb within complement | Complement within the complement |
|---|---|---|
| a train to Bear Mountain | to look at | the bridge |
| a pill | to get rid of | a cold |

A similar sort of nexus can occur within the subject, although it is less common there.

> *To make a start toward understanding the filing system was obviously my first duty.*

To say that *to make* is the subject is to talk very little sense. With the complement *a start* added, the subject becomes more adequate, but this complement, *a start*, becomes the subject of *toward understanding*, which requires its own complement, *the filing system*. That is, this subject can best be explained by interlocking nexus.

To return to complements, we might notice that they involve complicated variations in order. Instead of the sentence we considered earlier, *Jimmy made a grab for a goldfish*, we cannot say, *Jimmy made the goldfish for a grab*. If we say *Grandma gave Jimmy the goldfish*, Jimmy gets the goldfish, but if we say *Grandma gave the goldfish Jimmy*, the receivers are reversed. If we insert a *to* and say *Grandma gave the goldfish to Jimmy*, the receivers are again reversed, although *the goldfish* and *Jimmy* are in the same positions as in the previous sentence. That is, the word *to* here combines with position in the sentence to determine what sort of complement *Jimmy* becomes. But *to* can so function only within rigid patterns. We can say *His mother talked to Jimmy*, but not *His mother talked Jimmy*. We can say

*His mother gave Jimmy a talking-to,* but not *His mother gave to Jimmy a talking.*

Now let us turn to modifiers, that is to elements which are somehow subordinate to nexus. Many modifiers are easily recognized. In the sentence *Mary had a very red face,* *red* modifies *face* and *very* modifies *red.* To say that these words modify and do nothing else might be precarious; if the sentence means that Mary was embarrassed, not that Mary's facial cuticle was abnormally pigmented, then *a very red face* would seem to be the complement. Similarly, other modifiers will be found to become parts of subjects and verbs, and thus the function of modifying could be conceived within the other four categories. My personal impression is that a passable grammatical analysis could be made either way, but since I am trying to make this analysis as conventional as possible, let us retain the function of modification. Anyhow, modifiers probably come as near to modifying and doing nothing else as can be expected in a distributive language, where most words have some complication of function.

Some modifiers are not easily distinguished, because their function is readily confused with that of complements. The difference will become apparent as we look again at sentences we have already identified as containing complements. In the sentence *The boys lie on the beach,* we have identified *beach* as a complement because with *on* and *the* it determines the meaning of *lie.* In the sentence *The boys lie like troopers,* the word *troopers* modifies because, taken with *like,* it combines with *lie* to indicate the degree of the verb, but does not change its meaning. *Lie* has roughly the same meaning in *The boys lie* and *The boys lie like troopers.* Similarly, we call *wage scale* a complement in the sentence *He talked about the wage scale* because it is involved in the meaning of *talked about,* but in the sentence *He talked about an hour,* the word *hour* modifies because it does not change the meaning of *talked* from the meaning it has in *He talked and talked.* That is, functioning as complements, words are so intimately related with verbs and so interreliant upon them that they change the meaning of the verb; when words modify they

indicate something about the degree to which other words function, but do not fundamentally alter them; they are subordinate
in function to nexus.

Order is extremely interesting in modifiers. Obviously some
modifiers have their position rigidly determined by their function.

> *The small boy stepped on a black snake.*
> *The black boy stepped on a small snake.*

The position of the modifiers *small* and *black* determines their
functional application; furthermore, they must appear immediately before the words they modify, not after, nor elsewhere.
To notice what order does to modifiers consider the plight of the
political group which petitioned for an increase in salary, expecting to mention the high cost of living, but gave as their reason
the "cost of high living." Only a few modifiers of subjects and
complements can appear after the word modified, and usually
the transposition marks a specialized meaning. I recall now that
this principle was thrust at me in my childhood, although in the
manner of children I did not recognize it. My parents bought
their groceries from a rather prissy gentleman named Hammersmith, and I heard my mother say, "The steak should be all right
today. The last time the butcher boy cut it, but I got this one
from Mr. Hammersmith proper." I was intrigued by this remark,
and by the word *proper*, which was relatively unfamiliar to me
at the time. Accordingly when I was next sent to the grocery store
I remarked on my return, "I got the crackers from the proper
Mr. Hammersmith." Considering the reputation of the gentleman, my family thought the remark funny, but I did not know
why they laughed. I had learned the basic pattern of modifiers
in English, but I had not yet learned the variations for cause.

Modifiers like these may be called *fixed modifiers*. They have
strictly determined position. But we have already noticed that
there are some other modifiers which are not fixed.

> *By the window Grandma was peeling apples.*
> *Grandma, by the window, was peeling apples.*
> *Grandma was peeling apples by the window.*

In each of these sentences Grandma, the peeling, and the apples
are all by the window, and *by the window* can best be thought
of as modifying the whole predication, and is accordingly called
a *sentence modifier*. It can appear almost anywhere. A fixed
modifier, on the other hand, cannot be moved with impunity. A
child wrote, "Being several months old, my mother decided to
start putting me on solid food"; she treated a fixed modifier as
though it were a sentence modifier. In the wrong position, the
modifier attaches to the wrong idea.

Constructions are sometimes ambiguous because we cannot
distinguish the modifier from a complement. In *Get the truth
behind the iron curtain,* we are trying to obtain truth if *behind
the iron curtain* is a modifier, but we are trying to disseminate
truth if these words are functioning within the verb and complement.

We should perhaps pause to notice that a number of words
which would not customarily be called modifiers function as
modifiers, and in the system here being described must be called
modifiers. In the sentence *Swedesburg is my home town, home*
would normally be called a noun, but unless it is part of the
complement *home town* we must call it a modifier. In *Swedesburg folk patronize their home-town industries, Swedesburg* and
*home-town* look even more like modifiers. Thus modifying, as a
function, can be a property of words having many sorts of meaning, and words which function as modifiers can come danger-
ously close to functioning as other things, subjects and complements, for instance. And we noticed long ago that all verbs are
modifiers, at least of the subject.

And now for what I have called relationship terms. They are
not readily definable. All the words in the subject-verb-complement sequence are in some kind of relationship. But words like
*and* and *of* are almost exclusively concerned with showing relationships; they have little meaning. Other words much concerned with relationships are also so much concerned with doing
something else that they combine functions within themselves.
If they are relationship terms, they also clearly are Pooh-Bah
words. In *He is the man who takes candy from babies, who* is a

relationship term, but it is also the subject of *takes candy from babies*. Thus relationship must be thought of as a function, a function which may be a property of a word but not the only property of the word, not the only way in which a word can function. Naturally, relationship terms include many of the words commonly called conjunctions, prepositions, articles, and the like. Pronouns are likely to function both as relationship terms and as something else, as subjects or complements most frequently.

*Linguistic*
*Cast-off*
*Clothing*

ANYONE checking over a conventional list of grammatical terms will notice that there are no phrases in the system I have proposed. The prepositional phrase probably has no individual existence in English, although words in what are conventionally called prepositional phrases are among those in which a function is spread over several words. The so-called prepositional phrases break up into verbs, complements, and modifiers. In a sentence we noticed earlier, *He talked about the wage scale*, the word *about* seems to be part of the verb *talked about;* in the sentence *He talked about an hour*, *about* indicates relationship, relating the modifier *hour* to the verb *talked*. All prepositional phrases, carefully considered, disappear into one or another of the functions we have discussed.

In the same way, I have not thought it necessary to set up a function for what are commonly called *verbals* and are perhaps better called *verbids*, the words which are conventionally called infinitives, gerunds, and participles. They function in complicated ways; clearly, they are what I have named Pooh-Bah words. Determining how much of their use contributes to one function and how much to another may become, in any given construction, a complicated assignment. These words often indicate relationships. They can be modifiers—participles are conventionally defined as modifiers, and he would be a bold man who would assert that gerunds and infinitives cannot modify,

also. They can function as subjects; *to go* functions as subject in
*To go under those circumstances was impossible.* They appear
in a great variety of uses in the complicated verb forms which
a distributive grammar provides, and as we have already seen
these verbs are so intertwined with complements, both of them
involved in interlocking nexus, that we have difficulty determining where the verb ends and the complement begins. Notice the
two following sentences.

> *I hope to be able* to go.
> *I asked him* to go *to town to get that medicine to stop
> the baby's throwing up her dinner.*

In both, the idea *to go* is central, and in the first sentence it is so
central that a grammarian might plausibly call it the essential
part of a future verb, and *hope to be able* auxiliaries. In the second sentence, on the other hand, *to go* seems to be the first verbal
element in one of those complicated interlocking complements,
beginning with *him* and ending only with *dinner*. But, personally, I should not care to undertake to demonstrate that the reverse is not true, that the first *to go* is not part of the complement,
and the second *to go* not part of the verb. That is, words like
*to go, going,* and *gone* can serve in any or several of the five
functions we have discussed, but they do not seem to introduce
anything not comprised in these functions.

So much for the grammar of sentences, and beyond the grammar of sentences I propose not to go. Just to indicate that there
is grammar not comprised in the sentence, however, we should
note that grammar can be conveyed in oral speech by gesture,
tone of voice, speech rhythm, and the like, and that in written
English there are various sorts of nebulous grammar, including
a grammar of non-sentences, and grammar that arises between
sentences. Consider the following:

> *"Home?"*
> *"Not yet. Appointment."*
> *"The boss?"*
> *"Nope. Boss's secretary."*

Obviously there is a great deal of grammar in this exchange. Much meaning has been communicated with very few words. Grammar of this sort is subtle, flexible, and while clear in meaning, it often relies upon grammatical devices the workings of which are not well understood. In a sketchy survey we can scarcely conclude much about it, except to observe that it is there, and that it should be studied, even though for centuries it was dismissed as "bad grammar," unworthy of serious attention. At last it is receiving attention, and perhaps some such methods as those being employed by Professor Fries will help us to understand it.

Some of this grammar works between and among sentences, and is surely involved in them. For instance, I have suggested above that the words *The boys lie* imply that the boys tell lies, and that unless the verb is completed, these words do not imply that the boys continue in a prone position. But the verb *lie*, though uncompleted, can mean "to be prone," provided it is in appropriate relationship with another sentence. For instance, consider these sentences:

> *What do the boys do on the beach all day?*
> *They just lie.*

That is, there are grammatical functions associated with non-sentence elements, and functions between sentences. They are nebulous, or they seem so in the present state of our knowledge. Perhaps we can do no better in a book of this sort than to notice that when we have examined the grammar of sentences we have not examined all the grammar, and let it go at that.

Thus, when we examine our grammar in any detail we find ourselves in the shifting uncertainty of the functions into which a distributive grammar resolves. All grammars are bewildering in detail and usually in concepts. But in its broad outlines our grammar may be simpler than we have supposed. It employs both form and position, but mainly position, which it does through the employment of relationship words and word patterns. Words may be fixed or movable, but if movable they move within rigid restrictions. The core of our functioning grammar seems to be nexus, nexus of several sorts, supplemented with subordination and co-ordination. The grammar of sentences seems to break into five functions: being a subject, being a verb, completing a verb, showing relationships, and modifying. And we might, if we wish, dispense with modifying.

*The Pudding, Can It Be Eaten?*

A PREVIOUS chapter embodied the assertion that our traditional statement of grammar is unreliable because it will not analyze ordinary prose. This assertion was coupled with the charge that the conventional grammar seems to work at all only because it is applied exclusively to sentences made up to demonstrate the truth of the supposed grammatical rules, and that when even these devices failed, sentences were changed to fit the rules. But will the system just described work any better? The explanation of it has been based upon sentences chosen for the purpose although, the author hopes, not distorted for the purpose.

In short, a grammatical system should be tried upon ordinary prose, and since I have no chance to let you see me placing a finger on a random passage, we might take the present sentence, which is being written to communicate, not to serve as a grammatical example, and analyze it.

In short — relationship words tying sentence to previous sentences; sentence modifiers, subordinate to subsequent clause

a — relationship word indicating that what is coming is to be thought of as a particular representative of a class or group (subsequent occurrences of *a* will be ignored)

grammatical — modifier; modifies *system*; *grammatical system* could as well be thought of as the subject

system — subject of first main clause

| should be tried upon | —verb in the passive voice; a future obligatory form, general aspect |
| ordinary | —modifier; modifies *prose* |
| prose | —complement, serving with verb to complete first predication; *ordinary prose* could be thought of as complement |
| and | —relationship word indicating co-ordination, that something grammatically equivalent to previous clause is to follow |
| since | —relationship word indicating subordination, that prior to the clause signaled by *and* there will be a clause giving the reason for the subsequent clause |
| I | —subject of the causal clause, which clause is itself a sentence modifier, subordinate to the main clause to follow |
| have | —verb, immediate present; the verbal function continues into the complement |
| no | —relationship word, indicating that the verb and complement are to be taken negatively |
| chance to let you see me placing a finger on a random passage | —one of those complicated complements employing interlocking nexus which are difficult to distinguish from the verb; *chance*, the complement of *have*, becomes the subject of *to let*, which requires the complement *you*, which is the subject of *see*, which in turn has the complement *me*, which serves as the subject of *placing on*, which having a separable suffix takes the involved complement, *finger ... random passage*; *random* could be treated as a modifier, and *random passage* |

itself could be treated as a modifier, with *on* a relationship word

| | |
|---|---|
| we | —subject of main clause forecast by *and* |
| might take | —verb; future polite imperative |
| the | —relationship word indicating that the word coming has particular use |
| present | —modifier; modifies *sentence* |
| sentence | —complement with *might take; present sentence* can be conceived as complement |
| which | —relationship word indicating subordination, that a clause immediately following attaches to an important word before it; a multiple-purpose word, it functions also as subject of the clause |
| is being written | —verb in the passive, continuing aspect |
| to commu-nicate | —complement; could be conceived as part of the verb |
| not | —relationship word implying negative co-ordination; what is to follow is grammatically similar to that which preceded but semantically opposite |
| to serve as a grammati-cal example | —relatively simple interlocking complement, *to serve as* functioning as complement of *is being written,* and in turn completed by *grammatical example; grammatical* can be treated as modifier |
| and | —relationship word indicating that word to come is to be co-ordinated with a similar previous word in a like grammatical position |

analyze     —verb, co-ordinate with *take*

it          —complement

This analysis is not foolproof. It is rough and could be considerably expanded if this book were concerned with detail. I hope, however, that it does not defy the logic of the sentence in any outrageous way. Conventional grammar could not be applied to this sentence without defying logic, that is, without asserting that words do what they do not. And I, at least, have not been able to apply conventional grammar to this, nor to any sentence having any complexity, and come out with a statement which does not both defy logic and fail to describe most of what seems to be happening in the sentence.

## ⚜ 14 ⚜

# THE BUGS AND IMPS IN OUR LANGUAGE

THE BUGS WHICH PRESERVE CIVILIZATION—THE INFINITESI-
MAL BUGS—BACON AND THE BUGS—ORTHOGRAPHY, HOME-
LAND OF THE IMPS—IS THERE NO EXORCISING THESE IMPS?

*The Bugs*
*Which Pre-*
*serve Civil-*
*ization*

IN THE previous chapters we have discussed major aspects of communication: meaning, and the way in which meaning becomes associated with symbols (words); sound, and the way in which it is the medium and the instrument of language; grammar, and the way in which it permits organizing symbols of meaning into connected discourse; human nature and society, and the way in which they express themselves through language. We have now to consider some lesser and yet very important matters, the manner in which the little bugs which inhabit papyrus, old matted rags, and the dried paste of wood pulp preserve written language, and along with it much of our cultural heritage. That is, we must consider the alphabet and punctuation, which, through systems of spelling, writing, and printing, become the media of preserving language and culture in written form.

The notion of an established body of alphabetical symbols which can be used to express sound, and in combination to represent words, and even in rapid reading to represent meaning without the reader's being conscious of the word, is so familiar that only by a deliberate effort can most of us recognize that an alphabet represents an extremely sophisticated notion, and that we can have a workable alphabet only as the result of a long and complicated tradition. No alphabet is early. Primitive peoples have no use for alphabets, and during most of the time that there have been languages, people were primitive, language was oral, and nobody had, needed, or wanted any means of making language anything but oral. Racially and culturally, written language is late; but historically it is early, mainly because recorded history could not exist until we had a written language in which to record it. Our own alphabet is so old that its origins are obscure.

The origins are obscure, but they permit some plausible guesses. Like so many other things our letters seem to be rooted in human experience and to have been disseminated by international trade. Our alphabet (that is, our *a-b*, from Greek *alpha* plus *beta*) stems from Phoenician, and the Phoenicians spread their writing symbols so widely that, with the help of such agencies as the Indo-European family of languages and the Hebraic religions, most of the world today uses an alphabet stemming from Phoenician symbols. There is no reason, of course, to suppose that the Phoenicians devised this alphabet from nothing, however much they may have had to do with changing a syllabary into an alphabet. Where they got their symbols we do not know, perhaps from Egypt; more probably from Crete, where there was an important early culture to which archaeologists are attaching more and more importance. Whether all forms of writing, the Chinese characters, the Egyptian hieroglyphs, and the Sumerian hieratic writing, stem from one original invention we do not know. We can only remind ourselves that most great inventions now seem to have been unique.

Perhaps we can understand alphabets best by looking with some detail at one letter, and we may as well choose the first, *A*. All our letters, including *A*, come from the form of the capital, a design suited to carving, the lower-case forms having come from the rounded, cursive designs developed in the course of script. Presumably all writing is based upon pictures, the picture being used for the object, eventually becoming the symbol for the word, and finally for the sound associated with the word. The pictures represented familiar things like parts of the body (head, *Q, R*; hand, *I*; palm, *K*; mouth, *P*; teeth, *S*) or objects of daily use (house, *B*; fence, *H*; fish, *N*; water, *M*; door, *D*).

Our *A* comes from the Phoenician *aleph*, which stood on what is now the apex of the letter, like this: ⋎. We suppose it was intended to represent the head of the ox with his branching horns. It may have come from the Babylonian *aleph*, which also represented an ox. The Phoenicians acquired their papyrus from Egypt—it is thus that Bibles are named from the Phoenician city of Biblos—and they may have obtained the symbols to write on the papyrus along with the writing materials. *A* may have come from Egyptian *apis*, the sacred bull, and as sound it corresponds to the Egyptian hieroglyph for *eagle*, a picture-word of which it could be a stylized simplification, although we have little reason to suppose that it is. *A* may have come from any of these sources, or it may derive from an earlier, undiscovered source. Clearly, the civilizations of the Eastern Mediterranean area had back of them some kind of culture with common characteristics. One of the characteristics may have been the ancestor of our symbol for *A*.

The letter was taken by the Greeks as *alpha* and turned upside down, although as a matter of course the juggling did not take place with the careless nonchalance that these words suggest. The Greeks made, in time, many changes in the Phoenician alphabet. They increased the symbols from fifteen to twenty-four, stylized and balanced the characters and adapted them to their own style of writing. Phoenician had been written from right to left; early Greek was written back and forth across the page in a manner called "boustrophedon," that is, as the ox plows, like this: ꙅ. The Greeks had no hesitation about changing the form of the letter so that it no longer suggested an ox. *Alpha* does not mean *ox* in Greek. The letter took several forms in various Greek dialects—in Dorian, for instance, it was represented by *eta*, which resembles our capital *H*—but the Ionian form was approximately our *A*. The Ionian form was brought to the Italian peninsula through a Greek colony at Suma, and thence to the Italic colony at Rome. The Romans acquired the Greek alphabet, but did not borrow the Greek names; they called the letter [ɑ] instead of *alpha*, and the name has progressed to the sound in English of [e]. Thus the Phoenician and Old Hebrew word for *ox*, however it may or may not have been related to the Egyptian hieroglyph for *eagle*, has given us our letter *A*.

The history of most of the other letters is comparable. Presumably they all came from pictures of objects which were stylized and which eventually became symbols. The crucial point, of course, was that at which a symbol which had once stood for a word became the symbol for a sound, a free agent which could be used to represent a sound wherever the sound occurred, in an old word or a new one. The Phoenicians either made this discovery, or they had the sense to make use of it. It was known to the Egyptians, who were able to spell out a word if they liked, but Egypt never made the transition from a series of pictures which had become symbols to a series of symbols which represented sounds and nothing else. In Egyptian an *A* could be a symbol for *eagle;* with a human head, it could represent *soul*. *AB* spelled out could have a score of meanings, which in turn could be distinguished by more pictures. For instance, if *AB* meant *thirst*, it could be followed by a dog jumping up, by wavy lines to suggest water, and by a man pointing to his mouth; the same usage could be suggested by other pictures. Thus, the Egyptians had the idea of an alphabet, but they never learned to use one. The Phoenicians did. They were practical fellows; they made fortunes by extracting crimson dye from mollusks and by making and selling everything, especially slaves, apparently untroubled by Hebraic ethics or Greek philosophy. But they needed the simplicity of an alphabet in their business, and they either learned to use it from some other culture which has not left us the record, or they themselves simplified an alphabet out of some such confusion of symbols as that devised by the Egyptians. No one made this discovery in other systems of writing, and Chinese is plagued today because it inherited a style of writing based upon characters, not upon an alphabet. The bulk of Modern English letters come to us from the Phoenician through Greek and Latin, as will be apparent in the accompanying chart.

This main stream of alphabet has been influenced by the needs of the peoples through which it passed. For instance, the Greeks took the Phoenician *tau* (a mark), which was the cross made by a man who could not sign his name, and made of it two letters, *tau*, which gives us our *T*, and *upsilon*, the ancestor of *U* and *V*. The Romans produced the two letters *U* and *V* from *upsilon*, presumably because the first was more convenient in writing, the second in carving. The two forms did not become standardized as two letters with two pronunciations for centuries. One scribe used *V* consistently as a vowel, and *U* consistently as a consonant; another reversed the process, and some others seem to have used both symbols with a splendid nonchalance. That is, *love* could be written *luv* or *lvu*, or even *lvv*.

The Germanic peoples, who encountered Greek before they did Latin, had a sort of alphabet based upon the Greek alphabet which we call *runic futhark*. They could not write much in it; they used it for inscriptions and engravings on swords for the magical properties that the mysterious symbols were thought to have. The fact that the Anglo-Saxon word for *beech* is also the word for *book* suggests that our ancestors may have carved more on perishable wood than now appears, but certainly they did not write much. When the Anglo-Saxons later learned to write they learned by means of Latin, and they then wrote their native language in Latin letters, using a script developed in Ireland by Celtic scribes. But the Latin language did not possess the sounds now written with *th*, in IPA symbols [θ, ð], and accordingly the runic thorn (þ) and crossed d (đ) were retained for both the voiceless and voiced variations upon this sound. The symbols may once have had distinct uses, but they are indistinguishable in extant manuscripts, all of which are late. When the Normans took over England, Norman spelling and writing habits replaced the Anglo-Saxon practice. French, however, had no linguo-dental fricative, and consequently no letter for it. The new scribes tried to approximate the sound with *t* plus *h*, using a ligature which some Anglo-Saxon scribes had also employed, and which gradually superseded the native forms. But not entirely. In script, *y* looked enough like the Anglo-Saxon thorn ( *Ƴ* ) to be mistaken for it after Middle English ceased to be written or well understood, and thus *Ƴ* replaced *y* in certain archaic uses. In *Ye Olde Tea Shoppe*, the *Ye* is not *Ye* at all; it is *The* with the Anglo-

## Genealogy of Our Letters from the Phoenician Alphabet 1300 B.C.

| Phoenician 1300-1000 B.C. Form, meaning, name | | Greek 700-500 B.C. Form, name | | Roman 50 B.C. Form, sound | | Evolution of small letters 300 to 800 A.D. | | | Gothic 1200 AD | Italic 1500 AD | Script 1600 AD |
|---|---|---|---|---|---|---|---|---|---|---|---|
| ∀ ⋈ | = ox Aleph | A A | Alpha | A | Ah | ⋏ ⋏ a | | | a | a | a |
| ⋻ ⋻ | = house Beth | ⋻ B | Beta | B | Bay | b b b | | | b | b | b |
| 7 7 | = camel Gimel | 1 Γ | Gamma | C | Kay | C c c | | | c | c | c |
| ◁ △ | = door Daleth | △ △ | Delta | D | Day | ᴅ ᴆ d | | | d | d | d |
| ⊟ ⋛ | = window He | ⋏ E | Epsilon | E | Eh | E E e | | | e | e | e |
| ⅂ Ч | = hook Vau | Y F | [Digamma] | F | Ef | F f f | | | f | f | f |
| [*see footnote] | | | | | | G g g | | | g | g | g |
| ⊟ ⊟ | = fence Kheth | ⊟ H | Eta | H | Hah | H h h | | | h | h | h |
| ⋰ ⋰ | = hand Yod | ⋰ I | Iota | I | Ee | I ι ι | | | i | i | i |
| | | | | | | | | | j | j | j |
| ⋏ ⋏ | = palm Kaph | ⋏ K | Kappa | K | Kah | K k k | | | k | k | k |
| L L | = whip Lamed | ⋏ Λ | Lambda | L | El | L l l | | | l | l | l |
| ⋈ ⋈ | = water Mem | M M | Mu | M | Em | M m m | | | m | m | m |
| ⅂ Ч | = fish Nun | Ч N | Nu | N | En | N n n | | | n | n | n |
| O O | = eye Ayin | ⊙ O | Omicron | O | Oh | O o o | | | o | o | o |
| 7 7 | = mouth Pe | ⅂ Γ | Pi | P | Pay | P p p | | | p | p | p |
| φ φ | = monkey Koph | φ φ | Koppa | Q | Koo | Q q q | | | q | q | q |
| ◁ ◁ | = head Resh | ◁ P | Rho | R | Air | R r r | | | r | r | r |
| W W | = teeth Shin | ⋛ Σ | Sigma | S | Ess | S ſ s | | | s | s | s |
| X ⅂ | = mark Tau | ⊥ T | Tau | T | Tay | t t t | | | t | t | t |
| | | V Υ | Upsilon | V | Oo | V u u | | | u | u | u |
| | | V Υ | | V | | V v v | | | v | v | v |
| | | | | | | wen 11th Cent. Anglo-Saxon } W | | | w | w | w |
| ⋣ ⋣ | = post Samech | X Xi | | X | Eex | x x x | | | x | x | x |
| | | V Υ | Upsilon | Y | ü | y y y | | | y | y | y |
| ⋣ ⋣ | = weapon Zayin | I Z | Zeta | Z | Zayta | Z z z | | | z | z | z |

© N.T.A.M.     O.F.EGE

* Until the 3rd Century B.C. the character *c* represented the sounds of both *g* and *k* when a slight modification of the character *c* was made for the *g* sound.

From *The Story of the Alphabet* by Otto F. Ege. Copyright 1921 by Norman T. A. Munder & Company. Reprinted by permission of Mrs. Otto F. Ege.

Saxon spelling retained. Somewhat similarly, our *w* is a ligature of *vv*, introduced by Norman scribes. The sound had been represented by *uu* in early Anglo-Saxon, and later by wen ( $\omega$ ), introduced from runic futhark.

*The Infini-* PUNCTUATION, literally, "putting in
*tesimal Bugs* points," has nothing like the orderly history which characterizes the alphabet. Early writing had no punctuation, not even in the sense that a space between words is punctuation; everythingwaswrittensolidandwassomewhathardertodecipherthanthiswouldbe. Some early languages used symbols resembling our punctuation marks as a part of the letter (they are still so used in Arabic and a number of related alphabets), and some early languages used no character at all for the vowel but only a mark which would look to us like a mark of punctuation. This use of marks, however, was not punctuation as we know it. It must be thought of as part of spelling, just as the accents in French and Spanish are part of spelling. The marks led to confusion, particularly since for a time only one mark was used for all the vowels and the reader had to guess which vowel sound it represented.

Even in the Middle Ages, when marks became common as punctuation, they meant relatively little because they were not used in accordance with any consistent system. Many extant early manuscripts are punctuated, but they are copies by scribes, not manuscripts in the sense that they came from the author's hand or that he ever saw them. Copies of the same work vary so widely in the manner of punctuation that, by and large, we have no reason to suppose that they use the author's system of punctuation, that they resemble the author's system, or even that the author had a system to use. Punctuation marks for this period seem to mean almost anything or almost nothing; in fact, punctuation for all authors of more than three or four centuries ago, and for most authors of two centuries ago, must be supplied by modern editors. Sometimes, clearly, the punctuation marks were intended to indicate the lines of poetry, since poetry was often written solid, like prose. Sometimes they indicated the ends of sentences; sometimes there was no punctuation at the end of a sentence, nor internally where one would expect it by modern standards. That is, many medieval scribes seem not to have conceived that the function of punctuation is to make the meaning immediately and certainly clear. The punctuation marks used during the Middle Ages include most of those used today, and some others. Periods were often put at the top of the space devoted to the line of writing. Marks which can be described as inverted semicolons and inverted commas appear in some manuscripts. Not until printing became widespread did punctuation approach anything like standard use; we have mainly the printers to thank for our modern system of punctuation.

Credit for the move to standardize punctuation in printing is usually given to the numerous and influential Italian family of Aldus Manutius, whose Aldine editions of the classics set a standard throughout Europe at the opening of the sixteenth century for scholarly editing and careful printing. But the Aldine system of punctuation was slow in winning its way. The first folio of Shakespeare, for instance, published more than a century later, had punctuation sufficiently different from modern standards so that it has become, quite incidentally, the basis of one of the most amazing sequences of blunders that have ever been piled up within a civilized country.

Whenever a group of students of literature meets in convention, if a reporter appears, he asks somebody if he thinks Bacon or Shakespeare wrote Shakespeare's works. The victim replies more or less seriously that he knows no reason to suppose that Bacon wrote Shakespeare, and this statement then becomes news. This event occurs every year, usually many times. It has been happening for a half century, and more. It promises to continue. Partly, of course, it represents the way of a city editor honestly trying to get something newsworthy from an important meeting which is not likely to sound very interesting to the average reader. But partly, also, it reflects the very widespread notion that Bacon did write Shakespeare, and the fact that neither the desk editor nor the reporter has ever seen *The Great Cryptogram* by Ignatius Donnelly. If they ever had, journalists being on the whole intelligent men and women, they would ask a different question.

*Bacon*    D ONNELLY was an engaging, if unorthodox
*and the*   creature. Unknown for two bad but orig-
*Bugs*    inal novels, he enjoyed in the late nine-
        teenth century a vast reputation for three
        other books. Employing a jumble of classi-
cal folklore he startled many a sober American with *Atlantis: The Antediluvian World,* and followed it with an indigestible concoction called *Ragnarök: the Age of Fire and Gravel.* His Herculean labor, however, and his supposed masterpiece was *The Great Cryptogram.* Donnelly assumed, as the rest of the world does, that Francis Bacon lived a busy life as a public servant and produced the monumental literary and scientific works associated with his name. As a Baconian, Donnelly believed, also, that Bacon amused himself by producing the further monumental works attributed to Shakespeare. There Donnelly started. He tried also to demonstrate that in writing Shakespeare's works Bacon devised a cipher so amazing in its complexity that the plays are at once the greatest works of art and a secret *Life and Times of Queen Elizabeth,* at least as important as the plays in which it is concealed. Nor did Donnelly stop here. He produced what he thought was evidence that Bacon wrote the works of such distinguished playwrights as Marlowe, Kyd, Massinger, Marston, Green, Shirley, Webster, and, as Donnelly says, "still others." At odd moments, Donnelly asserted, Bacon tossed off the works of the learned Thomas Burton, and wrote Montaigne's essays, which he then translated into French.

All this Donnelly discovered with the aid of the erratic use of punctuation and other printers' devices. He knew that Bacon was interested in ciphers—as he was interested in almost everything. Then he noticed what he believed were strained occurrences of *bacon, beacon,* and other words which might have been puns on *Bacon.* He became convinced that Shakespeare's works contained a cipher, but using the current editions of Shakespeare, he was unable to solve the mystery, and was, as he said, "lost in the wilderness." Then he obtained a facsimile of the folio of 1623 and made his great discovery. The folio was mispunctuated! Furthermore, he saw at once that this mispunctuation provided the key to the cipher, that words were hyphenated, italicized, and placed within what he called "brackets" (our parentheses) in erratic ways.

Now he could read the secret history of the *Life and Times of Queen Elizabeth*. First he determined a sequence of numbers by counting words from one point to another, from the top of a page to the end of a scene for instance, and varying this count to include or omit material which he felt was mispunctuated or printed in an erratic manner. If he ended with a word he wanted he wrote it down; if not, he used a different set of numbers and a different valuation for the supposedly misprinted matter. With a system like this, of course, he could have proved that Tallulah Bankhead was the paramour of Genghis Khan. He almost did.

Here, for instance, is the account of a lively scene at court, as Donnelly derived it by applying his cipher to Shakespeare's first folio:

> *The sullen old jade [that is, Queen Elizabeth] doth listen with the ugliest frown upon her hateful brows, too enraged to speak; but, rising up and starting forwards, took Havord by his throat and choked him. He took to his heels and was running off in the greatest fright, but the old jade struck my poor young friend a fearful blow with the steeled end of the great crutch, again and again. His limbs being now so weakened by imprisonment and grief, he is not able to stand the force of the blows; the hinges of his joints gave way under him; and he fell bleeding on the stones.*

As for the plays, Donnelly's cipher revealed that "Morelow or Shak'stspur never writ a word of them." In fact, Shakespeare "is a poor, dull, ill-spirited greedy creature . . . the son of a peasant," a "rascally, whoreson knave" and "a crafty fellow," who soon became "blasted with the dread disease the pox" (this last word being included through the cipher but delicately expurgated from Donnelly's text), who repented "the lechery of his young days." At the age of thirty-three he was so reduced that "His cheek is white, his voice hollow, and his hand dry, his hair grey, his step feeble; and his head wags as he walked." There is "a bunch as big as my fist upon the side of his throat," and a "great wen or gall . . . which every day grows greater, and his strength more feeble," until he "cannot 'scape the grave." Even so, the cipher revealed that Bacon had some affection for this unsightly creature, for although he was "a gross, fat, ontaught rogue," and "a glutton rather over-greedy than choice," still "I must confess there was some humor in the villain; he hath a quick wit, and a great belly; and, indeed, I made use of him . . . as the original model from which we draw the characters of Sir John Falstaffe and Sir Toebe." Similarly, Ann Hathaway was a hoydenish widow from whom "the churlish fat rogue . . . had fled to the Welsh." He was dragged back to marry her, "far gone in pregnancy." She was a "gross and vulgar woman; with a good heart, 'tis true, but a loud tongue and rough manners; a gossip with a giddy head, the model from which I draw Mistress Quickly."

Such were Donnelly's revelations. Unfortunately, he did not live to finish them. By Chapter XVI he was complaining that his publisher had said they had already set up 850 pages, and that he must be briefer. By Chapter XIX the publishers had written again that the book "looks like the Chicago Directory." After that poor Donnelly was able to add only another 150 large pages, during which he described Shakespeare, fleeing for his life with "his great round belly" and hoping to beat "the old jade" to the Continent. Donnelly apparently went to his reward aware that although he could copyright his book he could not copyright his supposed discovery of the cipher; thus what was there to prevent some interloping rascal from using his discovery to unlock the remainder of Shakespeare-Bacon's secrets, and thus deprive Donnelly of fame and the royalties which were rightly his? So far as I know, however, no one has.

Naturally, Donnelly's historical revelations have been received only with guffaws, and cryptographers dismiss *The Great*

*Cryptogram* as one of the most puerile masses of confusion ever presented in the name of their study. But curiously enough, although no competent critic has ever supposed that Bacon had anything to do with Shakespeare's plays, and almost any person who has ever read both authors thoughtfully has observed that the two men must have been very different sorts of human beings, the notion still lingers that Bacon wrote Shakespeare, and to a considerable degree it lingers because Donnelly did not know that there was no standardized use of punctuation and printers' devices in Shakespeare's England.

But the development of standards was well under way by Shakespeare's time. The folio of 1623 was apparently printed with care, and its handling of punctuation and other printing devices was relatively consistent, considering the apparent purpose, that is, to indicate the actor's pauses. A century later books issued by reputable publishers bore a strong resemblance to each other in their punctuation, although the standards were obviously not those current today. The colon, for instance, was in common use, and commas frequently appeared between subject and verb. Standardization continued, but even at the end of the nineteenth century the editors of the *Century Dictionary* could write, as though recording a relatively recent development, "There is still much uncertainty and arbitrariness in punctuation, but its chief office is now generally understood to be that of facilitating a clear comprehension of the sense." Even so, writers in the United States and Britain have not as yet agreed whether a comma before *and* in words in a series facilitates or discourages "a clear comprehension of the sense." But on the whole, punctuation of English is now a matter of agreement in theory, and very largely in practice.

In fact, the swing toward a concern with punctuation went so far that earlier in this century the study of the minute bugs of writing became a major concern, as had spelling in the days of the spelling bee. Many a youngster has grown up supposing that the study of his native tongue is mostly knowing what to do with commas. Happily, that day seems to be pretty well past. Good teachers of composition are now concerned mainly with more important matters than conventions in the use of the comma.

*Orthography,*
*Homeland of*
*the Imps*

AH, SPELLING! It has been the joy of many a man, and many a woman, and many a child, some of whom could do very little else well. At the spelling bee they were heroes. They became leaders in their communities, and champions for their communities when one town spelled down another, or when spelling bees grew into spelling contests. Tots have become state spelling champions because they could remember *phthisic*. Adults who sadly needed ointment for their egos found it in an uncanny sense for knowing whether words ended -*ance* or -*ence*. The "spelling demons," as the "hard" words were called, have played strange tricks in the land. One of these curious twists is that ability to spell has become one of the "marks" of a gentleman, of an educated man. One may know Hittite and the binomial theorem, but if he has trouble with spelling, many of his colleagues will feel that he is no gentleman and no scholar either.

We do have trouble with spelling. Some of us are bedeviled by spelling. We live in a world not yet exorcised of infernal visitants, and spelling has long been possessed of more than its share of imps. Modern English is peculiarly susceptible to demonic visitation, but before we go into contemporary circumstances, perhaps we should know something of how we got our spelling, and what makes it so whimsical, not to say perverse.

We have no adequate history of spelling, but in a general way what happened is clear enough. When the Anglo-Saxons learned to read and write, they learned Latin. That, mainly, was what education was, and what it remained for many centuries—the learning of Latin so that one could read all that was written in the universal language. This Latin they learned had an alphabet, made up of letters with phonetic values, and the language was generally spelled phonetically. True, in classical Latin the vowels were supposedly distinguished by length, not by stress or tense-ness, but there is much reason to suppose that stress had replaced length in Vulgar and ecclesiastical Latin. In any event, the Anglo-Saxons learned Late Latin phonetic values, and used them to write their native tongue. As we have seen, the Latin alphabet required some adaptation, but not much, and with their amended Latin alphabet the Anglo-Saxons were able to write their language, and they did write it relatively phonetically and in a relatively standard manner.

Not that there were no variations in the spelling of Anglo-Saxon words. There were many. Any Anglo-Saxon dictionary records several variant spellings for most words. To a degree these variants reflect variations in spelling practice, but to a degree also they reflect the fact that scribes were endeavoring to spell phonetically in their various dialects. Anglo-Saxon England was much broken up socially and politically, and transportation was poor; varieties in dialect went back to differences between Anglian and Saxon, and further dialectical divergence was encouraged by Anglo-Saxon life. The dialects differed, notably in pronunciation. West Saxon, for instance, had a whole sequence of diphthongs which were represented in Anglian by relatively pure vowels; thus where Anglian had *world*, West Saxon had a sound which scribes represented as *weorld;* Anglian *heven* was West Saxon *heofon*, and so on through most of the vowels, at least in certain positions. But even rather superficial study of Anglo-Saxon orthography suggests that the scribes tried to use letters as phonetic equivalents, that they endeavored to be consistent, and that they had some spelling conventions.

Remarkably, this sense for spelling shrank until it almost disappeared. When the Normans became the Anglo-Normans, they brought their spelling with them. The French spelling *ou* or *ow*, for instance, was the common indication of phonetic [u]. We have already seen that Middle English [u] became a diphthong in Modern English, [aʊ]. Once the French spelling tradition was established in English, however, it did not change with the pronunciation. Thus, French *ou*, *ow* for Middle English [u], a spelling which we later imported unchanged for [u] in French words like *bouquet*, has become the English spelling for [au] as in *house, browse*. This substitution of one system of writing for another may have had something to do with the decline of regularized phonetic spelling; naturally, for a time the two systems existed side by side, and in any event the French spelling was, to a degree, inadequate for the sounds of English. Meanwhile English dialects were becoming even more varied. Perhaps in all this welter scribes gave up in despair, but whatever the reason, the situation is clear: Middle English spelling is little more than confusion.

Certainly some of the confusion is a confusion of dialects. Many Middle English scribes, like their Anglo-Saxon predecessors, had a sense of phonetic values in letters, and tried to spell a word the way they pronounced it. But many others seemed to have spelled with the greatest abandon. We constantly see the same word spelled in two ways in adjacent lines, and I recall once having noticed one word spelled four different ways in four consecutive lines. We may probably assume that scribes sometimes copied what they saw and sometimes rendered words into a rough phonetic equivalent of their own dialects; clearly this diversity accounts for some of the confusion, but by no means for all of it.

Consider the following bit of evidence, which I blundered upon in a manuscript in the Huntington Library at San Marino, California. The work is a long collection of rhymed sermons in Anglo-Norman, written by one Robert de Greatham. The scribe who copied the manuscript finished a line which ended in a form of *pêche* (sin). Whether or not this particular scribe had some Freudian interest in sin, when he flicked his eyes back to the manuscript he was copying from he hit upon another *pêche* which was the last word in the seventh line previous. Accordingly, he copied the same seven lines twice, which was no wonder. No doubt Robert de Greatham was a faithful servant of his Lord, but he was a very dull poet, and the lines say so little that the scribe could be excused for not realizing that he had read this before somewhere. But now the curious fact. No two of these lines agree. Here was the same scribe, with the same copy, who copied the same passage twice within a quarter hour, and he does not produce one single line which is identical in both copies. Nor is he consistent in his own spelling of common words.

Was this man a bungler, or someone who scarcely knew how to write? No, for we know something about him. The manuscript is vellum, and accordingly worth money; no beginner would have been allowed to touch it. Furthermore, the manuscript is clearly the product of a professional scriptorum, that is, of a business establishment which produced manuscript copies commercially. A note on it tells what it sold for; it is written in a rapid, easy, careless hand, in the script of a man who wrote for a living and could keep it up all day. We can tell, for instance, when he started in the morning—his hand is fresh and vigorous—when he went to confection, and when he stopped for a few minutes' rest. He was a professional, and this was a routine, professional job. Everything about the manuscript attests to that. The obvious fact about the copying is this: the copyist felt no obligation to copy what was before him. He looked at a line, and wrote it as he pleased, changing the order of the words if he felt like it, even substituting a synonym now and then, and spelling and punctuating as the spirit moved him. People in the Middle Ages were not much concerned about spelling.

Of the few who were, the best known for his zeal is Orm, author of the *Ormulum.* Orm possessed an undeniable but perverse ingenuity. No man that I have read before or since was so adept and so patient in repeating a dull remark in nine different ways without adding anything to it. His ingenuity seems to have been limited to this ability, except that he devised a system of spelling and managed to write more than 20,000 lines of agonized verse in it, partly to bring God's light to the benighted and partly to demonstrate his system of orthography. He adjured scribes not to copy his work unless they were careful to reproduce his spelling, which he assured them was the only correct one. In this he may have had his wish. As far as we know nobody was so profligate of time and vellum as to copy Orm's poem with any kind of spelling, and the piece remains as a monument to the dullness of the ungifted human mind. It is also a linguistic document of great interest. Obviously, Orm was trying to record in a systematic way the pronunciation of his time, but since no one has figured out with entire confidence what his system was, we do not know with any exactitude what he was trying to record. The best guess I know of has apparently not been explored. The late George Philip Krapp, long professor of English at Columbia University and a one-man faculty of philology if there ever was such a phenomenon, believed that Orm was trying to indicate Latin quantity in the English vowels. This, of course, is just the sort of thing that a pedant like Orm would have done. Professor Krapp thought he had found a lead of considerable interest, but he died without completing his study, and I have seen no evidence that anyone else has taken up his idea.

Just how a zeal for spelling revived we do not know. Certainly it grew with the Renaissance, along with other revived interests in language, and like punctuation, orderly orthography was encouraged by scholars and printers. Some whimsical printers spelled variously, to make their lines of type of even length. They would spell *know* with an extra *e*, *knowe*, or even *kenowe*, but on the whole printers encouraged regularity. Gradually the notion returned and became popular that there were right and wrong ways to spell words. The conception grew especially in the authoritarian eighteenth century, and by the time Noah Webster in this country was trying to encourage a simplified spelling, rectitude in orthography had become almost as rigid and demanding as rectitude in sexual morality. Men fought about spelling. Webster was either a hero because he defended Americans in their right to speak and spell as they pleased, or he was a villain because he tried to corrupt youth into spelling good old British *soup* as dubious Yankee *soop*. Today there is more rigidity in spelling than in anything else associated with language. One may say [təmɑto, təmɑtə] or [təmeto, təmetə], but if a freshman spells *too* as though it were *to*, his paper may be failed for it.

So now we have the most erratic spelling of any of the great languages, and we are devoted to it with an enduring faith. Can nothing be done about it? Perhaps, but reform is not easy.

In the first place, our spelling is rooted in our history and our nature. Some languages have instituted successful spelling reforms and now continually adapt their borrowings to their own systems. We have done neither. The bulk of our common words comes to us from Middle English, and we spell these words with some kind of standardization based upon what they were in Middle English. But we have already seen that Middle English had no standards of spelling worth the name, and hence modern spelling is founded upon confusion only haphazardly regularized. We double consonants to indicate a short vowel— part of the time. We use any one of several devices to indicate a long vowel—part of the time. We spell *maid* with an *ai* because this was a spelling convention in the north of England, or because the *i* represents the remnant of an old [g], or for both reasons. We double the vowel in *keep* because this was a Midland convention.

Some modern spellings represent sounds which have disappeared or changed. We have noticed in Chapter 9 that the curious occurrence in Modern English of *gh* to symbolize [f], as in *enough,* and various sorts of nothing in *through* and *thought* represents the survival of an *h* which represented [χ] in Anglo-Saxon, and *gh* which was the Norman effort to reproduce the sound. Somewhat similarly, we spell *sea* and *see, hear* and *here* because the sounds were formerly different, although they have subsequently fallen together. The medieval confusion is with us in other ways, also, because for some words we have preserved a spelling which apparently reflected a pronunciation in one district, whereas another word which for us has the same sound was preserved from another district. For instance, we have kept a southwestern form *churl,* whereas we might as well have kept an eastern form *cherl;* we kept an eastern form *hill,* whereas we might have kept a western form *hull* or *hyll.* In Middle English one might find *on mons long lond* or *an mans lang land* or any combination of the vowels *a* and *o*. The modern *one man's long land* has a fine impartial mixture of them.

Into this medieval hodgepodge we introduced what is probably the largest body of words ever borrowed by one language from others. Furthermore, whereas some peoples have been disposed to borrow words and pronounce and spell them as though they were native growths, writers of English have shown a strong predilection for borrowing the spelling along with the meaning. The British have a fine sense for keeping a good thing once they have it, even in language. If Woodrow Wilson is a hero in Paris, the polite Parisians name a street for him, and change the name when he is well forgotten. Not so the British. I recall the experience of looking for a certain address in Cambridge. I was assured it was "right down the way, sir," and when I had gone down the way was again assured it was "right back up the way, sir." I went back and forth, always being told politely that my address was in the opposite direction, until I discovered that the "way" started with one name at the end of a short block, changed to another name in the middle, and had picked up a third name at the next corner. The good citizens of Cambridge had three names for this street as it traversed one block, and they saw no reason to dispose of any of them.

Similarly, in language British speakers have retained from their beloved past a large number of words, handsomely spelled more or less as their ancestors spelled them. Meanwhile they have imported from abroad large numbers of words to which they have accorded all due respect, and allowed the immigrants to bring with them their native dress. These words, despite their highly varied forms and ancestries, seem to be getting on pleasantly together, and a good conservative Briton would be likely to see no great reason to be too much concerned about changing them very fast—or at all, for that matter. The British colonies, too, in colonial fashion, have been inclined to retain what they have from the mother country. And the United States, which grew up with colonial attitudes, has not been revolutionary in its spelling. Webster instituted a few reforms; we have *labor* as opposed to *labour* thanks to Webster, but although he endeavored to reform our entire spelling system, and fought the fight most of his life, he succeeded with only a handful of words. Subsequent movements have removed a few *-ue's* from a few *catalogues*, but not from many. Some people now write *thru* and *nite* while other people frown upon them. We have never had any concerted effort to reform spelling in this country, and the sporadic sniping at a few conspicuous words has had conspicuously unimportant results.

The ancient imps have not been exorcised, and at the moment very few people seem disposed even to shake a cross at them.

## HENGIST TO MENCKEN: A SUMMARY OF WHY WE TALK LIKE AMERICANS

CAME HENGIST—CAME WILLIAM—CAME THE DAWN—CAME THE FOREFATHERS OF MENCKEN—CAME LINGUISTIC GEOGRA-PHY—LINGUISTIC LAW WEST OF THE ATLANTIC

*Came*
*Hengist*

IN THE previous chapters we have tried to ask the most important questions that can be propounded concerning language, and to suggest answers, mainly on the basis of the English language. In this process the English language itself may have become somewhat obscured. In the course of trying to understand the various changes in language we may have missed the consistent story of the growth of our own language. In case we have failed to see the language for the linguistics, here is a pedestrian account of what seems to have happened.

> *A. D. 499. This year . . . Hengist and Horsa, invited by Vortigern, king of the Britons, landed in Britain on the shore which is called Wippidsfleet; at first in aid of the Britons, but afterward they fought against them.*

So wrote an Anglo-Saxon chronicler some hundreds of years later, using such sources as he could get, presumably Bede. There is no reason to believe his account in any detail, but he must have been about right. Whether these gentlemen with the picturesque names did or did not arrive on "the shore called Wippidsfleet," during the fourth century and the early part of the fifth, the Romans were withdrawing from Britain; they were followed by German marauders, who gave way in turn to two main bands of Germanic peoples, Angles to the north and east, Saxons to the south and west. The Germanic peoples brought with them lowland dialects of the West Germanic division of the Proto-Germanic branch of Indo-European. These dialects partook, as a matter of course, of the common body of Indo-European vocabulary, and they preserved considerable portions of the complicated inflectional grammatical system characteristic of early Indo-European languages. In the late seventh century in the earliest survivals of the language, their grammar had already become somewhat simpler than the inflectional grammar of Anglo-Saxon's hypothetical ancestor, and was moving toward distribution as the basic grammatical principle. Their activities encouraged instability in language; they had been for two or three centuries in more or less continuous migration, in more or less continuous war, first with the Celts who had preceded them on the island, and later with each other, squabbling over the spoils they had taken from the Celts. They were semibarbaric people, who practiced a little agriculture and hunted, fought, and fished for what they could not raise by crude cultivation. They could neither read nor write, and their language, both grammar and vocabulary, was mainly what had developed or decayed from Primitive Germanic through West Germanic.

Sometime after A.D. 500, the invasion was over, and the fighting had become either desultory or dynastic. Christianity and civilization were moving in upon these people from two directions. The famous advent is that of Augustine, who arrived at Canterbury from Rome, supposedly in 597, but Irish missionaries were already well established in the north and moving south. With the Church came Latin, even Greek; channels opened which were to bring to the barbaric inhabitants of Britain a relatively steady flow of Mediterranean culture, a flow which continued for hundreds of years. One of the immediate results was that Anglo-Saxons acquired a notion of what a written language could be, and an alphabet with which they could record their own language. No manuscripts survive from anything like that time, but manuscripts dating about 1000 or after preserve works which must have been composed in the late seventh and early eighth centuries. The language embodied in these compositions consists mostly of native vocabulary used with a grammar which shows marked distributive tendencies, but which preserves an elaborate inflectional system.

In the ninth century the Vikings harried and finally overran the country. Alfred the Great (d. 899) finally beat them but could not drive them out. Large numbers settled to the north and east of England; they had little immediate influence upon the English language, but in time their presence led to the inclusion of a considerable number of Old Norse words in the English vocabulary, including the pronouns *they, their, them;* these people may have had something to do with the pronoun *she* and the *-ing* ending of the present participle. The Vikings, too, spoke a descendant of a Germanic language and theirs is the only language which seems to have had much direct impact upon English grammar. By this time, contact with the Continent was bringing in a few Latin and Latin-French words (French can hardly be said to have existed as yet), and changes increased in grammar and phonetics, perhaps hastened by the decay of education and learning during the Viking raids.

That is, a notable drift appears in the language, when Late Anglo-Saxon is compared with Early Anglo-Saxon. (The word *drift* is here used in the technical sense of a consistent change in the pattern of a language.) This drift appears in sounds, but most notably in a simplification of grammar and in a growing tendency to rely upon the position of the word in the sentence. Part of this drift must have begun on the Continent, although having no records we have little evidence. The continuance and acceleration of the drift account for many of the subsequent changes in English.

Came

William

In 1066 the Normans came. They took over the administration of the island and occupied the important positions; a dialect of Old French, which eventually developed into what we call Anglo-Norman, became the official language. The presence of the Normans had wide and lasting influence on English, but not mainly in the direct ways that are usually assumed. The main stream of French influence upon English did not come from the borrowing of Anglo-Norman into English while the two existed side by side in the two centuries following the Norman Conquest. Some direct borrowing there was, but the influences were mainly indirect, though pervasive.

Except for an occasional local bit, Anglo-Saxon disappeared as a written language. The Peterborough manuscript of the E Text, or Laud version, was kept in the native tongue until 1154; a few other scraps remain, and many must have been lost, but practically speaking Anglo-Saxon disappeared. It must have continued as the common speech, the only language known by the great bulk of the people, and probably even the home language of educated people who spoke French for official purposes. Official, literary, practical, and popular affairs which required writing were recorded in Anglo-Norman or Latin; learned and churchly affairs were conducted in Latin. Both languages had some direct influence upon English, and there was a growing tendency to import Continental French, since the ancient Mediterranean cultures were flowing into Britain, mainly by the channel through Italy and France. Some culture came through the Low Countries, bringing Dutch and Flemish words.

Extremely important for the history of the language are the cultural areas which now appear in the island of Britain. To the south and west, including the area that was the ancient home of the Saxons in England, the Anglo-Saxon traditions persisted in customs and in language. To a lesser degree Anglo-Saxon ways, mingled with Old Norse, hung on in the north and northeast. London was the center of the growing French influence; the southeast generally, and to a degree central lowland England,

was receptive to influences from the Continent. Thus the rural
areas (Anglo-Saxon to the southwest and in the mountainous
areas, Danish to the north and east) remained conservative. The
urban areas and the central plain moved toward a Continental
culture, with London as the focus. On this base subsequent English culture and language grew.

The friction which resulted from the Norman Conquest was
not long lived, and partly as a result of the Conquest, the island
of Britain ceased to be an isolated Germanic community, and
partook of the culture of western Europe. The Normans spread
rapidly and developed a great empire which, for a time, had its
southern capital in Sicily, its northern capital in London. The
more sophisticated portion of the island of Britain became involved in the politics and the socio-artistic movements of the
mainland. Both Henry II and Eleanor of Aquitaine had their
courts in London, and Eleanor was a great lady, for whom princes
fought and poets wrote verses. When the Norman empire fell
apart the question was not whether Gascony should rule England, but whether England should rule much of what is now
France. With the wars which re-established the Straits of Dover
we are not here concerned; for us the important fact is that during the twelfth and thirteenth centuries England ceased to be the
home of certain outlandish islanders from the Germanic forests
and became part of the culture of western Europe.

During this time English as a written language reappeared.
In the thirteenth century it was beginning to be used again for
writing. By the fourteenth century almost nothing was being
translated into French, and all important works were being translated into English. That was proof of the end. English became an
official language, and the king addressed Parliament in English.
By the end of the fourteenth century John Gower was still so
uncertain as to what language might survive that he wrote a
long work in each of the three tongues, English, French, and
Latin, to insure his greatness in spite of the instability of languages. But Gower was a bit of a pedant. The courtly and sophisticated Chaucer must have spoken French fluently, but he wrote
English, and William Langland (or whoever wrote *Piers Plow-*

*man*) was composing poetry strongly redolent of Anglo-Saxon verse. Soon French was no longer a language in England; it was an accomplishment, or a jargon used in the law courts, which grew more ridiculous year by year.

Meanwhile English had become a different language, a language that would have been quite unrecognizable to Hengist and Horsa, or even to Alfred the Great. It retained most of the words of common living from Anglo-Saxon, and it retained also words having grammatical use—pronouns, articles, relatives, prepositions—but these were no longer used as they had been. The inflected grammar which Anglo-Saxon had inherited from Indo-European had mostly disappeared. Many endings remained on words, some few of them unchanged from Anglo-Saxon, especially in backward areas like the mountainous northwest, but most of them were so reduced that they were completely incapable of supporting a system of inflection. By 1400 most of the endings were spelled -*e*, and were probably pronounced [ə], or were not pronounced at all. To say that these endings could not support a grammar is to speak a truth, but one which is probably misleading. Supposedly they could no longer support a grammar because they no longer had a grammar to support, and they had atrophied from disuse. By Middle English times English had developed, during its period underground as an exclusively oral tongue, a distributive grammar which was quite capable of filling the needs of communication without much help from inflection. Since some time after the Norman Conquest, English grammar has been mainly distributive.

Nor did the language sound as it had when Hengist and Horsa spoke it. It had been breaking up into dialects, as unhindered language always does, and this tendency to fracture had been aided by the diversity of the original invaders, by the advent of the Vikings and their relatives the Normans, and by the uneven rate at which various areas of Britain took on Continental culture. But meanwhile a great change had rolled over all the language. One of those great shifts which occasionally and inexplicably alter the character of man's speech was sweeping through English. It probably began in some vowels in Anglo-

Saxon times; for a few vowels it was not complete until a century or two ago. But the great body of change occurred during Middle and Early Modern English. Through this change the tense vowels in English all moved forward and upward in the mouth, more or less regularly. That is, [ɑ] became [æ], [æ] became [e], and [e] became [i]; a word which would have the sound we in the United States now give to *hot* changed so that it had the sound we now use in *hat;* the sound in *hat* became the sound we now use in *hate;* the sound in *hate* became the sound we now use in *heat,* and so forth. There were a few other changes; [i] and [u], which could not move forward, became diphthongs; the Anglo-Saxon *h,* now frequently spelled *gh,* either broke up or disappeared. Probably rhythms of speech changed, but speech rhythms are hard to study; we know little about them.

Spelling had become confused. French scripts replaced the Anglo-Irish scripts, although curiously enough much of the Continental writing was Irish in inspiration; the Norman alphabet was used, rather confusedly, for Middle English. For some reason in all this welter, people ceased to bother much about spelling, which became whimsical to the point of fantasy. Punctuation was conspicuous, but not very helpful. There were clearly some conventions; there are always conventions. Obviously, many words were spelled with a final *e* because so many nouns and adjectives had the remnants of old declensions on them that people thought of nouns as ending in *e* and they put *e*'s on where no *e*'s had been. But if there were local feelings of right and wrong in such matters as spelling and punctuation, these feelings had no currency.

Analogy was at work standardizing, as it always is. Some endings from the Anglo-Saxon nouns and verbs were retained, not always uniformly. For instance, northern England inclined to standardize upon the Anglo-Saxon plural ending in *-n;* Midland and London English preferred *-s.* If York, not London, had been the political and cultural capital of England it is possible we would now be writing "The planen dropped bomben on the generalen," for "The planes dropped bombs on the generals." London won, and we now make all plurals on the London basis; the northerners managed to save a few of their verb forms, and to introduce three Old Norse pronouns. Native pronouns were reduced as the importance of case disappeared; on the whole, all forms of the personal pronoun were lost except the nominative, genitive, and dative; forms of relative and interrogative pronouns were sharply reduced.

The relationship words showed a great increase. Early Anglo-Saxon had needed very few; later Anglo-Saxon had developed more. Now a whole new crop was needed, particularly since some of the old ones had disappeared. Anglo-Saxon þ e, a sort of maid-of-all-work relative conjunction, was lost somewhere, and replaced by all sorts of new relatives impressed from other forms of speech: *that* had been a demonstrative, *who* and *which* interrogatives, *while* a noun, and the like. Prepositions had increased mightily, and from miscellaneous sources; *of* comes from the word which survives also in *off; under* had developed from an adverb already in Anglo-Saxon; *like* had been a word for *a body* (*litchfield* means cemetery), and had become a modifier in Anglo-Saxon.

Thus, the controlling changes in the English language took place during and shortly after the time in which English was submerged by Anglo-Norman. These changes do not suggest that English was borrowing much from Anglo-Norman—how could English borrow a distributive grammar from a language which did not have one? Anyhow, languages borrow words, but they seldom borrow sounds or grammar. Just why English underwent a shift in sound and moved rapidly toward distribution in this period we do not know. Knowing why things happen in language is often difficult even when we know how they happen; and our knowledge of how these changes came about is limited. We have little written English from the twelfth and thirteenth centuries. Quite possibly Anglo-Norman influenced English most just by submerging it for two or three hundred years.

How did English become a distributive language? A good guess—but it is only a guess—might be something like the following. A tendency is observable in most of the Indo-European languages to get rid of their clumsy inflections and move toward a more simplified, distributive grammar. This drift is observable, for instance in Medieval Greek as opposed to Classical Greek, Vulgar Latin as opposed to Classical Latin, and the like. The change had been going on in West Germanic, and continued in Anglo-Saxon. When Anglo-Saxon ceased to be written, when it was simplified by being deprived of any stabilizing element in formal language and existed only on colloquial and vulgar levels, when the language was spoken badly by official Normans who did not bother to learn the local tongue, a "drift" which was already under way was accelerated. Thus changes were effected in two centuries of submergence which might otherwise have required a millennium or two.

Meanwhile, because we have noticed movements peculiar to the Middle Ages, we must not forget the constant working of the basic forces in language. While the Danes were slaughtering the adherents of King Alfred, while the Normans were triumphing over Harold the Saxon, basic principles of language were functioning with a calm that ignored blood, rape, and arson. Men's minds worked by generalization and specialization then as now; from Hengist to James Joyce people have loved to play with language. Words go in and out of fashion; if people are not prudish about their bathrooms, they will be squeamish about something else—mentioning the deity or the devil, for instance. All of the ways of the mind, of society, and of man's vocal cords must be taken into account at all times, during the Middle Ages as during the twentieth century.

One of the feeblest of linguistic tendencies during this period was the concern for standards. People used English, but they seem not to have thought much about it, nor to have tried to police it. It was, after all, an outlandish tongue even though they loved it, a poor thing but their own. They showed some surprise when in the fourteenth century wealthy people started having their children educated in English, forsaking the then traditional French. They were grateful to Chaucer for having proved that the language was good enough to write poetry in—after all, it was nice to have some local poetry. Some people even read it or heard it read. But most speakers of Middle English let their language alone with a nonchalance that would have delighted many modern linguistic apologists. Anybody who studied language seriously studied Latin or Greek.

*Came the*        WITH THE sixteenth century the movement
*Dawn*          in Europe which we call the Renaissance,
             the "rebirth," was developing rapidly in
             England. "Rebirth" is not a very exact
             word, not nearly so exact as it was supposed
to have been when it became attached to the period. The Middle Ages were anything but dead; even philosophy and the arts were not dead; even the classics were not dead. Nothing was dead, although for a time our understanding of the Middle Ages was closer to being moribund than was the Middle Ages itself. The knowledge of Mediterranean culture, however, the knowledge especially of Latin and Greek, classical thought, art, and study— all of which had been filtering west and north for centuries—was now greatly augmented. In a growing degree, classical rhetoric became rhetoric, classical grammar became grammar, classical vocabulary became an ideal, at least with the more learned individuals. Of course there were sensible folk who scoffed at "inkhorn terms," and other sensible people who just ignored them, but the acceleration of learning and study during the Renaissance meant in part an acceleration in the borrowing of and influence from Latin.

Our debts to Latin in this way are incalculable. Many terms we borrowed; they can be traced. Other classical influences can only be guessed at. Latin was the core of the growing school system, and it was the ideal of cultured people. If a man knew Latin, everyone knew that he must be a man of parts. If a man of pretensions did not know Latin, he took pains at least to be well ticketed and branded with Latin tags from the choice authors. Thus, Latin seeped into the language in all sorts of invisible ways.

Medieval style had been influenced by Latin, because all men who wrote knew the language; especially they knew Jerome's Vulgate version of the Bible. Writers like Marlowe, Milton, and

Burke were deeply influenced by their knowledge of and their admiration for Latin style; orators tried to orate like Cicero and editors tried to write editorials in the shadow of the Roman tribunes. Surely there was causal relationship between the fact that men of the eighteenth century paid at least lip service to the classics in a degree never before or since equaled in England, and the fact that Dr. Johnson wrôte "like a whale," and that the imitators of Johnson wrote like little whales. Influences of this sort were learned; they had nothing of the power of linguistic movements which grow from daily life, but still they were widespread and they lasted for centuries. For a long time, and in many ways, English has been borrowing from the classical tradition as that heritage has come to us from Greek through Latin through French, and directly from each of the three.

During the Renaissance, also, and partly through classical influence, partly through the growth of printing, Britons endeavored to put their language and the knowledge of their language in order. They constructed grammars on the basis of Latin grammars, and by the eighteenth century these grammars had sired handbooks of usage, in which various authors, usually ecclesiastics, hotly ridiculed each other and informed the public as to what was right and what was wrong, usually quite arbitrarily and often in anything but concord. Spelling and punctuation became subjects for scrutiny, for determination of "right" from "wrong," and even, in the United States, for national necessity. Noah Webster was widely honored, at least by his own faction, for having struck a mighty blow for the unity of the growing republic; had he not provided a spelling book by which all of us, natives and immigrants alike, could learn to spell like Americans? During this period, also, dictionaries got started. There had been lists of "hard" words, and as Anglo-Norman became scarce, of Anglo-Norman words with English equivalents, and thesauruses of Latin and Greek, but not until the eighteenth century was lexicography sufficiently understood so that makers of dictionaries tried to include all words, and to rest the usage and definition of a word upon written practice as it was observable in careful users of the language.

One other important development needs to be related to this time. As England embarked upon her long career as a maritime and colonizing power, the colonizers encountered intimately peoples and their languages which had not previously impinged much upon English people or English speech. Where there was cultural contact there was linguistic transfer. Thus English acquired words from the Low Countries, from the maritime countries, from colonial areas; the largest recent body, of course, is Anglo-Indian vocabulary, particularly that brought back by English soldiers, officials, and traders in India. Trade followed the flag, linguistics followed trade, and the British flag during the last two centuries has been everywhere.

*Came the*
*Forefathers*
*of Mencken*

WE HAVE now to consider the results of the second great Anglo-Saxon invasion. The first carried a Germanic tongue from the coast of Europe to a new home on the off-coast island of Britain. The second carried the descendant of this Anglo-Saxon speech from England to the continent of North America. In some ways, from a linguistic point of view, the conquests were similar. Both conquests were slow and consequently thorough; the Celtic language was obliterated, except for scraps, mostly place names, in the portions of Britain taken over by the invaders. The Indian tongues were obliterated in North America except where scattering groups of Indians have been able to maintain some kind of integrated life, mainly in the Arctic Circle and on reservations.

But there were also differences. The Germanic invaders came in relatively few waves, and once they were established they maintained only scanty relations with the Germanic peoples on the Continent—in fact, they were more frequently at war with them than collaborating with them. The invaders of what is now the United States, in spite of some unpleasantness after 1775 and 1812, have always maintained close connections with Europe, have most of the time until very recently been reliant upon

Europe, and have always felt that their closest ties were those with the English-speaking people. Americans have always heavily imported British goods and British ideas, so much so that even Continental ideas have usually come to us through England. Both the United States and Canada were culturally and socially colonies of Britain long after the United States ceased to be politically a colony. The urban parts of the northern United States —Philadelphia, Boston, New York—and the plantation aristocracy of the South maintained unusually close relationships with the British motherland.

Consequently the transplanting of English to North America was a relatively long, slow, and involved process, although not so long as the immigration figures might suggest; the bulk of our linguistic habits seem to have been imported in the eighteenth century. Nor was the importation simplified by the fact that immigrants to this country brought with them a great variety of dialects, including those from Scotland, Ireland, and Wales. There were also speakers of other than English, of course, but they have influenced the growth of English in this country less than might have been expected. The early comers were preponderantly English-speaking. Later, when immigrants came from other areas, more than a million in some years, the speech habits of the country were well established. The newcomers did not all come from one country, and they were as foreign to each other as they were to speakers of English. Furthermore they came with a great desire to conform; the immigrants themselves were usually incapable of speaking the local language without peculiarities, but their children grew up speaking a dialect indistinguishable from that of other native-born citizens. These second-generation immigrants showed a zeal, which was probably generally harmful, to dispose of all vestiges of their foreign origin; our society is the poorer for having lost so much of what the immigrants brought with them, but our language is the more uniform, and currency is no small virtue in language. There are exceptions. The German spoken by the so-called Pennsylvania Dutch has had some impact on vocabulary. Near New Orleans

French has been important, and Mexican Spanish influenced the Southwest, but looking at American speech generally, the exceptions are still exceptions.

Immigrants to the United States presumably had at least one influence. If they did not transmit many of their speech habits to their new homes, they did constitute a continuous body of unstable speakers. From the earliest days in the white occupation of North America, there has been a mingling of dialects, partly because speakers of various British dialects were relocated in this country side by side, and partly because there was always a body, sometimes a very large body, of speakers who were compelled to speak a tongue to which they were not native. This provided a milieu in which speech could change rapidly. American speech has changed rapidly—and here we can use the word *American* in a manner not to offend our southern neighbors, for Spanish and Portuguese have changed more rapidly in Latin America than they have in Europe, just as English has changed more rapidly in the United States than it has in Britain. One suspects even that English has changed more rapidly in the United States than in Canada, partly because the States have generally had the larger foreign populations.

We have already noticed that the transition from Anglo-Saxon to Middle English was a rapid and violent change, as changes occur in language, presumably because Englishmen were speaking French badly and Normans were speaking Anglo-Saxon outrageously, and neither language found itself in the normal linguistic situation, that of being the common medium for all the people for all purposes of communication. The speech situation in the American colonies and in the United States later was never so unstable as this, but it was sufficiently unstable to encourage change, and change there was.

Now, having said so much, we need to make one further observation. American dialectal speech, on the whole, rests upon British dialectal speech. We have already noticed that language exists, and can exist, only on a dialectal level. Just as Hengist and Horsa brought their own dialects with them to the island of Britain, James Oglethorpe and Roger Williams brought their

dialects with them to America. That Georgia was a penal colony
and that Boston, Massachusetts, was named by those who came
from Boston, England, are significant linguistic facts. Naturally
the tracing of all dialectal waifs which came as stowaways to the
New World would require more evidence than has survived, but
even so, a careful student like Professor Krapp clearly felt that
the evidence is overwhelming for the supposition that every pe-
culiarity of American speech is an importation of a British locu-
tion, or an understandable development from an importation.

The variations of the word *idea*, which in efforts to reproduce
dialectal pronunciations are spelled *idear*, *idee*, *aidy*, *ahdy*, and
the like, can all be paralleled in British dialects. The sort of variation common in earlier American speech, and continuing in
some areas, represented by spellings like *bile* for *boil*, *ile* for *oil*,
*gwine* for *going*, are survivals of a widespread difference in the
pronunciation of vowels in these words in seventeenth- and
eighteenth-century Britain. We have already noticed the American dialectal substitution of *born* for *barn*; in fact, when a
dialect-speaking Briton says something which sounds like standard American *barn* he may mean *barn*, *born*, or *bairn*, depending upon his dialect, and all of those pronunciations have been
brought to this country. Perhaps the most notable set of variations
which grew as dialectal distinctions in the New World, resting
upon dialectal distinctions in the Old, appears in the differences
between what is sometimes called General American, a group of
dialects which spread in a great fan from the northern Appa-
lachians south and west, and dialects to the southeast and northeast of this speech.

| | |
|---|---|
| *Came*<br>*Linguistic*<br>*Geography* | To UNDERSTAND all this we must take ac-<br>count of linguistic geography, a study<br>which is relatively new in this country,<br>although its principles were worked out in<br>Europe some decades ago. Linguistic geog- |

raphers endeavor to study the distribution of languages, including language on a regional or dialectal basis, to determine the

spread and changes in language. They do this by studying the occurrence of a relatively small number of words, pronunciations, and grammatical structures, and by plotting their distributions. The result takes the form of dialect maps, with isoglosses which show the spread of certain speech characteristics. In Europe the method has revealed the mingling of languages, the development and movement of dialects, and has even thrown light on the ancient relationships within the Indo-European language family. In this country we may hope that linguistic geography will tell us a great deal about how we developed an American English, and something about how we developed an American people.

To see how linguistic geography works, we might turn to the Linguistic Atlas for the eastern United States, the first of a series of linguistic geographical studies which are now being conducted as far west as the Pacific Coast. It maps, for instance, various ways of referring to a bull. In Vermont and New Hampshire he may be a *male critter*, a *toro*, or even a *seed ox*. In a belt running south and west from Chesapeake Bay he may be a *stock beast*, a *brute*, or a *masculine* (the last syllable pronounced to rhyme with *fine*). This distribution must mean something, but before a linguistic geographer tries to make too much of it, he compares his results with the spread of other linguistic phenomena in the same areas. For instance, take the word for a plank balanced on a fulcrum and used to amuse children. It can be called *teeter board*, *tinter*, *hicky-horse*, *cock horse*, *tilting board*, or *tippity-bounce*, and in Rhode Island it can be *dandle*. That must mean something about Rhode Island, and the other variants must mean something, also, since they are scattered in patterns, and the patterns show some similarity to the distribution for such words as *critter*, *toro*, and *seed ox*.

The working out of this sort of data naturally becomes complicated, but when the isoglosses begin to pile up, when word after word shows similar configurations, important directions of movement and important lines of contact begin to appear. For instance, isogloss after isogloss begins just south of the Dutch

settlement around New York, moves west and a little north
through New Jersey and Pennsylvania to Lake Erie. The line
marks the border between *teeter* and *teeter board,* between
*whiffletree* and *whippletree,* between *spider* and *frying pan.* In
short, it is the line between the Westward movement of New
England and Midland dialects. (What is sometimes called the
Midland dialect is the speech of the Eastern central seaboard.)
This concurrence of isoglosses is a central fact for the study of
the English language on the American continent, and a central
fact also in the study of the American people. It shows us something of how language and culture came west. When people
move, they take their dialects with them. and scatter regionalisms along the route, as though they were migratory Hansels and
Gretels. The cultural way west seems to be well marked from
Jamestown, Philadelphia, and Plymouth Rock, all the way to the
Golden Gate. Linguistic geography is perhaps our best means of
identifying the way.

When the Linguistic Atlas of the United States is complete
we shall know more than we can now, but even now we can
make some approximate estimates, because the word geography
for the eastern coast identifies the dialects which moved west,
and plots them as they make their first moves. A preliminary
guess as to what happened would read something like the following. There were many minor variations, but in general, three
dialect areas built up on the Eastern seaboard in the eighteenth
century, one in New England which extended down to the Dutch
colony in New York, one south from Chesapeake Bay, and a
middle, or Midland, dialect between. The Southern dialect moved
west, fanning up a little into the Ohio Valley; it has its descendants from Maryland to Missouri to Texas, and in the areas to
the southeast. When New England expanded, much of the expansion went into ocean commerce, trade, and industry. Agri-
culturists from western New England moved west, and had their
effect, but they were not in sufficient numbers to establish char-
acteristically New England dialects in the northern parts of Ohio,
Illinois, and Indiana, nor in Wisconsin and Iowa. The Mid-

land dialect, centered on Pennsylvania, became the basis of the dominant speech of the Great Lakes area, and the determining dialect in the westward movement of language to the Pacific Coast.

Those are the broad outlines. Now we should add that the early colonists in this country, those who settled New England and the area from the Chesapeake Bay south, came mainly from the south and southeast of England, that is, from London and the areas immediately to the north. These immigrants brought with them the dialects which became established in New England and in the South. The Midland group, centered upon Pennsylvania, represented northern England much more extensively. Furthermore, when the Midland group moved west, somewhat later than the New England and southern movements, it was greatly augmented by the later immigrants which included large numbers of people from Celtic areas—Ireland, Scotland, Wales— all of whom spoke English with characteristics suggestive of northern British speech. Thus, as the three basic seaboard American dialects moved west, the central dialect was characteristic of northern British speech, the northern and southern dialects characteristic of southern British speech. That is, the difference between the pronunciation of Boston and Chicago is to a degree the difference between the pronunciation of southeastern and south central England as against the speech of northern England. For instance, the softening of the terminal *r* and the *r* before a consonant in words like *mother* and *hard* is characteristic of southern British speech and of northeastern and southeastern American speech, but not of northern British speech, east Midland American speech, or Middle-Western speech. And so rather generally. Even many particular details seem to fit. Some investigators have felt they could trace the so-called New England drawl to certain valleys in Essex, and there seems little doubt that this pronunciation came as part of our Puritan heritage. The New York City variant of *doy* for *die*, *boy* for *buy*, *thoid* for *third* suggests forms in Yorkshire, which are reflections of the strong influence of the old York upon the New York.

*Linguistic
Law West of
the Atlantic*

THUS THE solid fact of American speech seems to be that three dialects grew up on the Eastern seaboard and went west along with those who took Greeley's advice. The other permeating fact is an obvious one, although one which can be overlooked. Language is language and human beings are human beings, in the United States as elsewhere. Language in America has reflected human nature, human vocal systems, and human society; perhaps it has reflected these fundamentals even more intimately here than in most places because, our circumstances being what they were, American speech grew in a linguistic climate which encouraged change, all the sorts of change we have discussed in previous chapters, and all of these together. Once British dialects were established in this country they moved west. They mingled. They developed their own peculiarities when they became isolated. They acquired new words and new meanings for old words as a new way of living required new expressions. They encountered speakers of other languages and borrowed a little here and there, from French *coureurs de bois*, from Mexican *vaqueros*, from Seminoles, from Chickasaws. Americans played with words, and lived through experiences which engendered or altered words. The dialect of any given area in the United States today shadows the history of the area, and the linguistic history of those who live and have lived in the area.

Thus, current differences in American speech reflect what has happened in this country along with distinctions brought to this country. Sometimes developments abetted the old dialects; sometimes they confused them. The South, for instance, has been relatively conservative in language as in politics; much Southern speech is what it is because Southern speakers have preserved seventeenth and eighteenth century southeastern British pronunciations. Into the Middle West, meanwhile, millions of Celtic speakers were bringing with them great quantities and varieties of r-sounds. This difference was abetted in curious ways, even in the way children were tended. While there were Irish nursemaids in Cleveland, speaking English with a strong *r*, Negro mammies in Memphis were talking a dialect based upon a highly conservative form of dialectal British speech, and a dialect which the Negroes had learned as foreigners. Nor is the influence of nursemaids to be despised, for as we have seen, to a considerable degree the bosom that offers the nipple rules the language.

Conversely, there was no lack of influences to obscure the dialects of the Eastern seaboard. The great urban centers like Philadelphia, Boston, New York, and Charleston became influences of themselves. These centers and the Southern planters continued to be importers of British English after other parts of the New World had pretty much lost touch with the Old.

There are, of course, minor peculiarities. That the New Englanders were for many years schoolteachers to the nation has certainly spread more New Englandisms, and generally rather colloquial New Englandisms, than would otherwise be prevalent. A sophisticated Hudson Valley man like Cooper had the greatest contempt for the New England boor who was the local schoolteacher, if we may so interpret Cooper's picture of a New England schoolteacher in *Satanstoe*. But in most parts of early America a New England schoolteacher was a learned man, relatively speaking, and his influence was out of all proportion to his numbers. The impact of the frontier also changed American language. Frontiersmen were tough fellows, and tough fellows incline to vulgar talk; but the tough fellows became the solid citizens of a new land, and thus all sorts of curious speech, new and old, was dredged up and established as the frontier moved west, for tough fellows might come from any place, bringing their dialects with them.

And after all, the New World was a new world, inevitably colonial. Careful people wanted to speak correctly, but how could they know what was correct? In the Old Country, any commoner who wanted to be correct had only to try to talk like his lordship—or more probably like her ladyship—but in the New World there were no lords and ladies. The only standard for most people was the printing of the word in the spelling book— since spelling books were more common than dictionaries. Thus a tendency to try to be "correct" on the theory that "That's the way it's spelled," has influenced many American pronunciations. Some speakers are careful to pronounce *often* to sound like *off-ten*, *toward* to sound like *to-ward*, *forehead* to sound like *fore-head*, although these words had not been so pronounced for hundreds of years, and there is no more reason to pronounce *often* as *off-ten* than there is to pronounce *lord* as though it were spelled *hlaf-weard*, which it was some hundreds of years ago. Many Americans call a financial official a *comp-troller*, though the *p* never was pronounced historically, and was inserted at all only on the basis of a mistaken guess at the etymology of the word. But if we want to pronounce *often* like *off-ten*, there is no reason why we should not do so. And from present indications, quite possibly we all shall some day.

Nearly a quarter of a century ago Henry L. Mencken gave up many of his journalistic and critical activities and devoted himself to collecting American speech as it had never been collected, and defending it against all comers, especially against British comers. If we now combine his contributions with others, the essential facts concerning the growth of Mencken's mother tongue seem to be these. We imported British dialects, from various areas and over a number of years, but mainly in the eighteenth century. These dialects were separated and divided in this country in accordance with the vagaries of immigration and human history. Once British speech was established in North America, it went the way of speech everywhere, except that the circumstances of time and place encouraged at once strong conservatism and rapid change. As a colonial people we had the peculiarities, social and linguistic, of colonials; as pioneers, we had the characteristics of invaders who move slowly into a strange land.

# ℳ 16 ℳ

## THE KING'S ENGLISH IN A DEMOCRATIC WORLD

RIGHT AND WRONG, ARE THEY TRUTH, NECESSITY, OR FASHION?—EVERY WOMAN HER OWN WEBSTER—THE HARMLESS DRUDGES—THE BUSINESS OF BEING A DRUDGE

*Right and*
*Wrong,*
*Are They*
*Truth,*
*Necessity, or*
*Fashion?*

IF YOU mispronounce an American Indian word in an Indian household the adults will probably be polite enough not to laugh, but the children are likely to giggle. Ethnocentrism is so strong in the human animal that most of us assume, until and unless we have the assumption ironed out of us, that our way of doing things is the right way, that strange ways are inevitably wrong ways. A laugh is a powerful tool of social control, perhaps the most powerful, and thus from the earliest days strong forces have promoted standards and control in language.

Language always changes slowly. Even when it changes rapidly in historical perspective, it changes so slowly that the speakers of it are not usually much aware of the change. Thus unconscious controls upon language are sufficiently lax so that language can usually change freely even though it is subject to constant and quite exacting pressure the aim of which is to standardize it and keep it fixed. But as society becomes more complicated, as the users of a language become more numerous and more varied in their spread and occupation, as the necessities for communication become greater, and standardization becomes more and more the pattern of social living, the pressure to impose standards, rigid standards, upon language increases.

We are forced to ask ourselves very seriously, what are the relationships of language and life, and how much do the requirements of human welfare at home and abroad require that we police our language? Who is to do the policing, and how?

We have already noted that medieval speakers of English were apparently highly tolerant of variations in language. A Middle English poet mixed up his dialectal forms in any manner that gave him the rhymes and rhythms he wanted, and we have little evidence that anyone thought this practice exceptionable or even unusual. During the Renaissance correctness was much discussed, but apparently not much enforced. During the authoritarian eighteenth century, however, the *ipse dixit* pronouncement, the fiat which assumes that "it's so because he says it's so" reached its height, a height from which it has till now not much declined in some quarters.

A grammarian like Robert Baker, for instance, as the late Professor Sterling Andrus Leonard of the University of Wisconsin has observed, would blandly condemn all sorts of expressions with a positive, "There is no such word," "This is an expression of great barbarity," "This is not English," "That is a deformity in the language." But of course what was a deformity to Baker was not necessarily a deformity to Baker's contemporaries, Lowth, Murray, or Webster. Baker even admits—though he seems unaware that he is making an admission—that the reason one usage is "not English" and another one is unexceptionable "would be perhaps no easy matter to tell." It would have been no easy matter, but the difficulty seems not to have deterred those who set themselves up to do the telling.

Many of these policemen of usage were not close students of the language. If they appealed to linguistic history they were inclined to assume that there was a universal grammatical truth as there was a universal religious truth—indeed, a number of them were divines, and Lowth was a bishop—and that universal grammar was for all practical purposes embodied in Latin grammar. Thus, if they appealed to authority at all, they appealed to Latin. But most of them did not appeal. They asserted. The reviewers of Baker's grammar, even the favorable reviewers who applauded his methods and most of his conclusions, found Baker's composition, as Baker found others' compositions, replete with barbarisms, "vile phrases," and locutions which made "one inelegance necessary by another." Many pronouncements of this sort were drowned in the mutual recriminations of the self-constituted justices of the peace in language, but others became commandments from the linguistic Sinai, to be copied or miscopied blindly thereafter into handbooks of usage.

The supposed distinction between *shall* and *will* as future auxiliaries provides a pleasant example of eighteenth-century dictatorial procedures and modern echoes in language standards. A mathematician who signed himself Johannis Wallis when he wrote in Latin decided that *shall* and *will* should be distinguished in usage, and asserted that *shall* was properly used to indicate simple futurity in the first person, determination and purpose in the second and third persons; that *will* was used for determination in the first person, and for simple futurity in the second and third. There seems to have been no justification for this dictum among Wallis's contemporaries in seventeenth-century England, nor among his eighteenth-century followers; as Professor Leonard has observed, not even Lowth, who fought for the rule, observed it himself. Nor was there any historical justification. This distinction had never been made between *shall* and *will*, nor has there ever been a time, apparently, when *shall* and *will* were consistently distinguished by Englishmen as signs of different sorts of futurity.

In Anglo-Saxon the words were not used to signal a future; Anglo-Saxon used the simple present, as we do to a degree, to imply future. *Sculan*, from which we get *shall*, meant "ought to," and *willian*, from which we get *will* meant "to desire," "to wish," "to expect." They were not signs of the future, but they became so, very much as *ought to go*, *have to go*, *want to go*, and *expect to go* are becoming future forms. They retained their original meanings, in part, but they never became consistently divergent in any way to confirm the arbitrary rule proposed by Wallis. But once the new rule had been announced, nothing could stop it. Joseph Priestley doubted its validity, and said so; his contemporary, Withers, condemned it. But Priestley was a dissenting divine as well as a dissenting grammarian; that he was also a schoolmaster and a chemist did not save him. His voice, along with Withers's, was drowned beneath the authority of Lowth, Murray, and dozens of others. Grammarian after grammarian copied Lowth and Murray; generations of schoolteachers endeavored to enforce the rule and generations of groaning children tried to learn it—or to learn just the opposite, for some handbooks managed to reverse the rule in process of copying it. Until today, ability to follow a dictum concocted by a seventeenth-century teacher whose business was mathematics, has become one of the tests of knowing one's grammar, although on this basis very few have ever known their grammar, or know it now. Most of us who try to be consistent are not. Seemingly we can resist very stubbornly dicta for which we have no native feeling.

Latterly the procedures of a pontiff like the grammarian Baker have found little favor among thinkers about language. We have been inclined to ask why one man more than another has the right to decide what is and what is not "barbaric" or "vile." What makes a vile word vile, or a barbaric construction barbaric? If language grows from the nature of human beings and by the experience of all sorts of people, who is to decide what the language is to be, except those whose minds and lives make the language? If language has always grown and always changed, why should that which has been "right" necessarily continue to be so? If language always has changed and apparently always will change, why should anybody try to stop it?

These are pertinent considerations, but not the only possible ones. Language must not only have flexibility to live and grow, it must have currency to be understood. Like money, it is no fit medium for exchange unless it has sufficient currency so that he who gives the coin values it in roughly the same terms as he who receives it. And like money, it must have sufficient stability so that what is given today has approximately the same value tomorrow. Without stability we might never learn to speak, because the language could be changing faster than we were able to learn it; without currency, even if we learned to speak we could not communicate widely, because our medium of exchange would not be acceptable to enough others to make it usable. We understand each other only because large numbers of people over great areas of the earth have lived in mutual if unconscious agreement that certain words are symbols for certain meanings and not for other meanings; that strictly determined ways of handling these symbols reveal their relationships. We agree that the symbol *table* stands for a flat surface supported from beneath, that it is not a container used to enclose fire for heating purposes. We agree that in the construction *the red table, hot from the red-hot stove*, the table has a permanent color and the stove a temporary one, and that this distinction is apparent in part through the varying positions of *red* and *hot* in the sentence.

Thus there is a fundamental inconsistency in language and in the way in which we make it and use it which forever prevents the establishment and the upholding of any standards from being entirely logical. Language is a living thing. It must survive in men's minds and on their tongues if it survives at all. In so doing, it changes with minds, lives, and the use of vocal apparatus. But at the same time, language can function only if it has stability in time and place. Change is inevitable in language, and yet all change damages language, although it may at the same time revitalize it. We may be able to minimize the effects of this inconsistency, but we cannot remove it.

*Every Woman Her Own Webster* THUS IF students of language were to be guided only by the logic of the situation, they would find themselves neatly spitted on this dilemma, that stability and change are both imperative in a living, serviceable language. How can the difficulty be avoided? Surely not by allowing any man who can print a book to decide questions of standards by his own whim, as some commentators of the eighteenth century tried to do, and many authoritarian people would like to do yet. Surely not by appealing to Latin grammar or to some other supposed universal grammar. As far as we know, there is no universal grammar. There may be universal principles in language, but the laws of grammar, if they can be called laws, are descriptions of what human beings do with language. They are not pronunciamenta concerning what is "right" and what is "wrong." All words and ways of using words are right if the users of the language want them that way; they are wrong if the users of the language do not want them. If they are right now they will be wrong when the users of language want them no longer.

Obviously questions of standards must depend upon usage. In language, whatever is, is right—provided it "is" enough so that enough people want it that way for a long enough time. In short, in his own small way, every man is his own Webster, deciding what language is and what it is not. Even more, every woman is her own Webster. For as we have seen, the great arbiters of language are the women who speak it in the presence of children. There is a theory that men have made all the great innovations in language. Whether or not this hypothesis is sound—and there might well be women who would point out that the theory was propounded by a man—there is no question as to who preserves the language, through what medium language is handed on to the next generation, by whom some language is allowed to die and other parts saved. Mainly, women do it. What the women pass on to the next generation is "right" and what they do not bother to pass on to their children sooner or later becomes "wrong."

*The Harmless Drudges*  THE authoritarians of the eighteenth century, however wrong they were, did not lack for sound counsel. There had been wise men enough from Aristotle to John Locke who seem to have understood the nature of language. Plenty of men from Horace to Priestley had said quite clearly that standards must be based upon usage. And a considerable portion of the grammarians of the eighteenth century themselves, including authoritarians like Lowth and Johnson, paid at least lip service to the importance of usage while condemning "vulgar use, in which the caprice of Custom is apt to get the better of analogy." Even Webster, who asserted that "The business of a grammarian is not to examine whether or not national practice is founded on philosophical principles; but to *ascertain* the national practice," nonetheless found himself relying upon "the principle of analogy" and "the rules of the language itself," and condemning what he called "the well-nigh universal misuses of English." If the usages were "well-nigh universal," and the rightness or the wrongness of a use was to depend upon currency, how could they be "misuses"?

Perhaps one should remind oneself of the nature of the times. Few people in the eighteenth century, presented with the necessity of answering a difficult question, thought of going about to collect evidence, expecting thereafter to extract the answer from the evidence. This is the scientific procedure and it serves us well; it has served us so well and so long that most people can now think of no other way to attack a problem, and they assume that there is no other way. But if the scientific method serves us well, it also blinds us. Surely it must be obvious that we make the most egregious blunders, national and international, public and private, because we do not sit down and think long and seriously about things. We like to work things out, not think them out.

Men of the eighteenth century used, on the whole, the latter method; they liked to think things out. It was the method beloved of Socrates and Plato and of many who came after them. It was the method which seemed to be suited to an orderly world created and run by a Supreme Being in accordance with good, sound logic. Eighteenth-century seekers after the truth liked to use their minds in perceiving the order of the world and in telling the world how to continue to be orderly. Furthermore, it was a habit with them. It was one with respect for God, King, and Country. It was like the British climate and strong, black tea with milk; good or bad, eighteenth-century Britons had grown up with it, and it was a part of their lives, something to be loved and to be done automatically, not to be questioned, surely not long to be deviated from. Thus writers upon language, even when they professed other faiths, reverted mainly in their daily practice to authority in grammar as in theology. An occasional maverick like Priestley, who with some consistency tried to submit questions of standards to the court of usage—whenever he could convene the court—was not very influential. Lowth and Murray, not Priestley, were the accepted grammarians.

As a matter of practical fact, the court of usage is not readily convened. How is one to know what is the national practice concerning the multifarious details of language? How, to use Webster's phrase, is a grammarian "to *ascertain* the national usage"? Webster solved the problem neatly, and apparently to his own satisfaction, by assuming that the practices of Noah Webster and his neighbors in Connecticut were, for all practical purposes, "the national usage." This method had its obvious limitations, but Priestley, who made a more serious effort in England, fared in the end not much better. Even when he could shake himself sufficiently free of the shackles of the time to seek the national usage he had little machinery for discovering it.

And yet, in his century the machinery was being developed, and in the very seat of authoritarianism, in the bulky person of Dr. Samuel Johnson. The good doctor's own discussion of grammar allowed but twelve lines to syntax, which is obviously the heart of English grammatical usage, and his pronouncements come clothed as in the voice of Jove. But Johnson was known mainly as a lexicographer—it was he who, in one of those moments of whimsy and self-deprecation which make the Great Bear a charming fellow, defined a lexicographer as "a writer of dictionaries, a harmless drudge." He was authoritarian to a fault, and yet his work became a foundation for the modern practice of resting standards upon usage.

Johnson spent many of the prime years of his life making a dictionary, employing the best theory that had been worked out by the French and Italian academies, and resting his definitions not upon the usage of his day, but upon the best usage he could discover in the great writers of the British past. The French had made use of the practice, albeit with a different purpose. On the theory that the French language had now become a perfect linguistic instrument, the French Academy endeavored, in the interests of France and civilization, to collect their perfect language and put it in a book so that it should not decay. They thereby attested their ignorance of one of the fundamental principles of language, that a living language always changes and will change however authoritarians try to stop it. But they did advance lexicographical knowledge and practice. Johnson advanced them still further—his friend Garrick jubilated that "he beat sixty Frenchmen, and could beat sixty more," and there was some truth in the boast. Johnson, almost single-handed, created one of the best works of its day in any language, a book which saw the British Empire in and very nearly saw it out. Adapting French techniques, he relied upon usage, even though past conspicuous usage, not as a means of preserving a perfect language, but as the instrument for refining a faulty one.

After Johnson the next step was obvious if onerous. If enough people could be found to read carefully all the important writings in the language, from the earliest documents to today, a whole history of the language could be built upon citations from these writings. The result was the *New English Dictionary on Historical Principles*, the so-called *Oxford English Dictionary*, and accordingly known as the OED or the NED. Begun in 1858, it required three-quarters of a century to prepare and edit, killed off editor after editor, required the ungrudging labor of hundreds of scholars on both sides of the Atlantic, and was finally printed with the aid of the Almighty himself—the printing bill having been guaranteed by the Oxford University Press, relying upon its lucrative privilege to print Bibles in England. Beyond all comparison the *New English Dictionary* records the English language as no other language has ever been recorded, and it has sired a whole sequence of more detailed dictionaries, of which the *Dictionary of American English*, and what might be called its progeny, *A Dictionary of Americanisms*, are now in print; the *Dictionary of Middle English* is announced, and *the Dictionary of Early Modern English* has been in the editing almost a quarter of a century; the *Dictionary of the Older Scottish Tongue* and the *Dictionary of Later Scottish* are in process.

But our concern here is not with wordbooks, except incidentally. Samuel Johnson presumed not only to define words but to endeavor to remove from the language "improprieties and absurdities." In this, Noah Webster, in spite of his theoretical professions, followed him. But the *New English Dictionary* established, apparently for all time, that dictionaries are henceforth to be made by harmless drudges, even more harmless and more faithful drudges than Johnson conceived. The job of lexicographers is now to discover usages, sift them and record them, not mainly to legislate among them. Dictionary editors work on what are called "historical principles," as follows: if a word is recorded in writing it belongs in the dictionary; until it is recorded it will not be entered in the dictionary; when it is entered it will be defined and described in accordance with its usage in printed citations. This procedure, like any other, can occasionally be a bit ridiculous. We thus have the spectacle of a lexicographer refusing to put into a dictionary a word which he knows quite well because he cannot find it used in some piece of published writing. Recently one of our greatest lexicographers, the soundness of whose practice is amply attested by the excellence of his publications, wrote to an American language journal thanking them for publishing a certain article because it contained words which belonged in his dictionary, but which he had been troubled to find published anywhere. And so we have a man greatly learned in the language deliberately disenfranchising himself; though he knew quite well these words existed, and what they mean and how they are used, he could not put them into his dictionary until he could catch somebody using them, even though the user knew less about the words than he did. But even in spite of an occasional absurdity of this sort, the principles and practice of modern British and American lexicographers have given us dictionaries which are justly the envy of the world.

Perhaps we should notice at this point the dilemma of the modern lexicographer endeavoring to deal with grammar. He has troubles to which Johnson was immune. Johnson thought he knew what the grammar of English was, and he said so. The modern lexicographer may think he knows what the grammar of English is, but he will presume to say so only if he can find that there is agreement among those who should know. Johnson thought that making decisions in grammar was part of his business, but the modern lexicographer no more endeavors to decide what are the essentials of English grammar and how our grammatical statement should be formulated than he presumes to decide what are the essentials of chemistry or what is questionable in the quantum theory.

As we have seen, however, grammarians do not agree. The grammatical thinkers of our day are sharply at odds with the accepted grammatical statement. By the tenets of his profession the modern lexicographer should employ the accepted grammatical statement as the basis of his grammatical classifications. But modern lexicographers are learned people, learned especially in language. They do not need me to tell them that adjectives often cannot be distinguished from adverbs and that words like *up, out, off,* and *by* are frequently not prepositions but some part of the verb or complement. But where will they find a grammatical statement sufficiently standardized so that they can use it as the basis of the grammatical treatment in their dictionaries?

There is no such statement. Lexicographers are, on the whole conscientious men and good. Hence, one can almost hear them, like Launcelot Gobbo, listening to an angel with one ear while listening even harder to a devil with the other, and agreeing with both.

"Record faithfully the conventional statement," warns the angel of traditional grammar.

"Angel, you counsel well," says Launcelot Gobbo Lexicographer.

"But you will be printing nonsense," says the little devil, the modern grammarian.

"Devil, you counsel well," says the lexicographer.

And so in the end the lexicographer runs off with the devil of modern grammar, but he does not feel entitled to run very far.

Anyone who wishes to observe this little morality play may do so by examining carefully the desk dictionaries which have recently been put on the market—and there have been excellent ones.

Consider, for instance, the entries under *preposition*. *Webster's New Collegiate Dictionary* says that a preposition is a word showing any of various abstract relations "used to connect a noun or pronoun, in an adjectival or adverbial sense, with some other word." This definition would seem not to stray far from the conventional statement. Since an adverb is elsewhere defined as a modifier or a qualifier, presumably there is no intent here to suggest that the so-called prepositions can become involved in verbs or complements. (The *New International Dictionary*, however, upon which the *Webster's Collegiate* is based, has an entry *prepositional object* which suggests that a preposition can be "felt to be a loose affix giving transitive force to a verb." This entry was dropped from the *Collegiate*, presumably for reasons of space.)

The *American College Dictionary* goes several steps farther. The definition of *preposition* there reads, "(in some languages) one of the major form-classes or 'parts of speech,' comprising words placed before nouns to indicate their relation to other words or their function in the sentence." Another usage makes clear that a preposition need not be one word, but "any construction of similar function or meaning, as *on top of*." Here are considerable changes. Not only have the editors made clear that they do not much trust the notion of parts of speech by putting these words within quotation marks, they have asserted that a preposition may indicate the noun's "function in the sentence." There is no mention of "adjectival or adverbial." Presumably if the user of the ACD wishes to assume that a noun after a preposition can "function in the sentence" as a complement of the verb he may do so.

Similarly the most recent desk dictionary, and one of the most liberal, *Webster's New World Dictionary of the American Language*, defines a preposition as a "relationship word" or "any construction of similar function (e.g., *in back of*, equivalent to *behind*)" that "connects a noun, pronoun, or noun phrase to another element of the sentence, as to a verb (e.g., he went *to* the store) . . ." Here again, although the words of the definition suggest the conventional statement, they leave the reader free to call *store* the complement of the verb if he wishes.

That is, the editors of all three of these dictionaries are aware of the inadequacy of the conventional statement upon which they must, as yet, mainly rely. Being aware, each lexicographical staff has written a definition which does no violence to the accepted practice, but each insofar as he dares has framed a statement which permits a grammatical interpretation which is relatively liberal. As such an editor recently wrote me—he prefers to remain anonymous—"We like to imagine that we are infinitesimally avant-garde in our treatment of purist notions and especially in our inclusion of thousands of phrasal units constituting 'ungrammatical' idioms." A handsomely chosen phrase that, "infinitesimally avant-garde." It suggests at once the liberality of lexicographers as a group, and the strain they labor under these days in endeavoring to find their way among the uncertainties of grammarians and the differences among grammar books.

The same problem and a similar difficulty arise with questions of usage. Lexicographers now agree that just as words mean what they mean by common consent, so a given spelling, pronunciation, or construction is "right" or "wrong" depending upon its currency. Should we say "all the boys" or "all of the boys"? Must we say "Everybody took his hat" because *body* is singular, or may we say "Everybody took their hats" because *everybody* is popularly felt to be plural? Formerly such questions were decided by thunders out of grammatical Sinais. Now they are determined by mild-voiced drudges, with ears attuned to the mumblings of the multitude.

How can the drudge do this? Admittedly, he has his problems. Written work can be read, if the publisher will supply a sufficient staff of readers, and all good dictionary-makers do some reading, or at least some sampling. But language, including usage, is basically oral, and how can the drudge listen to all the babblings of the world? Partly, he can use scholarly studies of oral speech, and does. Partly, he has had to guess. Just now there is promise that he may soon have great help. A national study is in progress, sponsored by the National Council of the Teachers of English, the Modern Language Association, the American Dialect Society, the Linguistic Society, the Speech Association of America, and perhaps others. Soon there will be hundreds, probably thousands of students of language all over the country, looking and listening for the currency of certain usages, and some day the results of all this industry will be accumulated in a monumental *Dictionary of Current American Usage.*

Students of language are more and more becoming harmless and faithful drudges in search of what George Campbell, in his own declaration of independence in 1776, his too-much-neglected *The Philosophy of Rhetoric*, defined as "national, reputable, and present use."

*The Business*　　How FAR is it desirable to standardize
*of Being a*　　speech? Granted that standardization is de-
*Drudge*　　sirable, how much can it be standardized?

Of course questions like this cannot be answered with any exactness, but in a general way the first almost answers itself, and the second is being very practically answered for us. Obviously language should be allowed to change without great restriction. It always has changed, and it needs to change if it is to fit our changing lives. Quite as obviously it should not change so fast that it loses its currency and its relative stability. Slang is fun, but we should be worse off if the Constitution of the United States had been written in slang; we should be worse off if a candidate for the presidency could not talk to all the people, confident that his words would be understood. No one can well deny that the language should be allowed to change, but that it should be discouraged from changing too rapidly.

We can perhaps agree then, without necessarily agreeing about the details, that language should have restrictive but not coercive standards. There are two requisites for such standards: we must have some way of determining them, and some way of enforcing them. The second would seem the harder, but it is not. There are dozens of regulatory agencies, organized and disorganized. A very large part of our population is under considerable pressure to be "correct." All sorts of people are under all sorts of pressures not to be caught doing something "wrong." I lately heard a man giving a speech before an educated group. He was discussing the action of a committee, and you could see him hesitate before he used a pronoun. Should he refer to the committee as *it* or *they?* But he dared not hesitate long. He had to say something. He took the plunge with *it*. Then you could see him scrutinizing his audience to discover whether or not they were laughing at him. After all, there were five men on the committee. Were they not plural? People in the audience were not visibly laughing, but they were polite. He went on. He was still discussing the action of the committee, and we could see him trying to frame sentences in which he would not have to say either *it* or *they*. But he could not go on saying, "The committee . . . the committee . . . the committee." When he sat down, probably sooner than he meant to, he was red and sweating.

We are all subject, more or less, to pressures of that sort, and in addition there are planned and organized means of supporting standards. Parents correct their children, teachers rebuke their pupils, employers scrutinize their employees. Publishers have style sheets and copyreaders to enforce them. Broadcasters endeavor to police the pronunciation, diction, and grammar of language they send out upon the air, particularly language for which their employees are responsible. Various agencies will enforce any dictum in language if only they can believe that they have a touchstone by which they can determine what is "right" and what is "wrong." In fact, most regulatory agencies are so zealous to regulate that they embarrass the experts on whose authority they endeavor to act. They want to consult "the dictionary," and to ignore that dictionaries, being the products of human beings, differ. If they then find that two pronunciations, two spellings, two constructions are approved, they wish to know which one is preferred, and they wish to admit only the preferred.

Thus there are regulating agencies aplenty, even though we have no official ones. Do these regulating agencies depend upon sensible advice, sensibly arrived at, founded upon usage? In this we are not doing badly. The best dictionaries have all been edited at great expense, and several publishers of dictionaries maintain more or less permanent staffs of considerable size, composed of highly trained students of language, whose function is to determine current usage by wide reading, by consultation with specialists in geographical areas and technical fields, and by relating apparent shifts in language to the known linguistic practices of our past. Modern dictionaries are planned to take account of changes in language as these can be discovered from sampling of current practice, but to admit no change as accomplished until a new form gains considerable currency, and has maintained this currency for a reasonable period of time. Dictionary-makers endeavor, also, to determine levels of usage by observing who uses the language and how. In general they endeavor to distinguish three levels of speech as follows: (1) formal English, that is, the language of scientific and academic composition, of official documents, of the more dignified platform speech, and the like; (2) informal English, that is, the sort of language which cultured people use in their daily speech, which serves as the medium for most broadcasts, and which appears in written form in popular periodicals; (3) vulgate English, that is, slang, neologisms, barbarisms, and all locutions confined to the use of illiterate persons.

As with dictionaries, so in a lesser degree with handbooks concerned with grammar. Thus far the makers of dictionaries have gone much further than the makers of grammar books in resting standards upon usage, although even the dictionaries vary in the hospitality which they show to new words. Some are more conservative than others, so that anyone who cares to compare two dictionaries, even two dictionaries which have been recently edited (and not all dictionaries with recent dates are recent dictionaries), can find words which are accepted in one dictionary and frowned upon in the other. But all good dictionaries, even the most conservative, are today supposedly based upon usage. Until recently most handbooks of composition were authoritarian, although no thinker about language for generations has given makers of handbooks a shadow of authority for their authority. But now the tide has apparently turned. Most of the good new books rest standards of grammatical correctness frankly upon usage; the old books are dying out, even though they die a stubborn death.

The study and control of our medium of communication require both scholars with brilliant insight and harmless drudges with a great love of language.

# ❦ 17 ❦

## MAN DOES NOT THINK WITH BRAINS ALONE
### THE HANDMAIDEN OF CULTURE—WORD-HOARDS: THE FOUR VOCABULARIES—WORDS, THE BIG BOSSES—LANGUAGE, A SERIOUS BUSINESS—MOTHER TONGUE AT HOME—MOTHER TONGUE ABROAD

*The Handmaiden*
*of*
*Culture*

OF SUCH is the kingdom of language. Without language, no humanity. Without written language, no civilization. So much for the past. Need anything be said of the present and the future?

Perhaps the most important remarks to be made about language in the world we know are the obvious ones. But the obvious is sometimes the most ignored. Language is, and since its invention or discovery always has been, the most important tool man ever devised. Man is sometimes described as a tool-using animal; language is his basic tool. It is the tool more than any other with which he makes his living, makes his home, makes his life. As man becomes more and more a social being, as the world becomes more and more a social community, communication grows ever more imperative. And language is the basis of communication. Language is also the instrument with which we think, and thinking is the rarest and most needed commodity in the world.

But these are generalities. How does language promote thinking? Very much as one might expect; since there are two main aspects to language, meanings expressed in vocabulary and relationships expressed in grammar and rhetoric, language promotes thinking by both means. Let us take the first. Brains think with words. Perhaps they need not. Supposedly if we had no words,

269

we should still be able to think. But it is the nature of human brains that they think so much better with words than with any other medium—with mental pictures, for instance—that, words being available, we learn to think with them, and rely upon them so much that for practical purposes most people think only about things for which they have words and can think only in the directions for which they have words.

Perhaps an analogy may help. Most people can swim a narrow river. Water is an alien element, but with labor we can force ourselves through it. A good swimmer can cross a wide river, a lake, even the English Channel; no one, as far as we know, has ever swum the Atlantic Ocean, or is likely to do so. Even a champion swimmer, if he had business which required him to spend alternate weeks in Paris and London, would not expect to make the trip regularly by swimming the English Channel. Although we can force ourselves through water by skill and main strength, for all practical purposes our ability to traverse water is only as good as our ships or our airplanes. And so with the activities of our brains. Thinking is probably as foreign to human nature as is water; it is an unnatural element into which we throw ourselves with hesitation, and in which we flounder once we are there. We have learned, during the millenniums, to do rather well with thinking, but only if we buoy ourselves up with words. Some thinking of a simple sort we can do without words, but difficult and sustained thinking, presumably, is completely impossible without their aid, as traversing the Atlantic Ocean is presumably impossible without instruments of marine or supramarine transportation.

Now ships, from homemade, scowlike tubs to ocean liners, are highly varied, and they offer the passenger a variety of transportation. But they are not more varied than vocabularies. We have already noticed that the Anglo-Saxons had a fine phrase for giving information, "to unlock the word-hoard." In modern terms we might call a vocabulary an intellectual checking account, an instrumentality by which we bank our learnings and draw upon them at will. But intellectual checking accounts are infinitely assorted; they vary not only in size, but in the nature of the assets they contain, and in the readiness with which we can use them.

Consider first the size of the vocabulary. Some of us drag out our meager mental existences with only the few hundred words that we can be quite sure we have in the bank; others can be profligate with tens of thousands. How sharply our thinking may be circumscribed by our vocabularies we do not know, but this we do know, man does not think with brains alone. Psychologists find a closer correlation between intelligence quotients and vocabulary tests than between intelligence quotients and any other kind of test. Partly of course we must assume that good brains learn large vocabularies, but pretty clearly, also, good brains are in part good brains because they have large vocabularies to work with.

To say that learning to think is learning words with which to think is of course too simple. But perhaps not so overly simple as the statement might at first seem. Presumably there is a limit to each individual's capacity to think; presumably, also, most people never reach this limit. We can reach toward it, however, by increasing our mental checking account. But is this not extremely difficult, unless learning words "comes easy" for us? If a good vocabulary consists of tens of thousands of words, what chance do most of us have?

More than might at first appear. To understand why most of us can have good mental checking accounts we need to look a bit into the question of vocabularies.

*Word-Hoards:*
*The Four*
*Vocabularies*

As LITERATE beings we all have several vocabularies, commonly at least four.

    *The Speaking Vocabulary*—For anyone who can read and write, the speaking vocabulary is the smallest, usually much the smallest. Some few highly articulate individuals have speaking vocabularies running into the tens of thousands, but most of us have speaking vocabularies of only a few thousand, perhaps a few hundred words. They are the words, of course, which come readily to the tongue in conversation; what passes with most people for conversation employs only a very limited vocabulary. Consider the following:

"Hi, howsa boy?"

"Not too bad. How's yourself?"

"Okay, I guess. Say. About that deal."

"Yeah. Just goin' t' call. What's the pitch?"

"Here's the dope. You contact Jim. See? He'll give ya the picture."

"Okay. I'll contact Jim."

"Okay. You do that."

"Sure."

"Got it?"

"Sure. Well, okay. See ya in jail."

"Sure. Be seein' ya."

This may be a moderately important transaction, but it has required, and stimulated, the use of very few words. Had the conversation concerned the buying of a new car, who hit how many home runs, or who has been seen out with whose wife, not many more words would have been required, and, surprisingly, not very different words. The lives and talk of most people run in such narrow ruts that their speaking vocabularies are not cultivated, or even kept in repair.

*The Writing Vocabulary*—For many people the writing vocabulary does not much exceed the speaking vocabulary, for most people write very little except business letters in a highly formalized and routine vocabulary, friendly letters which are roughly transcripts of their talk, bills, simple lists, checks, notes on a memo pad, and the like. Asked to write anything more than this, they have the greatest difficulty, partly because they have not at their command words sufficiently varied and exact to make any precise expression possible. People who write much and carefully, or even people who write little but write carefully when they write, may have at their command tens of thousands of words.

*The Reading Vocabulary*—Anyone who reads at all is almost certain to know the meaning of words when he sees them which he would not be able to recall and use with facility when he is speaking or writing. Thus for literate people the reading vocabulary includes the speaking and writing vocabularies, with some additional words; for omnivorous and receptive readers, the reading vocabulary may contain tens of thousands of additional words.

*The Recognition Vocabulary*—This vocabulary may be very large, considerably above a hundred thousand words. It includes the words a person has heard in speech or seen in writing enough so that they have a familiar look, even though the person would never use them himself. He could not define them when he encounters them in reading or speech, although he probably would not feel the need of doing so, since he would think he could if he had to and he can guess the sense of a sentence without knowing the meaning of the word very exactly.

*Words, the Big Bosses*   But vocabularies vary not only in size. They vary also in usability, and, curiously enough, their usability varies with the way they are used. Like most tools, unused they rust or decay, but unlike most tools, used carelessly they never become good for anything except careless use. For vocabularies are self-sharpening. The more they are used, the better they become. No man owns more of a word or controls more of the power of the word than he has learned and learned to use. All words have uses that most of their users never suspect. For instance, let us imagine two people, each of whom knows the word *contract*. One of them is a corporation lawyer, and for him *contract* is the key to great bodies of law and life. The other is a bored woman of circumscribed existence for whom *contract* is only another way of saying *bridge*. Obviously, the lawyer owns more property in *contract* than the bored woman does, and the word is for him a better tool.

But tools can also be lethal instruments. We need no Lizzie Borden, taking an axe to give her progenitor forty whacks, to tell us that. For many centuries, however, men seem not to have much recognized words as tyrants and murderers. Lately we have done better.

To see how this sort of thing goes, consider the following incident. The local newspaper in the town in which I happen to be living printed the following:

### U. N. EMPLOYE
### HISS TIES TOLD

Former Diplomat
Named in Inquiry

Washington, March 23. (AP)—A security officer today described the state department office of Alger Hiss as "the reservoir" from which names of more than 477 American job seekers were sent to the United Nations.

William L. Franklin, special assistant to the department's security director, testified to a house judiciary subcommittee that of 49 who landed jobs with the U. N. at least five became "public issues."

CALLED AS WITNESSES

By public issues, Franklin said, he meant they were actual or scheduled witnesses before a New York grand jury or a senate subcommittee both of which investigated charges of Red infiltration of the United Nations.

Hiss was assistant director or director of the state department's office of special political affairs in 1946 when the names were submitted. He is in jail now, serving a term for lying about passing documents to a wartime Soviet spy ring.

I mimeographed this account, and distributed it to a number of classes of what seemed to be average second-semester freshmen, and asked them to check any of the following statements which they could infer to be true from the account:

Franklin's evidence proves that Hiss recommended
communists to the United Nations                          ———

Franklin's evidence proves that Hiss was endeavoring to overthrow the government                           ———

Franklin's evidence proves that Hiss recommended bad security risks                                    ———

Franklin's evidence provides us reason to believe that Hiss recommended public nuisances              ———

Franklin's evidence proves that Hiss was endeavoring to aid Russia                                      ———

Franklin's evidence proves that Hiss's candidates were either carelessly chosen or willfully mischosen  ———

Franklin's evidence tells something, but relatively little, about the character of candidates recommended by Hiss                                          ———

Franklin's evidence allows us to infer nothing about the candidates recommended by Hiss                 ———

*(Before we discuss this newspaper account, you may want to try the test yourself.)*

Now let us look at the account. What does it say? It says that of forty-nine individuals recommended by Mr. Hiss's office, and employed by the United Nations, five became "public issues." Obviously, we do not want "public issues" in office; the words have a dangerous sound, although it certainly is true that President Eisenhower, George Washington, and Jesus Christ have all become public issues. What is a public issue? Fortunately, in this instance, Mr. Franklin defined what he meant by "public issues," and some smart desk editor—many desk editors are liberal persons with a keen sense for words—saw to it that the definition got into the account which went out over the wires. "By public issues, Franklin said, he meant they were actual or scheduled witnesses before a New York grand jury or a senate subcommittee. . . ."

What evidence, then, does this account provide of guilty action on the part of any of these five people? None whatever. So far as this account tells us, none of these people was found guilty of anything; we are not even told that any of them was ever accused of anything. Presumably some of the five were called to testify, and were not merely "scheduled witnesses," but even if they were, is every witness at a murder trial guilty of murder? The five were "actual or scheduled witnesses," and the mere fact that they may have been only scheduled to give evidence—any kind of evidence, evidence for the government perhaps—is sufficient to associate them in print with "charges of Red infiltration of the United Nations" and "passing documents to a wartime Soviet spy ring."

I am not here concerned with who these five people are, or whether they are innocent or not. I am concerned with the effect of an article of this sort, considering the way we do and do not use words. Within the limits of this account, we are entitled to imagine several sorts of situations, including the following: The "public issues" are A, B, C, D, and E. Public issue E has a cousin, F, who is suspected of having communist connections, although the rumors about F are unfounded. E is a conservative Republican who hates F and always has, and disagrees with him about almost everything, but since E is a congenial sort of person who dislikes squabbles, especially family squabbles, he tries to avoid F, but inevitably sees him occasionally. Accordingly somebody on a legislative subcommittee determines to call E as a witness, and in order to evaluate the testimony of the witness, calls also upon A, B, C, and D, who have worked in offices with E. That is all that need have happened.

But what effect did this account have upon my freshmen? Obviously, only one of my statements was correct: "Franklin's evidence allows us to infer nothing about candidates recommended by Hiss." But of the freshmen who took this quiz, not one in one hundred checked that answer and no other. A fair percentage checked all of the first six, that is, that Hiss recommended communists who were bad security risks and public nuisances, and that he was endeavoring to aid Russia and overthrow our government. Franklin's testimony provides no evidence for any of these charges. The story does mention that Hiss "is in jail now, serving a term for lying about passing documents to a wartime Soviet spy ring," but this statement depends upon the verdict in Hiss's trial, and has nothing to do with Franklin's evidence as here reported. A favorite answer was the sixth, "Franklin's evidence proves that some of Hiss's candidates were either carelessly chosen or willfully mischosen." Of course there is no more evidence in the newspaper account for this answer than for any of the others, but apparently the students were intrigued by a sense of restrained justice in the charge, and the handsome words in the phrase "either carelessly chosen or willfully mischosen." Watching them as they filled in their answers, I could almost see them saying, "Where there's so much smoke there must be some fire, and this sounds like a good, conservative answer."

Admittedly, the results of a test of this sort are not accurate. But the sad fact is that an accurate test would probably produce even more dismal results. These students were not average Americans in an average situation. They were selected by the entrance requirements of the university, and further selected by having survived the first semester of college, including one course in English. They knew that this was some kind of test, and that the test had to do with their ability to read accurately—that was the subject of the course that week. They did not read as newspaper readers usually do; they were given all the time they wanted in which to read the account again and again.

Probably an accurate test for this sort of thing could not be administered. The following test, if it could be given, would be much more reliable. Select people who had read the newspaper article, and were sufficiently interested in it so that, say a week later, they would remember having read it. Engage them in conversation in such a way that they would have occasion to recall the article. It is a safe guess that, with a week in which to forget the details, almost all of them would have the conviction that in one way or another the article showed that there had been communist infiltration of the United Nations through Alger Hiss. In fact, I would wager that the only people who would remember the article without that notion would be the few readers who had been horrified and disgusted at the misuse of a phrase like "public issues," and had noted the article as a bad example of "either careless or willful" perversion of the public mind.

Fortunately, there are people who are aware of just this sort of thing, and who are trying to make us aware of the fact that we allow ourselves to be tricked, and to a degree ruled by words. In this country the number of such people has grown under the inspiration of the late Count Korzybski. Their approach and purposes are usually known as General Semantics. The Semanticists (with a capital *S*, for semantics as a common noun refers to the study of meaning) are generally not professional students of language, although there are conspicuous exceptions. But their activities are not less significant for that. Here is a splendid body of men and women, whose business is something else than language, who are nonetheless concerned that all of us learn to make use of language for the betterment of ourselves and of mankind. No one on the side of the angels can wish them anything but good.

*Language,*
*a Serious*
*Business*

VOCABULARY, we have noted, is not the only aspect of language, nor is it the only one with which we might concern ourselves when we try to ask what importance language has for mankind. Grammar is a means of using the logical and creative aspects of the mind to reveal meaning and emotion through the use of known grammatical devices. That is, the use of language is the use of the mind. Learning to use language carefully would seem to be training in using the mind carefully, and it has long been considered so. The Greeks and Romans were careful students of rhetoric and grammar; during most of the history of Europe, the study of the classical writings was the basis of all education. Egyptian education was based upon composition; Chinese education was based upon study of the Chinese classics. In fact most of the great cultures of the world seem to have been developed by civilizations which attached the greatest importance to the study of language and choice pieces of writing. Many of us continue to believe in this training of the mind by language, even in the face of some devotees of metrics who will not concede that a mind can be trained with one set of materials so that it becomes apt with another set of materials. Many of us believe we see that a mind which can deal logically with one study—mathematics, or language, or biology—quickly learns to deal logically with the other two. We are inclined to believe that studies which train minds are the most practical of all, even in the narrow sense of "practical."

These are among the reasons for teaching language on a very serious level, both the knowledge of language and the use of language. I am here reminded of a teacher of English I formerly knew, now, unhappily for her friends, gone to her reward. She fought the good fight all her days, and for her the good fight was marking misplaced commas with large red *F*'s. She had judgment and considerable taste; she was devoted to her teaching. But she had gone through the mill in the day and in a section of the country in which a knowledge of the irrefragable rules of the comma was mistaken for a knowledge of language.

She might have done worse. At least she made her *F*'s one of the terrors of the campus. Morons imported to play football fled her as the plague. Those unwary freshmen who blundered into her classes worked with a feverish if limited purpose, to eschew any *lèse majesté* among commas, and in learning to respect the integrity of punctuation they usually learned to recognize a sentence when they saw one. But even at best the situation was tragic. Here were a number of young people who needed, as they needed few other things on earth, to learn to use the minds they had been given, but which they employed most bunglingly. They never got the help they needed. They were never even led to see that the scrupulous and copious use of language was one of the crying needs of the world, and especially one of the crying needs of bright young people in the world. They hated English because it was drudgery and it "didn't make much difference anyhow, just commas."

Happily, this sort of teaching is no longer popular. It persists but it is out of fashion. The English language is now generally taught as the medium of the meeting of minds, as the tool of the mind and the tool of civilization. It is not always so taught, partly because there is a notion about that anybody can teach English—

a spare football coach who happens not to be able to add, or an indigent widow out of a job. Teachers of English, like teachers of most other subjects, are not well paid; people who have good minds usually insist on good pay, and no one can teach the use of the mind well who does not himself know how to use a good mind. And language is the use of the mind. We need it well taught. The Lord and the departments of English be praised, it is now better taught than it was recently in this country.

*Mother*     THE VERY obvious use of language is to
*Tongue*     serve us when we want to make ourselves
*at Home*    understood, or to understand somebody else.
How well is American speech equipped to serve this eternal and daily use? There was a tendency for a time to look somewhat patronizingly upon English, to praise the classical languages for the exactitude which their elaborate inflectional systems provided to the user of Latin or Greek. The flexibility and precision of French have received innumerable encomiums. Even speakers of English were inclined to be modest about their native tongue; modesty, including national and regional modesty, is a becoming virtue, but the state of the English language requires of English-speaking peoples a modesty no more than becoming.

As a matter of fact, most languages, even primitive languages, prove upon objective examination to be remarkably capable of expressing any concepts that their users can conceive. Few languages can be condemned as incompetent. But if one were to start making comparisons he might have difficulty discovering any language now spoken or ever spoken for which more could be said than can be said for English. If the users of any other language ever had so great a body of words from which to choose as that which is available to speakers of English, the dictionaries do not reveal the fact. To all appearance, English contains overwhelmingly the largest number of symbols for meaning which any people have ever devised and collected. Furthermore the flexibility and precision of these words seem to be commensurate with their number. The more meaningful symbols a language has, the greater is the possibility of precision in the use of these symbols. Of course any comparison between the exactitude with which words are used in one language and the exactitude with which they are used in another must be highly impressionistic, but speakers of English are apparently not backward in their concern for using words precisely and well. Even those critics who have not, on the whole, admired English have conceded to it a very respectable body of vocabulary.

Adverse criticism of English has usually been leveled at its meager inflectional system. The argument has gone something like this: Greek and Latin, the classical languages, have elaborate inflectional systems which permit precise speech; English has no such extensive system, is accordingly not exact, and is hence inferior. The first of these statements is certainly true; the classical languages do use inflection and they can be precise. But the second statement does not necessarily follow from it. If English is to be accused of being imprecise it must be imprecise because it cannot be precisely used, not because it uses a system differing from that of Latin and Greek. Now the fact is—and it is quite an obvious fact—that English is capable of the most exact use. Our grammar—witness our verb system—is a marvel of flexibility, variety, and exactitude. We can say with precision whatever we want to say. If so, does it matter whether we use a grammar different from that of Pericles and Virgil? The grammar of Shakespeare and Abraham Lincoln would seem to be quite good enough.

But if one wishes to reason from analogy in grammar, then the analogy could easily be turned the other way about. Indo-European, a relatively primitive language, was highly inflected, as are the modern primitive languages, Bantu and Chinook. Most Indo-European languages (including the descendants from Latin and Greek) are steadily becoming less inflectional and more distributive. The language still in use by a great people, which has been spoken continuously by the largest number of highly civilized people for the longest period, that is, Chinese, is the most extensively distributive language we know. Thus, whether one looks among Indo-European languages or outside them, the use of position and sequence in grammar seems to be the advanced method of showing relationships, the use of changes in form the primitive one. This argument is not to discredit inflection as a grammatical device; obviously excellent languages can use it and have used it. But it is certainly not to discredit languages which have been graduated from inflection, as has English.

In fact, if we wish to be speculative and philosophic, we might go a step further, and see in this shift toward a distributive grammar evidence of one of those deeply pervading movements that are so profound they escape the perception of their participants but occupy subsequent generations. Admittedly, when one becomes speculative he also becomes uncertain, but for what the speculation may be worth, here it is.

We have seen that in subtle ways language and life, language and civilization have worked together, if each by its own means and in its own channels. Of late years many observers have felt that we are moving either into chaos or into a great new age of the world, depending upon the use we make of the forces which are being placed in our hands, forces which are social as well as scientific and industrial. Along with the increase in worldly goods there has been a great surge among many of the peoples of the world toward democracy and democratic living, and this in spite of powerful movements which are anything but democratic.

Similarly there seems to be a progression in types of grammar. Most primitive languages function by sticking words or stems together, or by sticking inflectional bits to words. That is, inflection seems to be the sophisticated form of which agglutination is the relatively primitive form. Thus, a highly inflected language like Latin or Greek seems only to represent the advanced sort of grammar of the same type as that which we find in a less developed form in the most primitive languages. The use of position and sequence for grammar, however, is essentially different, and its cultural distribution is different. It is not common among primitive languages. It is found scatteringly among backward people—Siamese and Annamite are distributive—but it is characteristic of modern peoples and advanced languages.

Not everyone will accept this last statement. Some Russians surely will not, for Russian has remained a strongly inflected language. But many scholars, and more particularly many anthropologists, would insist that a movement from inflection as a grammatical device toward distribution seems to be a movement toward a modern world, as the forsaking of fascism for democracy seems to be a movement toward a modern world. And who shall say, in the intimate relations of man and society, of language and life, that they are not related? Who, indeed, even though there remains the obvious retort, who shall say that they are related? Anyhow, the notion remains intriguing. if not demonstrable.

*Mother Tongue Abroad*  THE categorical imperative seems not to function in language. Immanuel Kant mightily impressed our forebears by asserting that the basis of conduct was the categorical imperative in the human being, which forced him to desire to act as though each action were to become the basis of a universal principle. Perhaps, but not in language. Few people would be willing to regulate their speech as if each utterance were to become the basis of a universal tongue. And yet we dreadfully need a universal language, or at least one that can be understood throughout the civilized world. Quite possibly unless we can learn to live with our neighbors we shall be condemned not to live at all. And admittedly, one very good way to live with one's neighbors is to establish some means of communication with them.

Is it possible to have a world language? If any large portions of the previous chapters of this book come anywhere near the truth, then a few facts must be obvious. Any world language must be a living language; if no local language can exist without a living core of speakers, then surely no world language can. Efforts to devise universal languages which could be adopted without prejudice and learned without trouble—languages like

Esperanto—represent a noble intent combined with an essential ignorance of what language is and how it works. Efforts to revive Latin are as obviously doomed as efforts to revive the dodo would be. Efforts to promote arbitrarily simplified dialects like Basic English and Basic Chinese are probably equally futile; Basic English may provide a ready way for a non-English speaker to make himself understood, but it does not provide any satisfactory way for a native speaker of English to speak his native language.

Presumably, also, if ever there is a world language, it will represent a world situation, a situation in which social, political, and linguistic circumstances have combined to make a world language natural, not a situation in which a few people have concocted a world language and have tried to legislate it into being. To see this, one has only to consider what would happen if tomorrow the United Nations were to decide to compromise on a "dark horse" language, and name Nahuat, a language of the Mexican isthmus, as the world medium of exchange. Nahuat seems to be an excellent language, and it need occasion no Romanic-Germanic rivalry, no conflict of the East and the West. But what would happen? Nobody would learn Nahuat.

What are the forces which might make one language common in the world, and what likely candidates are there? Obviously, one answer is primary. Language will follow power, all sorts of power. French became the language of diplomacy not because it was a beautiful and subtle speech, but because Talleyrand was a clever and subtle diplomat, because Napoleon was a powerful and subtle general, because Louis XIV was a grasping and subtle monarch. Or to speak more generally, French became the nearest thing we have had to a universal language because, in the formative seventeenth and eighteenth centuries France was the nearest thing Europe had to a dominant military and social power. During the heyday of Hitler, German grew mightily as a world language; if you wanted goods or money or freedom from attack you had best be able to talk German. The Nazi influence did not last long enough to elevate the language much, but had Hitler succeeded, German would certainly have increased in importance. And should the time ever come that the world goes to the

Kremlin for cash and instructions, the world will go, we may be sure, with Russian on its tongue—whether or not it is compelled to by edict.

At the moment, the world certainly is not willing to speak only Russian, and many peoples are determined to avoid any position in which they can be compelled to speak more Russian than they wish to. That leaves English. English is the native tongue of both the United States and the British Commonwealth of Nations. At this writing those two bodies of people control, and at least for a time promise to continue to control, more of the sinews of language than any other in what we call the free world, incomparably more. These countries have more political prestige, more military strength, more international trade, more productive potential, more wealth, more of almost everything that goes to support language than have half a dozen of their nearest competitors. If, then, the future of the world is shaping at all as we hope it will shape, toward a free world following the lead of the English-speaking peoples, English has by all odds the best prospect of becoming a world language.

How is it suited, relatively, for this role? What are the requirements of a good world language? Surely some of the principal requisites fall under these headings: number of speakers of the language, distribution of the speakers, population potential of areas in which the language is spoken, adequacy of the language linguistically, availability of the language as a world medium, and adequacy of the language as a medium of the world heritage.

*Number of Speakers of the Language*—Only three languages, Chinese, Russian, and English, are spoken by many more than a hundred million native speakers. Chinese leads with more than four hundred million, but Chinese is a welter of dialects, which might better be called separate languages. English is second with some two hundred and fifty million. Statistics for Russia are difficult, but estimates do not usually run above one hundred and fifty million for the speech of the Great Russians and dialects mutually intelligible. German may have passed one hundred million, but at present this language seems not in a good position to expand. Spanish is smaller, perhaps seventy-five million, but is growing rapidly. French is spoken by perhaps fifty million, and seems not to be growing.

*Distribution of Speakers*—Thanks to the British Empire, English is spread over the world as is no other language. French was widely spoken, but seems to be declining. Russian expands with the expansion of the Soviet, but as yet the expansion has been limited. Chinese is spoken only sporadically in the Orient outside China. English is the native speech of more than fifty million in Europe, the speech of North America north of Mexico, of Australia and New Zealand along with other spots in the South Pacific, of parts of Africa and bits of Asia.

Here we might pause for a somewhat curious footnote. A means of speaking which is not quite English, and yet is nearer to English than to anything else, has spread widely through the world in areas where otherwise there are only native dialects which will certainly disappear with the spread of civilization. This means of communicating has grown up through the prevalence of the British trader and the need of a language for trade in the more obscure areas in and about the Pacific Ocean. It is usually called *pidgin English*—*pidgin* is supposedly a corruption of business—and sometimes *bêche-de-mere* (by folk etymology *beach-la-mar*), after a trepang, or sea cucumber, which was an article of trade along several Pacific coasts.

As a sample of pidgin English we might take the following:

Big Name watchem sheepysheep. Watchum blackfella. No
*The Lord is my shepherd;*                                    *I*
more belly cry fella hab. Big Name makum camp alonga
*shall not want          He maketh me to lie down in*
grass.          Takum blackfella walkabout longa, no fight-
*green pastures; He leadeth me beside still waters.*
em no more hurry wata. Big Boss longa sky makum inside
*He restoreth my soul;*
glad; takem walkabout longa, too much goodfella.
*He leadeth me in the path of righteousness for His*
*name's sake.*

Pidgin occurs in two widely flung areas from independent origins, one along the coasts of southeastern Asia, one among the islands of the Pacific. It usually comprises some 300–400 nouns, 40–50 verbs, perhaps a hundred modifiers and relationship words, and a dozen or two native terms, usually local. With this limited vocabulary and a simple grammar making use of distribution and agglutination, the natives manage to express themselves quite remarkably, often vividly. For instance, whiskers become *grass belong face;* a pocket is *basket belong trousers,* and the sun *lamp belong Jesus.*

In fact, pidgin has become, for large areas of the world, a universal language. It is spoken by millions, and is the civilized means of communication which millions more will probably learn when they get around to learning a language which will link them with civilization. It is already breaking up into dialects of its own, living the sort of life we expect of any growing language. To date it faces only relatively minor competition through similar developments from other languages, Chinese and French notably, and must be weighed more heavily in any balancing of world languages than its humble origin might imply.

*Population Potential of the Areas in Which the Language Is Spoken*—Something is to be said for each of the great languages on this score. Russia has great undeveloped areas and resources. China is heavily populated, but industrialization would greatly increase the population, although what birth control may do in China and Russia is yet to be seen. The United States is still growing, and nations like Australia and Canada have great possibilities of growth. The greatest potential seems to lie before Spanish, which, except for some areas where Portuguese is spoken, is becoming the common language of all the Americas south of the Rio Grande. These countries are not sufficiently stable politically nor developed commercially and socially to further their common language greatly in the near future, but eventually Spanish may become one of the great world languages.

It faces at least one hazard, however. At this writing Latin-American Spanish is rapidly breaking up into Mexican Spanish, Cuban Spanish, Chilean Spanish, and the like, the new dialects differing in vocabulary, grammar, and pronunciation. Latin American Spanish is unstable; the large numbers of Indians who speak Spanish only as an acquired language, the inadequacy of the school systems and the low level of literacy, the rudimentary communications systems, all encourage rapid linguistic change along regional and dialectical lines. If linguistic change in Latin America continues at its present rate—and it seems not to be diminishing—Spanish may not remain the language of Latin America, but become the ancestor of a Latin-American linguistic family. If that happens, Spanish has no future as a world language.

German seems now to be circumscribed, Germany having lost most of her colonies after World War I. The potential of French outside France is threatened by the probable doom of what once promised to be a French empire.

*Adequacy of the Language Linguistically*—This question is complicated. English has a prodigious vocabulary and a simple grammar. Those are advantages; the fact that English is closely related to other Germanic languages and has borrowed extensively from Romanic languages makes it easy for many foreigners to learn. It uses the widely spread Latin alphabet. In fact, it seems to be as easy to learn as anybody can expect—no foreign language is easy for most people to learn—except for one shortcoming. English spelling is fantastic. We have already seen why; it has preserved all sorts of remnants, foreign and native, and it has never been reformed.

There have been movements for spelling reform, and there will be more. English spelling is very handy for anybody greatly interested in language and language change, because it embodies so much of its own history in its spelling. But undoubtedly a phonetic spelling would be easier to learn, easier even for natives, to say nothing of foreigners who inevitably endeavor to learn by rule—and we have no spelling rules that are worth much. The difficulty is that spelling is not easy to reform. The great body of the writing of the past is all in an established spelling; if we were to reform spelling in a thorough way we should have to start teaching two sets of spelling in order that children could read more than contemporary writing. Furthermore, anybody who has learned to spell one way is not anxious to learn another system—and at any given time most of the people living, and all of the important people, have already learned the old system. Most important of all, pepul hu hav lurnd tu spel wun wa du not lik tu se wurds speld anuthr wa—in fact, you probably did not like that.

Certainly, successful spelling reform would promote English as a world language. But unsuccessful spelling reform can be hazardous. The Scandinavian countries have tried it, for instance, not very successfully, although those countries are small and are on the whole adept at reforms. In some Scandinavian areas one spelling has been replaced by two; in others it has been replaced by three. That sort of spelling reform would not help much.

*Availability of the Language as a World Medium*—Here we have to think of the human and mechanical problems involved in a world language. Obviously, Nahuat would not be a good world language, partly because there are not enough Nahuat translators or Nahuat printing presses. Translators cannot be trained overnight, nor can great publishing houses be built in a day, nor transferred readily from one place or one language to another. English has a tremendous publishing industry behind it, and the ability to print and broadcast English is moderately well scattered about the globe.

The regularity of the language, also, is important. One limitation of the Chinese language is this: the Chinese themselves cannot agree as to how their language is to be spoken or written. English is the most uniform of all the great languages; it is spoken in a manner mutually intelligible in all societies and most areas. It has the best and the most numerous dictionaries.

*Adequacy of the Language as a Medium of World Heritage*— Civilization has been going on for a long time, and its past in thought and action has been recorded mainly in words. These words exist in a language translated from many tongues, printed on paper, bound in volumes, and cataloged in libraries. All this store of knowledge is essential to our civilization, to the continuity of our heritage. It represents a staggering investment in time, in skilled labor, in massed goods. Thus a world language should be one into which the written heritage of the world has already been well translated, well printed, and well distributed. Probably no other language has been the medium of such widespread translation and publication as has English.

*Summary*—The situation would seem obvious. If there is to be a world language in the relatively near future—say within this century—and this language comes from the supposedly democratic, relatively free world, then the language should be and probably will be English. There is scarcely a close competitor. The only serious limitation of English arises from its spelling, which, while it is pleasant for etymologists, is needlessly hard for most of the rest of us, especially for anyone who does not learn English as a native tongue. Should we then, in the interests of the safety of the world and of ourselves, try to do something to make our language more acceptable to whoever was not so fortunate as to be born to English?

Many of us would willingly make sacrifices for world peace, even to squirming in the presence of spelling which would suggest nothing more pleasant than the tracks of a demented bantam. But tinkering with language is uncertain business. Usually it does no harm because it has no effect, but sometimes it does have effect, as with the Scandinavian spelling. Everything we know about language suggests that it is uncommonly tough and resilient stuff. It is very likely to go its own way. It has a stubborn proclivity for reflecting the kind of people who make it, and resulting from the kind of world in which it is made. Certainly we can do much to promote English as a world language by promoting a world fit for one language and by promoting that world through the leadership of English-speaking people. We can promote the English language by improving the study of English, by improving our publishing in English, through whatever medium. And we might be able to do a little deliberate doctoring if we are careful. Greatly to its credit—not all reform bodies have shown such good sense—the Simplified Spelling Board, a subsidized body which exists for the reform of American spelling, has been careful. It has also been ineffectual. Against one's best wishes, it probably will remain so. Language lives on men's tongues, in their innermost beings, and in the totality of peoples. It has never responded very satisfactorily to little things, either to nostrum committees or to nostrum notions.

Mother Tongue is a very self-reliant female.

Formal bibliography and footnotes would seem unnecessary in a volume of this sort, the more because excellent bibliographies of several sorts are readily available. The standard complete bibliography of the English language, of course, is Arthur G. Kennedy's *Bibliography of Writings on the English Language from the Beginnings to the End of 1922* (Cambridge, Mass., and New Haven, 1927). Professor Kennedy has been working on a revision. The current bibliography in *American Speech* bridges the gap since 1922. Useful, also, is Clark S. Northrup's *A Register of Bibliographies of the English Language and Literature* (New Haven, 1925), also in revision. Excellent working bibliographies are available in Margaret M. Bryant's *Modern English and Its Heritage* (New York, 1948), arranged by author, and Arthur G. Kennedy's *Current English* (New York, 1935), arranged by subject. Briefer, but judiciously selected is the bibliography in Albert H. Marckwardt's *Introduction to the English Language* (New York, 1942). An excellent critical bibliography appears in Simeon Potter's *Our Language* (Harmondsworth, Middlesex, 1950). The forthcoming *Guide for Comparative Literature* (American Library Association) will contain a bibliography of the movements and contacts of languages by Margaret Schlauch.

Perhaps the best survey of language for general use is still that by Leonard Bloomfield, *Language* (New York, 1933). The most penetrating study of the nature of language, backed by a bewildering wealth and spread of learning, is Edward Sapir's *Language* (New York, 1921). The various volumes by Otto Jespersen should not be neglected, especially *Growth and Structure of the English Language*, 4th ed. (Oxford, 1923); 8th ed. (Leipzig, 1935); *Language: Its Nature, Development, and Origin* (New York, 1933); and *The Philosophy of Grammar* (London, 1935). The volumes mentioned above by Professors Bryant, Kennedy, and Marckwardt were prepared as texts, but are suitable also for general reading; they place emphasis on English, but concern principles of language as well. Professor Simeon's *Our Language* provides a very good survey, with the bias its title suggests. Margaret Schlauch's *The Gift of Tongues* (New York, 1942), Mario Pei's *The Story of Language* (New York, 1949), and George A. Miller's *Language and Communication* (New York, 1951) are broader in approach.

The standard histories of the English language are Albert C. Baugh's *A History of the English Language* (New York, 1935), a reliable and very readable volume which concerns all aspects of the language, and Henry Cecil Wyld's *A Short History of English*, 3d ed. (New York, 1927), an admirable work but sufficiently technical so that it is difficult for the lay reader to use. These should be supplemented with George Philip Krapp's *Modern English: Its Growth and Present Use* (New York, 1909) and *The Rise of*

*English Prose Style* (New York, 1915); the late Professor Krapp is here, as always, learned and penetrating. Indispensable for American speech is H. L. Mencken's *The American Language,* 4th ed. (New York, 1938), with *Supplement I* (New York, 1945) and *Supplement II* (1948). Professor Krapp's *The English Language in America* (New York, 1925), 2 vols., although less exuberant and somewhat out of date, is still useful. Embodying the three R's —readable, reliable, and recent—is Thomas Pyles's *Words and Ways of American English* (New York, 1952).

The *New English Dictionary on Historical Principles,* the so-called *Oxford English Dictionary* is superb and indispensable. It provides the only comprehensive view (to 1900) of the language based upon citations. A two-volume abridgement, the *Shorter Oxford,* comparable in size with the "unabridged" dictionaries, sells at a reasonable price, but lacks most of the citations. In some ways the most remarkable dictionary in English is Henry C. Wyld's *Universal Dictionary of the English Language.* It has made more use of modern etymological study than has any other general dictionary, and Wyld and his staff have shown gratifying acuity in distinguishing definitions. Good in spite of its age is the *Century Dictionary and Cyclopedia,* either the ten- or twelve-volume edition, out of print, but at this writing quite cheap at second-hand stores. The best of the so-called "unabridged" dictionaries is the *Webster's New International Dictionary,* followed, although rather remotely, by the Funk and Wagnall's *New Standard Dictionary of the English Language.* Smaller, but extremely usable, is the two-volume *Webster's New World Dictionary of the American Language;* it is the only general dictionary published in this country which gives Indo-European bases. At this writing, the best desk-size dictionaries—much the best—are the college edition of *Webster's New World Dictionary,* mentioned above, the *American College Dictionary,* and the *Webster's Collegiate Dictionary* (or the more recent partial revision called *Webster's New Collegiate Dictionary*). Since my name occurs on the staff page of one of them, I must reserve comment; each has its virtues. For American developments the *Dictionary of American English* and the *Dictionary of Americanisms* are excellent and engaging; I prefer the second. The best work on American slang to date is Lester V. Berry and Melvin van den Bark's *The American Thesaurus of Slang,* which makes delightful browsing. The *Dictionary of Americanisms* includes slang and colloquialisms, and monumental dictionaries of colloquialisms and usage are in preparation.

The conventional grammatical statement, liberalized by a historical approach, is well presented in the monumental work by George Oliver Curme, *A Grammar of the English Language* revised by Hans Kurath (Boston, 1931 —), of which vols. 2 and 3 concern syntax and accidence. Important, also, are Jespersen's *A Modern English Grammar* in seven parts (Heidelberg, Copenhagen, and London, 1904–1949), *An Advanced English Syntax* (London and New York, 1904) by C. T. Onions, and the grammars of E. Kruisinga and H. Poutsma. Two very sensible little books are those by the late Janet Rankin

Aiken, *New Plan of English Grammar* (New York, 1933), and *Commonsense Grammar* (New York, 1936). Mrs. Aiken's work has been carried forward by Professor Bryant, whose *A Functional English Grammar* (New York, 1945) embodies an excellent tempering of the historical approach with a clear grasp of modern grammatical thought; it is written as a college text, but it is also an important contribution to grammatical understanding. Recent and radical, but important, are Charles Carpenter Fries's *The Structure of English* (New York, 1952) and Harold Whitehall's *The Structural Essentials of Written English*, 2d ed. (Indiana University, 1951).

Indispensable for the modern linguistic approach is Bernard Bloch and George L. Trager's *Outline of Linguistic Analysis: Linguistic Society of America, Publications* (Baltimore, 1942).

The standard treatment of phonetics is Jespersen's *Lehrbuch der Phonetic*, 2d ed. (Leipzig and Berlin, 1913); for English see Daniel Jones' *An Outline of English Phonetics*, 6th ed. (New York, 1940). A basic statement for General Semantics appears in Charles Kay Ogden and I. A. Richards's *The Meaning of Meaning* (New York, 1923), but modern schools of semantics are now too numerous and varied to be analyzed here. A good survey with bibliography will be found in Professor Bryant's *Modern English and Its Heritage*, pp. 353–361. S. I. Hayakawa's *Language in Thought and Action* (New York, 1949) is readable and enlightening. Extremely interesting at this writing is the growth of American linguistic geography; for volumes published to date see the preface and introductory note to Hans Kurath's *A Word Geography of the Eastern United States: Studies in American English*, 1 (Ann Arbor, Mich., 1952). The *Linguistic Atlas of New England* has now been completed under Professor Kurath's editorship; atlases for the remainder of the country are projected.

# About the Author

CHARLTON LAIRD, scholar, linguist and Professor of English at the University of Nevada, is a novelist and the author of scholarly and reference works.

Born in Nashua, Iowa, in 1901, he received his B.A. degree from the University of Iowa in 1925. Further studies followed at Columbia University and as a Traveling Fellow in Europe in 1930 and 1931. He received his Ph.D. in 1940 from Stanford University.

Professor Laird has devoted most of his time to free-lance writing, journalism, and college teaching. He has taught at the University of Iowa, Drake University, the University of Idaho, Purdue University, Columbia University and the University of Nevada.

Among his books are: *Laird's Promptory, Thunder on the River, The World through Literature, Modern English Handbook* (with Robert M. Gorrell), and *West of the River*. He has also served as a special editor on *Webster's New World Dictionary of the American Language.*

He is married to author Helene Laird.

# INDEX

297